Brisling with guns, the U.S.S. *Pennsylvania* leads a line of battleships into Lingayen Gulf for the American return to the Philippines in 1945. Dearborn Countian Sylvester (Dutz) Neary was serving aboard this battleship in the Plotting Room of the Gunnery Department.

CONTENTS

	Introduction	2
Chapter 1	**On the Brink of War**	5
Chapter 2	**Pearl Harbor Bombed The U.S. Goes to War**	27
Chapter 3	**U.S. Expands Military to Fight Global War**	49
Chapter 4	**Fighting from Africa through Italy**	77
Chapter 5	**On the Home Front**	113
Chapter 6	**Women in the Military**	129
Chapter 7	**On the Offensive in the Pacific**	141
Chapter 8	**Assaulting Europe**	181
Chapter 9	**Final Victory**	229
	Book Donors	294
	Acknowledgments	295
	Bibliography	296
	Photo Credits	297
	Index	301

Turner Publishing Company

P.O. Box 6802
Evansville, Indiana 47719-6802

Pre-Press work by M.T. Publishing Company, Inc.
Graphic Designer: Bob Parker, Dearborn County Historical Society

Copyright © 2001
Dearborn County Historical Society

This book or any part thereof may not be reproduced without the written consent of the Dearborn County Historical Society and the Publishers.

The materials were compiled and produced using available information; Turner Publishing Company, M.T. Publishing Company, Inc., and the Dearborn County Historical Society regret they cannot assume liability for errors or omissions.

Library of Congress
Control Number: 2001088504

ISBN: 978-1-68162-389-4

Introduction

In introducing this book to you, to explain some of the production considerations, several emotions will probably surface. First and foremost is pride. We all can be proud of the Dearborn County people and the part they played in World War II. We are told by professional historians that the Second World War was the biggest single event in all of history. It was fought on most continents and on all the oceans. Over 50 million people were killed, hundreds of millions wounded, not to mention the incalculable destruction of property. Not only were political forms and boundaries altered, but social and economic norms were changed forever.

In America some 16 million men and women served in the armed forces, and others did their part on the home front. Unlike any other war, every single person in Dearborn County was touched by WWII. Everyone had a spouse, father, sibling, sweetheart or friend in the fighting services. Dearborn Countians served in all parts of the armed forces: infantry, artillery, submarines, battleships, tanks, Marines, Coast Guards, bombers, gliders and mountain troops. They served in all theaters: from Alaska, Iceland and Murmansk in the North to New Guinea and Australia in the South, and from Iran, India and China in the East to Germany, Central Europe and Yugoslavia in the West.

They were definitely part of "The Greatest Generation" as newscaster and author Tom Brokaw referred to them. We feel that it is important to preserve the memories of this time period in Dearborn County and the World. And so we have attempted to tell their stories against the background of the military phases of World War II. Our aim is to present local history in light of world events for a better appreciation of both. The younger generation today as well as future generations need to be reminded that their forebears once led this nation in a great struggle to defeat the forces of dictators who sought to rob the world of freedom and democracy.

While it gives us great pleasure in publishing this account, it differs from Volume I in that it only covers six years. We were constrained in doing this by the concentration of events and the multitude of Dearborn County people all interacting in this span of time. We are thankful to all those who loaned the Historical Society their photos, without which this book would have been impossible as a pictorial history volume.

Nowhere in our search was there a complete list of Dearborn County veterans of WWII to be found, not in the Armed Forces records nor in the Veteran Administration files on a national, state or local level. So, we drew upon three main resources for local information: the Aurora and Lawrenceburg newspapers of 1940-1945; the Dearborn County Recorder's office; and oral accounts of veterans themselves or their families if deceased. Resources used for the military history of WWII are listed in the Bibliography. In addition we made use of the D-Day Museum in New Orleans, the Air Force Museum at Wright-Patterson Field, and the Patton Tank Museum at Fort Knox.

Finally we feel a deep loss as well as gratitude for those who gave their lives in WWII. To these men, who made the supreme sacrifice for their nation, county, and you and me, we dedicate this book, Volume II of the Pictorial History of Dearborn County.

Robert Parker, Editor

A group of Dearborn County draftees and well-wishers, wait at the Courthouse for the bus which will take them to Fort Knox for entry into the military service.

CHAPTER 1

On the Brink of War

World War II began in Europe in September 1939, but it wasn't called that as yet. It began when Germany, in her plans for conquest, suddenly and unannounced invaded Poland. Poland counted on her allies England and France for help, but their forces did not reach Poland, and the Nazi blitzkrieg (German for lightning attacks) overran the Poles in a matter of days.

In America, in Dearborn County, this war and the one in China were overseas battles we watched on newsreels in movie houses, at the Palace Theater in Aurora or the Walnut or the Liberty theaters in Lawrenceburg. Like most Americans, we weren't convinced that these foreign wars across the seas posed a threat to the U.S. As Dearborn County entered 1940, life was lived at a fairly normal level, especially since The Depression was over locally and most Dearborn Countians were employed, many at the two major and one smaller distilleries in Lawrenceburg and Greendale.

A newspaper editorial at the time, summed up the hopes of most Americans: "We have a peaceful New Years. Let's keep it." A look at our peace then, according to the 1940 Census, showed that 1 of every 5 Americans owned a car, and 1 in 7 had a telephone. But 1 of 3 families got by without an indoor toilet, and 2 of 5 had no bathtub or shower. Most homes, however, had a radio. Besides listening to the President's fireside chats, millions turned in on Saturday nights to hear WLS's National Barn Dance, starring Lulu Belle and Scotty, and the Hoosier Hot Shots. On Sundays, the favorite programs were: "The Jack Benny Comedy Hour" and "The Kate Smith Show."

However, conditions in Europe continued to change rapidly, by May 1940, the German Army had smashed Denmark and Norway, blitzed through Holland and Belgium, and by June were in Paris. By now, most Americans had changed their minds about national security. President Roosevelt began to take steps to correct America's unpreparedness (the U.S., before WWII, ranked 18th in the world in terms of military strength, behind the tiny nation of Romania). At his urging, Congress passed the first peacetime draft, the Selective Service Act, in September of 1940. He also urged the nation to become an "Arsenal of Democracy", to help supply England - and eventually Russia - with planes, munitions and food they so desperately needed in their stand against Hitler and Mussolini. As the year progressed, the U.S took other defense measures. In particular, F.D.R., came up with a "short of war" policy to gain time for rearmament; to help keep Great Britain fighting the Axis; and to restrain Japan's aggression in China and Asia by peaceful means.

Congressman Eugene Crowe from Indiana's 9th District, which included Dearborn County, was sent to Panama officially to inspect the defense work performed on the Canal. Congress had appropriated funds for bomb-proofing the old locks, the construction of a new set of locks and increasing all U.S. military forces in the Canal Zone. Mr. Crowe reported the work was making this important area into a Gibraltar of America.

One of the first young men from Dearborn County, **CHARLES BENNETT**, from Greendale, enlisted in the Army during this period before the Draft was in operation. In July, others from Dearborn County followed: **GULLEY**, **STEVENS**, and **HULBERT** from Lawrenceburg, and **NELSON**, **ALLEN** and **MISIK** from Dillsboro. **ROBERT MARTIN** next followed these men to the Army Air Corps, **HARRY GODFREY** to the Army, **JOHN JACKSON** of Bright to the Sea Bees, and **PHILLIP REESE** of Logan to the Navy. Other Dearborn Countians, who were already in the Military Services or who would go in before the operation of the Draft began in November 1940, are noted in the following paragraphs.

David Loomis

DAVID LOOMIS was Dearborn County's oldest, in point of service, in any branch of the Military. He was a Chief Petty Officer in the U.S.Navy. He had enlisted in 1912, and was in a submarine patrol operating out of French ports during WWI. For three years before Pearl Harbor, he had duty at Manila and in Hawaii. In WWII, he would serve aboard the cruiser, U.S.S. *Astoria,* which would take part in the battle of Midway and the battle of Savo Island, where the ship would be sunk by the Japanese. David would be injured and sent to an Australian hospital to mend. After recovery and more combat duty, he would retire from the Navy as a Lt. Commander in 1946.

Arnold Cash

W. Lee Crouch

Walter Hallfarth

John W. Hughes

Carlyle Gulley

Woodrow Wilson Gulley

Francis (Ted) Fiorito

Clayton Wells

Leroy Baker

EDWARD GENTER, of Lawrenceburg, was also a Chief Petty Officer in the Navy. He had enlisted in April 1917. During WWI, he served with the Submarine Detector Division in Europe. During his naval career, Edward served in various types of ships, making ports in almost every important nation. In addition to WWI, he served in the Nicaraguan and Cuban uprisings. During 1940-1941 he was serving with the Navy submarine forces.

JOHN WYMOND, of Aurora, was a Lieutenant Commander in the Navy, having graduated from the Naval Academy at Annapolis in 1924. In 1940, he was serving aboard a new aircraft carrier, the U.S.S. *Wasp*, which would see action in the Mediterranean at Malta, and then in the Pacific. John would lose his life when the U.S.S. *Wasp* was torpedoed and sunk while taking reinforcements to Guadalcanal in 1942 (see Chapter 2).

JOHN CRAMER, of Lawrenceburg, had enlisted in the Navy in 1927, and became a Chief Petty Officer. He served on the cruiser, U.S.S. *Omaha*, and then he was sent to the Asiatic Station for duty on the U.S.S. *Pittsburgh*. He visited many Asian ports, including Tokyo and Nagasaki. His next duty was aboard a new cruiser, U.S.S. *Chester*, operating in European waters. His duty was then at the Recruiting Training School in Norfolk, after which he did recruiting in the Cincinnati area.

J. ROMAIN CLAUSE was a Chief Petty Officer in the Navy in the 1930s. He was from Aurora and had been stationed in Houston, Texas, and in September 1941 was transferred to the submarine base at Key West, Florida. Later he would become an officer at the Submarine School in New London and be commissioned an Ensign.

EARL WAFFORD, of Dillsboro, joined the Navy in 1930 and became a deep-sea diver. He would have duty aboard the U.S.S. *Mallard*, based in Panama, when war was declared. Later he would serve on the coast of Africa. When his ship was attacked there, he was caught in a deep dive, but was brought up without mishap. Later he would be assigned to the Philippines as a diving instructor. After the war he did dives to check the effects of the atomic bomb in the sea off Bikini. In 1948, he would make the deepest dive on record at that time. He would retire in 1950 as a Chief Petty Officer.

RALPH POUND enlisted in the Marines in 1940. He would take part in the initial landing on Guadalcanal where he would be wounded. He would be sent to a naval hospital in California where he would spend a year and a half recovering, and be discharged in 1943.

WALTER HALLFARTH, of Aurora, enlisted in the Navy in 1932. In 1935, while serving on the battleship, U.S.S. *Pennsylvania*, he answered a call for volunteers for submarine duty. He served on the submarine S-28 and then had recruiting duty in Redwood City, California. During WWII, he would have duty on the following subs: U.S.S. S-27, U.S.S. S-28 and the U.S.S. *Searaven*. He would make the Navy his career and serve during the Korean Conflict. Then he would serve in the Special Weapons Department for two more years and retire as a Chief Petty Officer.

FRED PHIESTER, of Lawrenceburg, enlisted in the Army at the age of 17 in 1934, finished his hitch and returned home. He re-enlisted to make the Army his career and would serve 20 more years. During WWII, he would serve as a Technical Sergeant in the Infantry in the ETO where he would receive the Bronze Star.

CARLYLE GULLEY, of Lawrenceburg, enlisted in the Army on July 15, 1940 and became a Staff Sergeant. He would fight in the ETO in the Rhineland and Central Europe until October 1945.

WOODROW W. GULLEY, of Dillsboro, entered the Army on August 2, 1940. He would become a Technical Sergeant serving in France and Germany. As a Radio Operator, he would serve with the 754th Tank Battalion.

Fred Phiester

MARION BRUCE, of Lawrenceburg, had enlisted in the Army in April of 1927 and became a Private First Class. In 1930, he served three years in Panama, and then was stationed in Utah. He re-enlisted and was sent to the Philippines with an Infantry Unit at Clark Field. The Japanese would take him prisoner when Corregidor and Bataan surrendered in 1942. He would be transferred to a POW Camp in Japan, where in 1944 he would die as the result of a broken hip.

LEE CROUCH, of Lawrenceburg, was serving in the Marine Corps. He had received an appointment to the Marine Officer's School in June 1936, after graduating from Purdue University. He served two years with the Marine Company aboard the battleship, U.S.S. *Colorado*. By 1942, he would be in action on Guadalcanal and Tulagi, and then on to the Central Pacific battles (see Chapter 7).

AUGUST (GUS) SCHREIBER, of Aurora, joined the Marines in March 1939. He qualified for a medal as an Expert Marksman.

He would spend five months of combat on Guadalcanal, taking part in the initial landings and the defense of the island's airstrip. As a Staff Sergeant, he would be in command of a telephone and radio communication section of 14 men. Altogether, he would be involved in five major battles against the Japanese in the Pacific Theater.

TILDEN (TIL) KARR, of Aurora, enlisted in the Navy in August of 1939, and became a Signalman First Class. He would serve in both the Atlantic and the Pacific, aboard the following ships: U.S.S. *Patoka* (an oiler), U.S.S. *West Point*, U.S.S. *Boyle*, and U.S.S. *Parke*. He would also participate in the landings in North Africa and Sicily.

CLAYTON WELLS, of Guilford, joined the Navy early in 1940. He would serve aboard the carrier, *Saratoga*, in the battles of the Guadalcanal Seas, the invasion of Truk, Marshalls and Iwo Jima. He would retire after 20 years as a Machinist Mate First Class.

JOHN W. HUGHES, of Aurora, enlisted in the Navy in June of 1940. He would make the Navy his career, serving at many stateside bases, in addition to sea duty aboard aircraft carriers in WWII in the Pacific. Later he would take part in Vietnam War when he and his son would serve together on the U.S.S. *Constellation*. John would advance to the rank of Chief Petty Officer.

ARNOLD CASH, of the Moores Hill area, enlisted in the Army on July 23, 1940. He would serve as a Truck Driver in a Field Artillery Battalion in the Italian Campaign, Southern France, and Central Europe. He would earn 5 battle stars and be awarded a Bronze Star for outstanding performance of duty in combat.

WESLEY B. TAYLOR, of Wright's Corner-Guilford area, graduated from Purdue's ROTC program in 1934 and was commissioned a Second Lieutenant. He was called to active duty in 1940 and sent to Panama for three years. As a result of contacting malaria, he would return to the States to train troops at Camp Crowder. He would later serve in Japan, Korea and Iran. He would retire in 1964 as a Lt. Colonel after a career of thirty years.

ISAAC C. POWELL entered the Merchant Marines in 1940, but would transfer to the Navy in 1944 and serve aboard the U.S.S. *Charles Carroll* in the Pacific. He would remain in the Navy until September 1945 when he would receive a medical discharge.

Isaac C. Powell

Wesley Taylor (middle)

LESLIE BECRAFT entered the Army in 1940, but he could only serve for three months.

JOHN R. JACKSON, of Bright entered the Navy in October of 1940. He trained for the Sea Bees at Camp Peary, Virginia.

JACK GOODPASTER, of Aurora, enlisted in the Navy in 1939 and would see action in the Atlantic by June 1941, even before the U.S. was at war with Germany. As a Torpedoman First Class on the destroyer, U.S.S. *Rowan*, he would be battling Nazi submarine packs. At that time, the U.S.Navy was protecting Allied convoys, carrying supplies to Britain and Russia. In November 1941, his ship sailed from Portland, Maine in response to a distress call from a convoy under attack sailing from Scotland. Goodpaster would also make convoy runs to Murmansk, Russia. He would later serve in the Pacific, altogether receiving 14 battle stars for engagements against both the Germans and the Japanese.

EARL E. BOCOCK, of Dillsboro, enlisted in the U.S.Navy in 1929. He served aboard many ships, which would include the battleship, U.S.S. *Missouri*, in the Pacific Theater during WWII. He would serve 25 years, retiring in March of 1951 as a Chief Petty Officer.

ROY CORNS, of Lawrenceburg, was commissioned a Second Lieutenant on the completion of several summers of Civilian Military Training Camps. In July 1940, he was ordered to active duty and sent to Panama. He was promoted to First Lieutenant and completed 14 months in the Canal Zone. After an illness, he would be transferred to inactive status. He would then enter the Canadian Army and serve in the European Theater.

HERBERT CASH served a hitch in the Army prior to the 1940s. He re-enlisted for WWII and would serve convoy duty in the Mediterranean in 1944.

STANLEY RUNYAN, of Aurora, enlisted in the Marine Air Force in 1937. After completing his hitch, he entered the Army Air Corps in 1942. He would fly P-38 fighter planes in the South Pacific where he would lose his life while searching for a downed comrade in the sea.

ROY REDWINE, of the Dillsboro area, joined the Navy on November 4, 1940, and became a Chief Turret Captain. He would serve in both the Atlantic and Pacific Oceans on the battleship, U.S.S. *Arkansas*, and the cruiser, U.S.S. *Astoria*.

Earl Bocock

HARRY GODFREY enlisted in the U.S. Army at Fort Knox in 1940 and served in WWII as a Private.

GEORGE OWENS enlisted in the U.S. Army in October of 1939. He would serve with an Engineering unit during WWII, building military roads in North Africa and Italy.

LOREN (HOBE) ELLIOTT, of Lawrencburg, began naval officer's training on November 2, 1940. Hobe went to New York and embarked on a training cruise in the Caribbean Sea. He would then become a member of the Reserve Battalion at the Naval Academy, complete a 90- day course and be commissioned an Ensign in 1941. During WWII, he would be assigned to the Engineering Department of the transport, U.S.S. *Orizaba*, and see service in the Atlantic, Pacific and Indian Oceans and the Mediterranean Sea, including the invasion of North Africa and Sicily. He would become Chief Engineer of the U.S.S. *Orizaba* and stay aboard temporarily when the ship was given to the Brazilian Navy after the war. For this service, he was given a letter of Commendation from the Brazilian Captain. During the Korean Conflict, he would be recalled to active duty. Afterwards he would command the Cincinnati Naval Reserve Unit, and then retire with the rank of Commander.

Loren (Hobe) Elliott and the Naval Transport, U.S.S. *Orizaba*, on which he served.

The Draft Gets Underway

The new Selective Training and Service Act, commonly referred to as the Draft, required all men between the ages of 21 and 35 to register with local draft boards on October 16, 1940. Every man registering received a draft number.

Two weeks after the registration, President Roosevelt, Secretary of War Stimson and other officials met in Washington to determine the order in which the registrants would be called for training. The officials used a glass fish bowl, which had been used for the same purpose in 1917 for WWI. The bowl contained 9000 capsules, in which were numbered slips of paper corresponding to the ones assigned each registrant by their draft boards. A blindfolded Stimson drew the first capsule and handed it to the President. F.D.R. extracted the paper and read the number, 158, into a battery of microphones. The process continued with other officials until all numbers had been selected.

Next, the registrants were called to appear before the local boards in the order of the selected numbers. They would then be given a preliminary physical exam and classified as to their fitness for military service. Boards could place a man in any one of a dozen classifications, ranging from 1-A (available for service) to 4-F (physically, mentally or morally unfit for service). Deferment from the draft was based on such reasons as: being a conscientious objector; employment in an essential occupation; and economic dependence of one's family. Marriage alone did not warrant deferment. Before the war was over, there was a total of 8 different registrations, and the age span changed to 18 years through 65 years of age, though only those between 18 and 36 were called. Three-member draft boards represented each county in a state, or each 30,000 of population within larger counties. Each board was supplemented with a government appeal agent and a physician. In Dearborn County, the first draft board appointed by Governor Townsend was composed of Clifford Edwards and Hewson Wright of Lawrenceburg, and ex-mayor of Aurora, Walter Kerr. Dr. G. F. Smith was appointed draft physician, E. G. Bielby appeal agent, and Arthur Ritzmann as Advisory Board member.

A Board of Appeals also represented each congressional district. Local people who were named to this board for the Ninth District were Dr. J.C. Elliott of Guilford, and Charles A. Lowe of Lawrenceburg. The Clerk for the board was Geneva Meyers, with Anna Kurtzman as assistant.

The man who had the distinction of being called first in Dearborn county was **JACOB KABAKOFF** 23, of Aurora. Jake, as he was known, had just returned with his new wife from their honeymoon in New York when he received the news of being called first in the draft since he held number 158. However, there is no indication that he passed the physical exam to be drafted.

Dearborn County's first draft contingent, the group who was actually the first to enter military training, consisted of only three men. This was Dearborn County's part of Indiana's first quota. Two of the three: **TERRANCE SMITH**, of Aurora, and **JOHN BIEKER**, of Lawrenceburg, went as volunteers; and **FLOYD STAMPER**, of Harrison, was inducted. They left for Fort Benjamin Harrison on November 19, 1940.

Of these first three young men, Terrance (Ted) Smith would be killed in action in the Battle of the Bulge in 1944 in Belgium. By that time, he had become a Master Sergeant and the holder of the Bronze Star medal for capturing a German officer and 23 enlisted men.

Richard Bieker was assigned to clerical work at Fort Harrison, but would be transferred, at his request, to the Army Air Corps at a station in California. He would advance to the rating of Sergeant.

Floyd Stamper, of Harrison Township, would serve with Terry Smith until April 1941. He would become married while serving in the Army, but little else is known about his experience in the war.

The second contingent from Dearborn County, consisted of 30 men. They left Lawrenceburg for Ft. Knox on January 17, 1941. Many wives, sweethearts, and relatives were present to bid farewell to the draftees. Judge Charles Lowe gave them a farewell speech. In future departing ceremonies, there would also be band music and, sometimes, fireworks.

These men, along with those listed previously and those listed in the following paragraphs, who entered the service before America declared war, were the vanguard of some 3,500 men and women from Dearborn County who served their nation in the military during World War II.

Dr. J.C. Elliott

Ellis Rees

Willard Ester

ELLIS REES, of Aurora-Lawrenceburg road, enlisted in the Navy on January 2, 1941. He would first serve aboard a battleship and then on other types of ships during a 22 year career in the Navy. Most of his duty would be in the field of sonar (sound echoing for distance determination). He would advance to the rank of Chief Petty Officer before retiring.

LEROY BAKER, of Aurora, who belonged to the Indiana National Guard, was called to active duty in January 1941. His unit would train at Camp Shelby, Mississippi. In 1943, they would be sent to Hawaii; and in May of 1945, Leroy would be assigned to General MacArthur's staff in the Philippines. In may of 1946, he would separate from the service with the rank of full Colonel.

LELAND TRESTER, of Aurora, enlisted in the Army Air Corps on January 28, 1941. As a Corporal, he would first serve as a radio operator, and later take training for medical administrative duty.

WILLARD ESTER, of Guilford, entered the Army in January 1941. He was sent to Fort Knox to become a member of an Armored Unit. In 1943 he would be commissioned a 2nd Lieutenant. In June of 1943, he would lose his life in an accident at Camp Polk, Louisiana. His untimely death would occur 8 days before his daughter's birth.

GILBERT NOLTE, of Farmer's Retreat, entered the Army Infantry in January of 1991, but was released after serving for eight months by reason of dependency. He was a Private First Class.

CHESTER PURVIS entered the U.S. Army in January 1941. As a Private, he would serve as a truck driver in the American Theater until November 1943.

CLYDE COMBS, of Dillsboro, enlisted in 1941 and served to late 1945 in the U.S.Army. He would see action in France and Germany.

RAYMOND RUBLE, of Lawrenceburg, entered the Army in February 1941 and would become a Technician 5th Grade as a Mortar Gunner, he would see action in Normandy, France and Central Europe, earning 3 battle stars.

CARL GEHRING, of Lawrenceburg, entered the Army in October of 1940. He would be among the first group of GIs to be shipped to England where he would serve in the Army Postal Service for 4 years.

JOSEPH (PETE) SMALL, of Aurora, entered the military in February of 1941. He would complete Officer's Training School in engineering at Chanule Field in November. He would be assigned to an air field in California as a Squadron Engineer; and serve in the South Pacific, attaining the rank of Captain.

MAURICE MILLER, of Guilford, entered the Army in March 1941 and became a Sergeant in the 176th Engineering Battalion as an auto parts Clerk. He had duty in the Pacific and the Philippine Islands.

IVAN CHAMBERS, of Aurora, entered the military in 1941. He would serve as a Cook with the 740th Ordnance Company in the southern Philippine Islands.

WILLARD FAWCETT, of Lawrenceburg, entered the Army Air Corps in March of 1941. He was appointed a Flying Cadet and sent to an air field in Missouri for training.

RALPH FURTRICK, of Greendale, enlisted in March of 1941 at Ft. Thomas and was assigned to Purdue University for aeronautical engineering training.

JOHN STRYKER, of Lawrenceburg, enlisted in the Army Air Corps in March of 1941. He graduated from Officer's Training School and was commissioned a Second Lieutenant. He would become Executive Officer for the 361st Fighter Group in the ETO. After WWII, he would be recalled for service in Korea and Vietnam. He would retire in 1970 with the rank of Lieutenant Colonel.

RUSSELL STEELE, of Logan, was drafted off his father's farm in northern Dearborn County in March of 1941. He would attend radio operator and radio electrician school at Fort Knox. After which he would attend Officer Candidate School and graduate as a Second Lieutenant. He would go to Europe to duty as Regimental Communication Officer. He remained in that capacity throughout five campaigns in Europe. He would be with the Third Armored Division under the command of General Hodges. This division would land on Omaha Beach on June 20, 1944 and advance across Europe to the Elbe River. Here they would meet the Russians just 50 miles from Berlin. He would receive the Purple Heart and Silver Star and the rank of Captain.

Joe (Pete) Small

Carl Gehring

Russell Steele

Oliver Boehler

Joseph Hartman

Charles Klump

MILLER KEITH enlisted in the Army Air Corps in March 1941 and became a Master Sergeant. He served in the Pacific Theater with a Troop Carrier unit in the Fifth Air Force in the campaigns in New Guinea, Dutch East Indies and the Philippines.

ELMER NEAL, of Dillsboro, joined the Army on April Fool's Day (April 1) of 1941. He would earn a sharpshooter badge at gunnery school at Ft. Myer. He would serve as a Corporal until discharged in May of 1945.

EDWARD BIHR was inducted into the Army in April 1941. He served as a Staff Sergeant in the Cyclone (38th) Division in an anti-tank company. In January 1944, the Division went to the Pacific Theater, serving in New Guinea, Corrigidor, Luzon and other parts of the Philippines which they helped to recapture.

JOSEPH HARTMAN, of Guilford area, was inducted into the U.S. Army in April 1941. He would become a Master Sergeant, earning 4 battle stars for combat in New Guinea and the Philippine Islands. He would serve until November 1945.

FRED ROACHE, of Aurora, entered the military service in April of 1941. He would be promoted to the rank of Major, serving in an Army Armored Unit in France and Germany.

OLIVER R. BOEHLER, of Lawrenceburg, served in the U.S. Army from April, 1941 to 1946. He was a Staff Sergeant in the Ordnance Department. After special training at Aberdeen Proving Ground, Maryland, he was sent to Camp Stoneman, California and thence to the Pacific Theater, where he served in the Philippine Islands.

CHARLES KLUMP, of New Alsace, served from April 16, 1941 to November 5, 1945. He was with the 150th Field Artillery in New Guinea and the Philippine Islands.

FRANCIS (TED) FIORITO, of Aurora, was inducted into the Army in April 1941 and became a Sergeant in the Infantry. In 1943 he would see action in New Guinea.

CHARLES W. FEHLING, of Aurora, enlisted in the Army in April of 1941 and became a Technician Grade 5. He participated in campaigns at Naples, Rome, Rhineland, and Southern France. He received 5 battle stars.

GERALD (TUG) MEYERS, of Aurora, entered the Army in April of 1941, and became a Staff Sergeant. He would serve as a Squad Leader in the 152nd Infantry in New Guinea and the Philippine Islands. He would receive a wound in the battle for Luzon.

EMMETT PARKER, of Lawrenceburg, joined the Army in April 1941 and would become a First Sergeant. He would serve as an Administrative NCO in France, Ardennes and Central Europe, earning 4 battle stars.

LYNDON MOON, of Lawrenceburg, was inducted into the Medical Department of the Army's 38th Division at Fort Knox on April 16, 1941. In January 1942 he would be transferred to the 128th Task Force Quartermasters as an Embalmer. He would be stationed on the islands of Aruba and Trinidad in the Carribean. In August of 1944, he would return to Carlisle Barracks and be discharged in September 1945 as a Staff Sergeant.

DR. PAUL MUELLER, of Lawrenceburg, who had received his medical degree the previous year from St. Louis University, entered the Army Medical Corps on July 2, 1941. He would attend the School of Aviation Medicine at Randolph Field, Texas, and the Command and General Staff School at Ft. Leavenworth. He would serve in Africa and Sicily. He would become a Lieutenant-Colonel and Executive Officer of the Ninth Troop Carrier Command medical section, which carried the wounded by air from the Normandy invasion to hospitals in Great Britain.

STAFFORD SEAVERS enlisted in the U.S.Navy in 1941 and become a Seamen First Class. He was at Manila when the Japanese attacked there, after the Pearl Harbor bombing.

EDMON (EDDIE) TUCKER, of Lawrenceburg, enlisted in the Army Air Corps in November of 1941. He would fly with the 8th Fighter Group over New Guinea and the Philippines, and in the bombing of Japan. He would be discharged in 1946, but stay in the Reserves and be recalled for the Vietnam War. He would retire as a Lt. Colonel in 1970.

Charles Fehling

Lyndon Moon

Irwin Miller

Roger Cormican

ROBERT WESTRICH, of Bright, was inducted into the Army in April 1941. He would serve in Hawaii and then with the 152nd Infantry in the retaking of the Philippine Islands where he would receive a Bronze Star medal.

ROGER CORMICAN entered the military in 1941 and served in the Army's 26th Coastal Artillery. He was stationed at Galveston, Texas, teaching the men in his unit how to fire the large coastal guns as protection against enemy submarines. He would advance to become a First Sergeant.

LEO STENGER, of St. Leon, was among the first young men to leave that community for the service. He entered the Army early in 1941 and became a member of Rifle Company G, 38th Division.

WALTER NEARY, of Lawrenceburg, entered the U.S. Coast Guard in 1941. He would have duty at the following stations and ships: U.S.S. *Wakrobin*, *Wolflake*, *Brooklyn*, U.S.S. *Love*, and then as a Cadet at the Coast Guard Academy in New London.

IRWIN MILLER, of Yorville, enlisted in the army in April of 1941 and was assigned to the Artillery. He would see action in New Guinea and the Philippines.

DR. LESLIE BAKER, of Aurora, in April of 1941, after completing his internship at Ball Memorial Hospital in Muncie, was called to active duty in the Army and was stationed at Carlisle, Pennsylvania. He was an officer in the Army Reserve, holding the rank of First Lieutenant. He would become a member of the 437 Medical Battalion of General George Patton's Third Army in its drive from Normandy across the Ardennes, Belgium, Rhinland and Central Europe. For outstanding service, Dr. Baker would receive the Bronze Star medal and attain the rank of Lieutenant Colonel.

JOHN LIPSCOMB, of Aurora, entered the U.S. Army in June of 1941. He would serve as a cook in a detachment in the Pacific Theater. He held the rating of Technician Grade 5.

DELMAR MANGOLD, of Aurora, entered the U.S. Army in June of 1941 and became a Private First Class with the 108th Quartermaster Bakery Company. As a Truck Driver, he would serve in Italy, France and Central Europe.

LESLIE FOGLE was inducted into the Army in July 1941 in the Infantry. In combat in France, he was reported as missing, then it was learned that he was a prisoner of the Germans.

LEROY SHILTON, of Dillsboro, entered the Navy in August 1941 and served at Corpus Christi and Norfolk Naval Stations. He was in the Navy 6 years.

KENNETH WALSH entered the U.S. Army in September 1941. He became a Military Policeman and a Private First Class, and served with the 165th Infantry in the Pacific Theater of Operation until June 1945.

GLENN ESTER entered the U.S. Army in September of 1941. He would serve with the Army and the Army Air Corps in the ETO. He would receive the Bronze Star medal.

JACK FINNEY served as a Captain in the U.S. Marine Corps, having entered the service in September of 1941. He would serve until March of 1945.

HAROLD MARKLAND, of Bright, was inducted into the Army in October 1941 and became a Private First Class. He would see action in the invasions of Africa, Sicily and Italy. He would be wounded twice and then killed in action in Italy on October 13, 1943. He would be the first from Bright to lose his life in WWII.

EDWARD THEETGE entered the service in October 1941. He would train for 5 months and then take part in the North African invasion. He would be killed in action in the North African Theater in April 1943. He was one of the early casualties from Dearborn County.

DR. MURL FOX, veterinarian of Aurora, had been at Camp Shelby for several months by December 1941. He received a commission as a First Lieutenant in the Army Veterinary Corps. In 1942, he would be placed in charge of the Kingham Packing Plant in Indianapolis. He would make inspection tours across the U.S. while stationed at Ft. Harrison.

RUSSELL CHEEVER, of Dillsboro, won his wings as an Air Cadet in July of 1941 at Kelley Field, Texas. As a new Second Lieutenant, he would report immediately for active duty as an Army Air Corps pilot.

WILLIAM SARTIN, of Lawrenceburg, enlisted in the Navy in July 1941. He would become a Seaman Second Class and was stationed at Naval Operating Base at Norfolk. He would receive a medical discharge after a year's service.

John Lipscomb

Walter Neary

Leslie Baker

Ralph Bentle

Leo (Doc) Seitz

RALPH BENTLE, of Greendale, was called to active Army service on May 12, 1941. He had graduated from Indiana University in 1936, and commissioned a Second Lieutenant with 4 years of ROTC training. He was assigned to the 83rd Quartermaster Company, training at Ft. Lee, Virginia. In April 1942, he would be sent to Hawaii to set up a hospital at Kaneobe. In 1944, he would serve with the Army Mobile Supply Base at Ulithi Atoll in the Pacific. In 1945, his unit would unload the Army Mobile Supply Base at Saipan, which would amount to some 8,000 tons of supplies. He would return to the states on V-J Day, and then retire as a Lieutenant Colonel.

LEO (DOC) SEITZ, JR., of Greendale, in May 1941, passed preliminary examinations for the Army Flying Cadets, at Ft. Hayes, Ohio. He would successfully complet his pilot's training; and, as a First Lieutenant, would become a flying instructor in the Army Air Corps at Lowery Field, Denver.

ARNOLD BRAUER was drafted in May 1941. He was in the 6th Infantry Division which went to Hawaii in 1942 and then moved to New Guinea. His unit would work their way up the coast and be involved in many skirmishes. From there they would go to the Philippine Islands, fighting until war's end in 1945. He would receive the Purple Heart and the Bronze Star.

TAYLOR COMBS enlisted in the Army on May 12, 1941. He was assigned to the 706th Tank Battalion as a Mess Sergeant. He would become a Staff Sergeant and be awarded the Bronze Star medal and 4 battle stars for service in the Philippine Islands and Okinawa.

RAYMOND THAYER, of Aurora, was a 1941 graduate of Purdue. He was commissioned a Second Lieutenant for a having completed the required ROTC course. He trained at Ft. Sill in August of 1941 and became a Captain with the Fifth Division Artillery and served in the ETO for over three years.

LOREN CANFIELD, of Aurora, entered the Army in June 1941 and became a Private First Class. He would serve 27 months in the Aleutian Islands, attached to an engineers group who did nost of the construction in that area.

MILBORN WESTRICH, of Bright, was inducted into the Army Air Corps in July of 1941. He would be stationed in England at an 8th Air Force base. He would become a Staff Sergeant with duties in the post office.

OSCAR PARKER, of Lawrenceburg, entered the Army in July 1941 and would become a Technical Sergeant in an Ordnance Company. He served in the European Theater as well as in the Pacific, earning 3 battle stars.

JAMES HUGHES, of Aurora, entered the Army in July 1941. He would become a Master Sergeant with the 9th Army and would spend 2 years in the European Theater of Operations, receiving the Bronze Star and the Purple Heart with two clusters for being wounded several times in action. He would see action in Ardennes, Rhineland and Central Europe.

ROBERT HASTINGS enlisted in the Navy in 1941. He served aboard the U.S.S. Griggs and saw action in the following Pacific Battles: Marshalls, Eniwetok, Carolines and Okinawa. He was recalled to duty for the Korean Conflict.

Edward Bihr

James Hughes

Kenneth Walsh

Leroy Shilton

Taylor Combs   **Maurice Miller**

Murl Fox   **Arnold Brauer**

The first five men to leave St. Leon for the armed services, with the blessing of their priest, are (l. to r.): Richard Andres, Leo Stenger, Albert Schuman, Edmund Andres, and Paul Andres. Father Adam Ebnet, Pastor of St. Joseph Catholic Church, is standing with these boys.

Clarence Cramer

Loren Canfield

CHAPTER 2

Pearl Harbor Bombed
The U.S. Goes to War

By the late 1920s, Japan faced two major problems: a growing population and a failing economy. Militarists in the government concluded that imperialism would provide the solution to both problems. Through an Army ploy in 1931, Japan seized Manchuria from the Chinese. She then began to nibble at other parts, and in 1937 was in full-scale war with China.

By 1940, the Japanese war lords decided to take advantage of the European situation to take over eastern Asia and the Indies to secure their resources of oil, iron and rubber. This was part of Japan's new "Greater East Asia Co-Prosperity Sphere" whereby she would control this part of the world. The only deterrent was the U.S. bombers at Manila and the fleet at Pearl Harbor.

In early 1941, President Roosevelt continued to condemn Japan for her aggression in China, and gave a loan and a number of aircraft to China. By June, embargoes were placed on all exports to Japan and their assets in the U.S. were frozen. Japan then signed a treaty with Germany and Italy to become the third member of the Axis nations.

In September, Japan held a war council before the Emperor. The plan that emerged included: (1) Prior to a declaration of war, destroy the fleet at Pearl Harbor, (2) Invade territories needed in the Pacific, (3) Establish a defense line from the Kuriles, north of Japan, to the Solomon Islands then south to Java on to the India-Burma border.

In February 1941, Admiral Yamamoto conceived a plan for a surprise attack on Pearl Harbor. He believed that only a quick, destructive blow on the U.S. Navy had any chance of Japan's invading the territories she wanted. On November 25, while diplomatic talks continued in Washington, Prime Minister Togo ordered the striking force to sail from Japan.

(opposite page) The battleship U.S.S. *Arizona*, engulfed in smoke and flames from Jap torpedoes and bombs, sinks during the attack on Pearl Harbor. Hit by several bombs, one in an ammunition magazine, she sank quickly, with the loss of 1,103 crew members, including the captain.

Shortly after dawn on December 7, some 400 planes took off from Japanese carriers. Without a declaration of war, Americans were caught completely by surprise as bombs rained down on their anchored fleet and nearby bases. By the end of two hours, the enemy had sunk 2 battleships, severely damaged 6 more and destroyed over 180 planes on the ground. Our Military forces lost some 2,600 dead and 1,150 wounded.

The next day, December 8, The President asked Congress to recognize that we were officially at war with Japan. Within three days, Germany and Italy also declared war on the U.S.; thus we became engaged in World War II.

Reaction in Dearborn County

News of the Pearl Harbor attack reached Dearborn County by radio about noon on December 7, 1941. Like the rest of the nation, people in Dearborn County were stunned and angry. It was unthinkable that Japan would pull a sneak attack on an American base without a declaration of war. It was a dastardly move that civilized nations wouldn't commit, for even war had its rules. But then it aroused a great sense of patriotism in Americans. Nothing brought our people, all over U.S.A., together in a unified front as this "day of infamy," as President Roosevelt referred to it.

Those who were the first to hear the news locally telephoned others, and radios were kept going far into the night. In Lawrenceburg, special editions of the Cincinnati newspapers appeared on the streets in the early evening and were hawked as "extras" with the latest news from Pearl Harbor, a place most people had never heard of.

Great concern, of course, was shown for Dearborn County people who were possibly in the Hawaiian area. These included people in the following paragraphs.

WILLIAM ANDERSON, of Lawrenceburg, was serving in a Coastal Artillery unit at Fort Shafter on Hawaii. He had enlisted in the Army in June. Before the war's end, he would serve 42 months in the South Pacific.

CARL BORDERS, also of Dearborn County, was serving as a Fireman 2nd Class in the U. S. Navy at Pearl Harbor.

Gene Seitz

Harry Gulley

Denver Gulley (right) with his father (center), a WWI vet., and his brother, Carlyle Gulley

Elmer Cook (left) and Howard McKee

Clarence Fondong

ELMER (PETE) COOK, of Greendale, was serving on the cruiser, U.S.S. *Northhampton* at Pearl Harbor when the Japanese attacked. Afterwards they were ordered to go after the enemy, to no avail. In mid-December, Pete's ship was sunk and he was assigned to the U.S.S. *Iowa* to take part in many battles in the Pacific.

ALEX GARDINER, of Aurora, who at this time was a Pay Clerk, with nearly 20 years of service in the Navy. Later, he would be promoted to officer status and serve in the Pacific.

In addition to these servicemen on Hawaii, there were three civilians, formerly from Dearborn County, in the islands. **EDITH FITCH**, of Lawrenceburg, who taught school in Hawaii; and **HERMAN HUGO** and **MRS. HUGO**, who had a business in Honolulu.

ROBERT DARBO, of RR2 Aurora, who was a Navy veteran, had recently left Pearl Harbor to spend some leave with his mother. He arrived in Aurora on Saturday, December 6; and received orders on Monday, December 8, to return immediately to his ship, the U.S.S. *Sabine*, on the Pacific Coast. Later, he would take part in the Battle of the Coral Sea, and become a Warrant Officer.

Two submariners, both from Aurora, had different experiences on the day Pearl Harbor was bombed. **WALTER HALLFARTH**, was aboard a sub that was berthed at Pearl, but he was unharmed during the bombing. **TOM (TUCK) RICE** was serving aboard the submarine U.S.S. *Skipjack*, which had left Pearl Harbor for Australia. He, of course, was not there for the bombing, but his wife and child were, but they escaped injury. They left Hawaii a few days later for Aurora where they would live with Tom's parents. Tom, an Electrician's Mate First Class, had been in the Navy for 8 years and would make it his career. During WWII, he would see action in the seas of Indo-China, Java, Borneo and many other places. When he retired, he had received a commission and the rank of Lieutenant (j.g.).

DENVER GULLEY, whose ship, the U.S.S. *New Mexico*, would ordinarily be at Pearl Harbor, had just received some repairs in the U.S. and was preparing to get underway on December 7, hence missed the Jap attack. Denver would spend his entire service on the *New Mexico* in the Pacific, taking part in many naval engagements there.

Part of the crew of the U.S.S. *New Mexico* with their mascot, an eagle

CLARENCE FONDONG, of Mt. Pleasant, had just completed his training for the Merchant Marines and was hitch-hiking home when the Pearl Harbor attack occurred. He returned to New York for duty on a tanker. By April, in the Atlantic, the tanker would be hit by torpedoes from a German sub. As the ship began to sink, the Captain gave the order, "Abandon ship." Clarence would be adrift for three days in a lifeboat before being rescued by a U.S. Submarine Chaser. Clarence would serve on two other tankers, which would also be sunk by Nazi subs, but he wasn't deterred from going back to sea. He would attend the Merchant Marine Officer's Training School and become an Assistant Engineer. His last ship would take supplies into Yohohama, Japan.

The very next day after Pearl Harbor, **EUGENE (GENE) SEITZ**, of Lawrenceburg, and his younger brother, **JEROME (JERRY) SEITZ**, of Lawrenceburg, went to the Recruiting Office in Cincinnati to sign up for the Military, as did others all across America. Gene entered the Coast Guard, was sent to Officer's Training to become an Ensign in time to serve in the seas around Guadalcanal where his ship was torpedoed. Rescued, he became a Lieutenant during 14 months in the South Pacific. Jerry Seitz enlisted in the Navy and would serve as a Pharmacist Mate.

Another young man who went to the Recruiting Office and enlisted on the day after Pearl Harbor was **HARRY GULLEY**, of Lawrenceburg. Harry was sent to Fort Benjamin Harrison. He would then go to Cooks and Bakers School. He would become a Cook on the troop trains that traveled across the U.S. He would be promoted to Corporal.

MATTHEW SEAVER, Seaman First Class, who had enlisted in the Navy in February of 1941, was serving on a submarine based at Pearl Harbor on December 7, 1941.

CHARLES FITZPATRICK, Private in the Army, was aboard a ship traveling from San Francisco, taking troops to the Phillipines, when news of the Jap attack was received, the ship returned to California to sail for Hawaii a few days later.

Leslie Boone and wife

George Bennett

Disaster Continues in the Pacific

The Strike at Pearl Harbor was not an isolated attack, but part of a larger plan that saw the conquest of two smaller U.S. bases at Guam and Wake, as well as the beginning of the fall of the Philippines. Within hours of the Pearl Harbor strike, Japanese forces throughout Southeast Asia began six months of conquest that brought them to the gates of India and the seas north of Australia.

The very next day, December 8, 1941, a group of Japanese bomber and fighter planes bombed and strafed the U.S. Army Air Field at Manila. In spite of having received news of the Pearl Harbor debacle, American planes, mostly B-17 bombers, were caught on the ground like sitting ducks and destroyed by the Japanese. Two days later, The Cavite Naval Yard, near Manila, home of the small U.S. Asiatic Fleet, was also destroyed, there being no U.S. air defense. A small group of U.S. cruisers, destroyers and PT boats were able to slip away to friendly bases in the Dutch East Indies.

With both air and naval forces out of action, no supplies or reinforcements could reach the American Army in the Philippines, and they would be forced to surrender by the spring of 1942. Upon orders from President Roosevelt, General MacArthur had escaped from the Philippines by PT boat, submarine and plane to Australia, vowing, "I will return" and retake the islands on his way to conquer Japan.

The Dutch and the British in the Pacific fared no better than the U.S. During the next three months, Hong Kong, Singapore, Java and the East Indies were taken by Japanese forces. Within four months of the Pearl Harbor strike, Japan has achieved many of her pre-war goals.

Naval Warfare Takes a Turn

In early 1942, The U.S. Navy with its few carriers could do no more than some hit-and-run raids at a few Jap bases in the Pacific. Then came the Doolittle-Halsey raid from the carrier, *Hornet*, to bomb Tokyo. This proved to be a morale-booster for Americans, an unexpected concern for the Japanese.

The first ship-to-ship battle took place in the Coral Sea, located between the northeast coast of New Guinea and the Solomon Islands, in May of 1942. The Japanese entered the Coral Sea to invade Port Moresby and the southeastern coast of New Guinea to threaten Australia. In the meantime, Admiral Nimitz sent a 2-carrier task force to spoil Japanese plans. The engagement extended over five days and was the first naval battle in which no ship on either side would be sighted by the other. Although the Japanese sunk more tonnage, the battle was won by the Americans as the Port Moresby invasion force was forced to retreat. The American's greatest loss was the aircraft carrier, U.S.S. *Lexington*.

A second naval offensive was launched by the Japanese in the late May to invade Midway and the Aleutian Islands. Japan planned to install bases in the Aleutians and to draw out and annihilate the U.S. Pacific Fleet before new construction could replace the losses of Pearl Harbor. On June 3, a prong of the Japanese forces struck the Aleutians, with the object of luring Admiral Nimitz into believing that this was the enemy's main force. Nimitz didn't take the bait, and ordered his carriers to search and engage the enemy closer to Midway. The battle, which followed on June 4, was an overwhelming American victory. The Japanese lost their entire modern carrier group and 250 planes. The Japanese Navy had never, in all its history, experienced such a defeat. The results of this battle changed the course of the Pacific war; although the U.S. Navy lost the carrier, *Yorktown*.

Paul Lemm

Phillip Reese

PAUL (WHITEY) LEMM, of Lawrenceburg Junction, had enlisted in the Navy in October of 1941 and trained as a Gunner's Mate. In February of 1942, he sailed for the South Pacific and saw action in the Battle of the Coral Sea. Later after making several voyages to Australia, the Solomons, South America and Cuba and into the Atlantic, Paul would be injured while at sea and be given a medical discharge in November of 1942. After surgery and recovery, he would be drafted into the Army, and see action in France, Belgium and Germany. In 1946, he would enter a third U.S. Armed Service, the Air Force, from which he would retire in 1967 as a Senior Staff Sergeant.

PHILLIP REESE, of Logan, also took part in the Battle of the Coral Sea. He was serving aboard the carrier, *Lexington*, as a Fireman 3rd Class. When the *Lexington* was hit, Phillip was knocked down by the explosion. Most of the

Roy Callon

Arlie Baer

men in his section were killed, but he was unhurt. When the Captain gave the order to abandon ship, Philip gave his life jacket to a shipmate who had none; then jumped into the water without a preserver. Since he was a good swimmer, he made his way to a life raft and about an hour later was rescued by the cruiser, *Minneapolis*. He was cited for bravery in helping the wounded. From the Coral Sea, he was taken to New Caledonia and then San Diego. After a recovery and a leave at home, he was reassigned to duty on a troop transport. Later, he reenlisted and stayed in the Navy until 1951.

The carrier, *Yorktown*, was damaged from a bomb hit during the Battle of the Coral Sea, but returned to Pearl Harbor for repairs which were completed in time for the Battle of Midway. Serving on the *Yorktown* were brothers from Dillsboro, **HAROLD** and **JIM DAVIS** who had enlisted in the Navy together in 1940. Harold's battle station was on an anti-aircraft gun. As the Japanese attacked, Harold's gun-mate was hit and killed. With the planes strafing the decks, Harold continued to keep his gun in action, doing the work of two men, until the ship was hit by torpedoes and began to sink. When the call for evacuation was given, Harold climbed down a rope into the water to be picked up by a life boat. Unknown to him at the time, brother Jim also escaped into the sea and was picked up by a destroyer. Harold was awarded the Silver Star medal for his courage and determination to duty in keeping the gun loaded and firing without help during the sinking of the *Yorktown* at Midway.

ROY CALLON, of Aurora, also fought in the Battle of the Midway. He received a commendation for bravery during the battle when he manned a leaking whaleboat to pickup survivors, keeping the boat afloat by bailing out seawater with his helmet. Roy was a boatswains's Mate 2nd Class.

JOE STERLING, of Aurora, was a Ship's Serviceman 3rd Class who served on the *Yorktown*. He would be reassigned, and by war's end he would have occupational duty in Japan.

Guadalcanal

In July 1942, Allied reconnaissance planes discovered that the Japanese were building an airfield on the island of Guadalcanal in the Solomons. Operations from Guadalcanal would not only threaten Australia but also the important sea lanes between the United States and Australia. Consequently, the Joint Chiefs ordered our first invasion; and on August 7, U.S. Marines landed on the jungle-clad island, to completely surprise the Japanese. Within two days the beachhead and the airstrip were secured. This was the beginning of the first American land offensive in the World War II.

The Guadalcanal campaign would be comprised of seven major naval engagements, ten pitched land battles and innumerable skirmishes in the dense, humid, disease-ridden jungle. It would be one of the most bitterly contested campaigns in American history since the Civil War.

ROBERT SCHWING, of Lawrenceburg, earned the prestigious Silver Star medal during the battles on Guadalcanal. Technical Sergeant Schwing, then a Corporal, crawled 250 yards up a beach, with another soldier, in the line of fire of enemy machine guns to bring back a wounded Sergeant. Because of enemy fire, they had to drag the wounded man on a shelter-half before putting him on a stretcher. Schwing was wounded in his shoulder by a shell fragment. He would fight on the island for some six months.

While carrying supplies and reinforcements to Guadalcanal, the aircraft carrier, U.S.S. *Wasp*, was torpedoed by an enemy submarine. Fire Controlman **ARLIE BAER**, of Moores Hill, was at his battle station and watched the enemy torpedoes slam into his ship. Arlie later said, "I never did a dive or a swim in my life, but on that occasion I did a 111-foot dive into the ocean where my lifejacket kept me afloat". After four hours in the water, a destroyer picked him up. Another crew member was Arlie's Division Officer, Lt. Commander **JOHN WYMOND**, of Aurora, who was a graduate of the U.S. Naval Academy. He was not as fortunate, for he was trapped below deck and, with 180 others went down with the *Wasp*.

KENNETH ZEH, of Aurora, a Sonorman 2nd Class, was on board another ship in the task force with the carrier *Wasp* and saw her go down.

JEROME FUGITT, of Lawrenceburg, was a Gunner's Mate First Class, serving on a battleship which fought in the naval battles at Guadalcanal. Later, Fugitt's ship would be an escort for the first carrier to bomb Tokyo; and later still, this ship would be at the Iwo Jima invasion.

Michael Klump

Marvin Schultz

Robert Schwing

Larry Schuler

CARL MOSLEY, of Moores Hill, was on Guadacanal as a member of the 230th Port Transportation Corps. As a Private First Class, he served as a Truck Driver.

JAMES (JIM) BECKETT, of Greendale, fought in the campaign for Guadalcanal. Later he would serve in the Northern Solomons and in the Philippines. While he was earning four battle stars, he would be wounded on Munda. He was a Technical Sergeant and would receive the Bronze Star medal for meritorious service in combat.

A letter from **SERGEANT WILLIAM GRIZZEL**, of Guilford, "from somewhere on Gaudalcanal," stated that three local boys were on the Island with him: **CLARENCE (RED) TIBBETTS**, of Lawrenceburg, **WALLACE BOYLES**, Technician 4th Grade and Private First Class **DONALD PALMER**, both of Guilford. Grizzel was in charge of two warehouses. Tibbetts was a Staff Sergeant serving as a Mess Sergeant with an Engineering Equipment company. Boyles was a Mechanic and Palmer was a Truck Driver. In addition to these three, he was on a photo with **CHARLES JOHNSTON**, of Lawrenceburg, and Army Sergeant **DALE KNIGGA**, of Dillsboro.

MICHAEL (MIKE) KLUMP, of New Alsace, enlisted in the Army Air Force on January 5, 1942. After basic training his unit was shipped to Sydney, Australia. They went through more training at Ipwich, and then moved up to Guadalcanal. Camping next to Henderson Field, his tent became part of the main target for Japanese bombers. Mike was in the 50th Fighter Control Squadron of the 13th Air Force which operated in the Pacific Theater until war's end.

ROBERT (BOB) CUTTER, of Aurora, was on Guadalcanal with the Sea Bees as a Storekeeper 3rd class. During enemy shelling he shared a foxhole with another sailor and described the experience as, "We were bounced around like ping-pong balls." In 1945, he would complete Officers Training at Notre Dame and be commissioned an Ensign.

The first young man from Dearborn County to die in the Pacific Theater was **LARRY SCHULER**, of Aurora. While serving on Guadalcanal with the 1st Marine Division he was severely wounded in action, and then hospitalized. Another home boy from Aurora, **JOSEPH HURD**, Navy Medical Corps, happened to be serving in that hospital, and had the privilege of being with Larry when death occurred.

Hurd remarked in his letter to Mr. and Mrs. Schuler, "Larry died as a brave and gallant as a boy could." Larry's was the third death of Aurora service-men since the start of the war. He was preceded by **LYTLE SMALL**, in Panama and **EMERY NOCKS** in the Atlantic.

THOMAS (TOM) HENSON, of Lawrenceburg, served as a Private First Class in the 25th Division, Engineering Corps, on Guadalcanal.

FERMAN WILLOUGHBY, served with the First Marine Division. They received the Presidential Citation for landing operations on Tulagi and fighting against the Japanese on Guadalcanal. Ferman was a member of the 14th Construction Battalion.

William Ritzman

WALTER EUGENE NOWLIN, of Bright, participated in the invasion of Guadalcanal with the Marines, and remained there until his unit was relieved. He was then sent to Australia for recuperation.

WILLIAM (BILL) RITZMAN, of Lawrenceburg, was a Staff Sergeant with the 17th Aerial Photo Reconnaissance Squadron of the 13th Air Force. Beginning at Guadalcanal, he would spend three years in the jungles of the South Pacific, fighting up through Solomons and New Guinea to the Philippines. Bill served in the Intelligence Department of his unit. He would inform the pilots about the types of photos needed of enemy installations, so the intelligence people could interpret the photos for planning purposes. Bill would earn seven battle stars for participation in major battles in the South Pacific islands.

Harry Lyness

MARVIN SCHULTZ, of Lawrenceburg, was also a Staff Sergeant who was involved in most of the Pacific campaigns from Guadalcanal to Iwo Jima. He would also serve at Nagasaki with the Army of Occupation of Japan.

HARRY C. (PETE) LYNESS, of Bright, served with the U.S. Navy at Guadalcanal in 1942-1943. He would become a Chief Petty Officer and later have duty in the Aleutians.

GLENN SORTWELL, served with the Marines in the Solomons, following a tour of duty in Iceland. He was a Corporal.

Nicholas Wittrock

EUGENE SEITZ, Ensign in the Coast Guard and from Lawrenceburg, had his ship sunk by the Japanese in the waters off Guadalcanal.

CLARENCE TIMBERLAKE, of Dearborn County, was a Marine Staff Sergeant who took part in the combat on Guadalcanal.

JOHN TRICHTER, Marine Private First Class, was in the initial engagement on Guadalcanal.

NICHOLAS WITTROCK, of Lawrenceburg, was a Rifleman with the Marines fighting on Guadalcanal.

ROBERT BOYLES, of Guilford, fought at Guadalcanal as a Tank Mechanic with an Army Engineering unit.

JOHN FUGITT, of Aurora, was a Private First Class with the first Marines to land on Guadalcanal.

WILLIAM JUSTIN, of Moores Hill, served with an Army Tank Battalion fighting on Guadalcanal. He would also see action on Bougainville.

CHARLES WHITAKER, of Lawrenceburg, was a corporal with an Army Infantry unit which fought at Guadalcanal. Later he would be part of the Americal Division in combat at Bougainville.

MELVIN CRAIG, of Lawrenceburg, enlisted in the Navy in 1942. He was a Fireman First Class in action at Guadalcanal. He was wounded at New Georgia and returned to the hospital at Great Lakes.

EDWIN METZ, of West Harrison, was a Private in the Marines serving on Guadalcanal and other sites in the Pacific Theater.

The China-Burma-India Theater

Back on the continent of Asia in early 1942, the Japanese pushed into Burma and beat back the British, Chinese and a small force of Americans. General Stillwell led a core group of Chinese and Americans through the mountains and jungles to emerge in Eastern India.

Jerry Seitz

In April, the Japanese had cut the Burma Road which was the Allies' overland supply route to China. To allow for the construction of another road; to stop the Japanese in Burma; and to continue to supply China, U.S. forces quickly established bases in India. The President felt it was important to continue the U.S. supplies to China, because their armies were holding down a million Japanese invaders within the mainland. So one of the most spectacular outfits of the war began in India, flying supplies over the Himalaya Mountains, or "the Hump," as the U.S. pilots called those mountains, some of which reached over 20,000 feet high. Nor were they the only obstacles, for Japanese fighter planes patrolled from bases in Burma. By August of 1944, General Merrill's Marauders recaptured northern Burma to shorten flights to China. In the meantime, the CBI was a blood-guts-jungle struggle that insured victory in the Far East.

Roger Taylor

WALTER FULTON, of Lawrenceburg, one of five boys from the same family who served in WWII, was a Corporal in the Army Air Force. He served with the 166th Liaison Squadron of the 1st Air Commando Group in the China-Burma-India Theater.

ROGER TAYLOR, formerly a Dearborn County school teacher, joined the fourth Ferrying Group Army Force at Memphis where he was in Officer's Candidate School. Graduating as a pilot and Second Lieutenant, he was assigned to the Air Transport Command in the CBI. He would fly 83 trips over the Hump, receiving the Air Medal and Distinguished Flying Cross, and become a Captain.

HARLEY HOLLAND, of Wright's Corner, enlisted in January of 1942 in the Army Air Corps. He was selected for flight training and graduated to receive his wings and Second Lieutenant's bars. He was sent to the CBI to fly B-24 bombers with cargo over the Hump, many times on instruments. Also he was one of the first flyers in the CBI to refuel in the air. Harley would retire as a Major in 1974.

Harley Holland and son David

WILLIAM AUST, of Yorkville, was an Army Corporal who served as a cargo checker in the CBI Theater.

EARLE BLACKBURN, of Lawrenceburg, was a Staff Sergeant, serving as a Air Operations Specialist in the CBI.

ELMER BENNING, of Moores Hill, graduated from Officer's Training School at Carlyle Barracks and was commissioned a Second Lieutenant. He served in North Africa

Mervin Brandt

Roy Neary

and the CBI with the First Air Command which received a Presidential Citation for excellent performance of assignments. He became a First Lieutenant and served with a Medical Detachment at Louisville at war's end.

MERVIN BRANDT, of Guilford, served as an Airplane Electrician with the Air Force in the CBI, earning 2 battle stars and the Distinguished Unit Badge. He was a Sergeant with 28 months on station in India.

GEORGE BENNETT was an Army Private First Class in the CBI Theater. In 1945, he would be killed in action.

MARVIN BRIGGS was a Technical Sergeant who served with a Supply Unit in the CBI. He helped his Unit win a Distinguished Unit Citation.

JONAS SLAYBACK, of Moores Hill, was a Staff Sergeant who served as a Gunner on a bomber based in India. He received the Air Medal when his plane shot down 3 Jap fighter planes.

HOWARD MOELLER, of Dillsboro, was an Army Staff Sergeant who served as a Supply NCO in the CBI Theater.

HARRY COTTINGHAM, of Moores Hill, enlisted in the U.S. Army and was sent to the CBI Theater. His unit helped to build Burma Road, bridges and air strips.

FREDERICK SPRONK, of Lawrenceburg, served as a Special Vehicle Operator in the CBI. He received 2 battle stars and Distinguished Unit Badge as a Private First Class.

ROY NEARY was the first Lawrenceburg man to lose his life in World War II. He entered the Army in 1941 and shortly thereafter transferred to the Army Air Corps. In July of 1942, he received his wings and was commissioned a Second Lieutenant at Lubbock Field, Texas. After spending the next several months of duty at Colorado Springs, he was sent to the CBI Theater as a P-38 fighter pilot in 1942. On March 31, 1943, he was killed in action over India and his remains were returned to the States, but with no other details from the War Department on the casualty. Since Roy was an outstanding athlete at Lawrenceburg High School, as well as at Xavier University, the new athletic field at Lawrenceburg High was named in his honor.

GLENN SHANKS, of Lawrenceburg, entered the Army in September of 1943. He was in the Field Artillery and served in the CBI where he instructed Chinese soldiers in the operation of artillery.

EARL SOMMER, of Dillsboro, served in the U.S. Army Air Corps in the Air Transport Command in the CBI as a Supply Sergeant.

VIRGIL HELLER, of Moores Hill, was a Staff Sergeant, serving as an airplane Instrument Mechanic in the China Offensive from the CBI, earning 2 battle stars.

HOWARD MUELLER, of Dillsboro, served as an Army Staff Sergeant in the China-Burma-India Theater.

EUGENE EVERETT entered the Army Air Force in 1942 and served as a Sergeant with the 760 Base Unit. He was then shipped to the CBI for duty as a Radio Operator.

JAMES BROOKS, of Aurora, was a Special Vehicle Operator in the Army. He served in the CBI, earning 3 battle stars.

JAMES DEATON, of Aurora, served in Burma and India. He was a Technical Sergeant and served as an Automotive Mechanic, earning 2 battle stars.

EDWARD BALES, of Dillsboro, was a Sergeant in the 12th Air Cargo Resupply Squadron. He served as a Truck Driver in the CBI.

ROY HINSON, of Bright, was a Sergeant in the Army Air Corps. He served with the 373rd Bomber Squadron in the CBI.

THEODORE ROBERTS, of the Sunman area, was a Private First Class in the Army. He served with the 743rd Railroad Operating Battalion in 1942. He was a Signal Operator in the CBI.

Wallace Boyles

Meanwhile in the Atlantic

While Americans battled in the South Pacific and Asia during this period, the Atlantic was anything but calm and peaceful. German submarines, or U-boats, had been active before our entry into World War II. Now that Germany had declared war on the U.S., the U-boats promptly attacked shipping along America's Atlantic Coast. With an antisubmarine fleet of only 3 subchasers, 2 patrol craft and 20 Eagle boats left over from WWI, the Nazis had a field day along our Atlantic Coast in 1942. Some sinkings were so close, they could be seen from the beaches.

The number of Allied, American and Neutral merchant vessels sunk by U-boats in the North Atlantic was also increasing. As yet, the Allies had not constructed the new destroyer escort vessels nor perfected antisubmarine warfare methods. In March of 1942, 86 ships, mostly tankers and merchantmen, were sunk in the Atlantic by German U-boats.

Naval gun crews were put on U.S. merchant vessels and better tactics were developed by convoys sailing across the Atlantic, but still the U-boats continued to be a menace. By the latter half of 1942, however, more effective countermeasures were adopted by the Allies and convoy travel became safer.

CLARENCE JAMESON, of Aurora, entered the Navy in January of 1942. He would have duty in the Atlantic and before long would be reported missing in action. **JACK HUNTER**, also of Aurora, was serving in the same ship with his friend, Jameson, and was reported missing at the same time.

CARL ROSS, of Aurora, a Merchant Marine sailor, was reported missing action in the summer of 1943, during his first voyage in the Atlantic. He had enlisted in the Merchant Marines on Christmas Day in 1942. Carl was a brother of Keith Ross, the first American casualty in WWI. Carl was widely known in Dearborn County for his athletic ability and refereeing of high school basketball games. He was 29 and left a young wife and infant daughter.

JOHN (BUSTER) EDRINGTON, of Aurora, enlisted in the Navy when he was 16, in September of 1941. He would be assigned to duty as a member of an armed guard crew aboard the merchantman, *West Chesswald,* in a convoy crossing the North Atlantic where mountainous seas and bone-chilling weather

John Edrington

were encountered as well as enemy attacks. The convoy, carrying materials and food desperately needed by the Russians in their stand against the Nazis, made their way around the northernmost part of Norway to northern Russia on the Murmansk Run. They underwent every type of air, surface and submarine attacks by the Germans. Five of the seventy-two ships were sunk, but the *Chesswald* made port safely. On the return voyage, Edrington's ship was not so fortunate. It was torpedoed and sunk by a German sub. John was thrown overboard into the sub-freezing water where he floated for some fifteen minutes before being rescued by a British trawler. Recovering from frozen hands and feet, he would make additional convoy runs, and receive a commendation for bravery under fire to drive off enemy planes from the convoy. Eventually John was transferred to the Pacific Fleet for the invasion of Okinawa as a crew member of the *Riverside*. In this action, he received three wounds to receive the Purple Heart. He would continue to serve in the Navy until 1961. Still, later in 1992, he and other crew members were awarded medals from Russia for their service to that nation during WWII, in a ceremony at Baltimore performed by the Russian Ambassador.

Lytle Small

Aurora's first casualty of World War II was **CAPTAIN LYTLE SMALL**, Army Air Corps, when his plane crashed in Panama on June 5, 1942. Words of praise of Captain Small's courage, daring and excellent service from his superior officers were received by his family. After graduating from Aurora High School in 1937, he received a scholarship to Purdue where he studied three years. He enlisted in the Army Air Corps and won his wings at Randolph Field, Texas. He was assigned duty in the Canal Zone and then in Ecuador for two months before returning to Panama. A military funeral service was held in Panama with his fellow-officers officiating.

EMERY LEE NOCKS, of Aurora, joined the Navy in June of 1940. He attended Submarine School at New London and upon graduation was assigned to the submarine, *Bass*, earning the rating of Torpedoman First Class. During a training exercise off the coast of Costa Rica in August 1942, the ship caught fire and Emery with thirty-some other sailors lost their lives. Emery was the third casualty in Dearborn County since the U.S. entry into the conflict; and the first listed as "killed in action." When the Aurora V.F.W. Post was established later, the organization was named in his honor.

Emery Nocks

Harry Cottingham

CLYDE SOMSER, of near-Logan, a Gun Pointer First Class, was reported missing, then officially declared dead following action in the North Atlantic in October of 1942. This was according to a communique from the Secretary of the Navy, Frank Knox. He enlisted in the Navy in December of 1941.

LESLIE BOONE, of Georgetown Ridge, enlisted in the Navy in 1942 and was assigned to duty on PT boats, then a destroyer and then a minelayer. He was a Radioman 3rd Class, on convoy duty in the Atlantic.

A View of the War by an Underaged Dearborn County Boy

The following was written by **JOHN R. HOLLAND** describing his feelings and actual events after contemplating a war involving his country, a war in which he wanted to be engaged. Actually, he was Dearborn County's youngest man to enter the military in WWII:

"Damn it was rough with a war going on and me being too young to go! Would I ever get a chance to do my part defending our country and protecting the people I love?

"My favorite cousin had enlisted in the Marines a week or two before Pearl Harbor. Other guys I knew had been drafted or had enlisted prior to and immediately after the attack. And here I was, a fourteen year old boy, big enough to do a man's job, wanting to do a real man's job, but held back by only a calendar.

"We were living on Possum Ridge and I was a Freshman at Aurora High School. The time between Pearl Harbor and Christmas break had been an absolute hell for me. I was totally consumed by world events. God, how I cried when Wake Island fell!

"By the 5th of January 1942, the first day of school after break, I had become determined to go, by hook or crook! That morning I was feeding calves from buckets. One of them refused to drink and I lost my temper with it and tried to kill it. Thinking I had, I used that as a trumped-up excuse to leave. As I went out the back door of the barn, my younger brother, Bob, said, "Boo where are you going?" I knew but I wasn't saying. I was going to join the Marines!

"Getting to Cincinnati on that cold, snowy day, being led from Fountain Square to the Marine Recruiting Office by a cop on the beat, and the lies I told are another story in themselves. The fact that I was still wearing my chore clothes (two pairs of pants, each covering the holes in the other, clod hopper boots still covered with manure, and an old jacket) sure didn't help my chances. Actually, I still believe the cop just wanted me off his beat.

"I told the recruiters that I was seventeen years old, and that I would be eighteen on March 1st, thus changing my birth year from 1927 to 1924. After getting a preliminary physical and some kind of mental test, I was given a bunch of papers and told that since I was only seventeen, I would need my parents' signatures. Get those and I would be on my way.

"I rode a bus from Fountain Square to Saylor Park for a nickel and walked through Addyston, North Bend and Cleves to Grandma Loomis' house in Hooven. It was zero degrees or below. I was really worn out, cold and hungry when I got there.

"My older brother, Harley, was there. He had been looking for me all day, but never thought I would reach Cincinnati. (He had already joined the Air Corps, and had to wait until February to go to Flight School.) Harley told me that Mom and Dad had decided that if I wanted to go, they would let me try. With that in mind, I went back to Possum Ridge to tell them goodbye.

John Holland

"On the morning of January 7, 1942, I reported back to the Recruiting Office, and with no further ado, I was sworn into the United States Marine Corps at fourteen years, ten months and seven days of age! Could I continue the bluff? Would I be dishonorably discharged? I had only one choice—keep going. Damn I was proud! Damn I was scared!

"I finished Boot Camp in March. Then I saw my first action during the mop-up stages of Guadalcanal, patrols to the interior of the island and air raids. Our first beachhead came at Bougainville, where our platoon was in the first wave. However, where we went ashore, there was no resistance, only machine gun fire from the Japanese positions a couple hundred yards away, and one lone enemy plane strafing our area.

"Moving off the beach, we hit knee and thigh deep swamp, and there we stayed for the next month or two. There we met the Japs in mortal combat, and, I believe, I held my own until malaria and Denge Fever placed their toll on me.

"I returned to the U.S. shortly after my seventeenth birthday, and spent the rest of the war recuperating in Naval Hospitals and rest camps. I was honorably discharged in May of 1945, and sent home with an 80% disability".

On December 7, 1941, Japanese carrier bombers struck American military air fields as well as the naval ships at Pearl Harbor. Two of the air bases bombed were at Ford Island and Kaneoke Bay. This action prevented American aircraft from pursuing the enemy planes and carriers.

The most famous of all WWII recruiting posters.

CHAPTER 3

U.S. Expands Military To Fight Global War

The year of 1942, especially the first part, was a bleak time for the Allies. The Germans were on the offensive in the Soviet Union and in North Africa. In the Atlantic, Nazi submarines were having a field day as pointed out in Chapter Two. In the Pacific, Japan continued her march of conquest.

In America, it was a busy time for building up the military forces to meet the demands of global warfare, but no longer was there much of an isolationist attitude. Pearl Harbor had brought all Americans together in the greatest effort of unity the nation had ever experienced. But the fact was that at this point, the U.S. was incapable of defending itself. And so the first priority was the converting of civilians into warriors as America accelerated her calls to arms and hurriedly trained her civilians as fighting forces on land, sea and air.

The general attitude was right for the occasion and everyone seemed ready to support the military. Army and Navy recruiting stations were deluged. Lyndon Johnson and Gerald Ford joined up. So did Joe Dimaggio and Gene Autry. Volunteers and draftees, including movie stars, farm kids, professors and students, Congressmen and factory employees were joining up all across the country. They went despite long absences from family, living a strange life in alien places and with an overwhelming feeling of loneliness. As one Dearborn County Soldier wrote to his parents, "and home to me now is pure heaven!"

The uniforms issued to the new soldiers were known as "government issue" and in no time at all, so were the men who

Richard Schulz

T. Ray Geisert

Elbert Bentle

wore them. They took on the label "G-I". In training camps, the recruits gave up their civilian identity for a serial number and a new kind of life, filled with marching, calisthenics, short hair-cuts, kitchen police (KP) duty, and barracks life. In the field, they learned to dodge bullets, to hug the ground and dig foxholes. Extensive maneuvers and simulated battles brought them to become a modern fighting force. In less than two years, our Army would grow from 300,000 men to 1.5 million men.

As the immense system for training civilians into military men and women, units completed training and began to head for the Pacific and England. Australia became the base for Americans and other Allied forces in the Pacific for further training and a jumping-off site for the first offensives in this region. Toward Europe, American forces were gathering in Iceland and the British Isles. Many of these troops would go into battle later in the year when the North Africa campaign got underway.

The year 1942 saw many young men from Dearborn County begin and carry on new lives in new and never-before-heard-of places. Many would leave the county and the nation in 1942, most to enter combat and some never to return alive.

RAY GEISERT, State Representative for Dearborn and Ohio counties (1940 -1945), received orders to report to active duty with the Army from reserve status on March 19, 1942. Ray was a veteran of WWI, having served with the Field Artillery in France, participating in the battles of Chateau Thierry and the Meuse-Argonne. In 1923, he was commissioned a Second Lieutenant in the Army Reserve Corps and took training each summer, advancing in rank to Major. After reporting for active duty, he was assigned to the Quartermaster Corps, and stationed at Fort Mason, California. In 1943-1944, he would be in charge of some replacement troops shipping out from the States to the South Pacific. Following his last voyage, he was hospitalized with pneumonia and an unknown fever, possibly contacted in the islands of the South pacific. Unfortunately, Ray would not recover and would die in a San Francisco hospital on March 14, 1944.

The second Dearborn County casualty in the armed forces of WWII, came early in August of 1942 when **PRIVATE FLOYD SHUMAN** was killed in a crash landing of an Army bomber at Columbia, South Carolina. Floyd was a Radio Operator-Mechanic assigned to that bomber crew. He had been in the Army for seven months when the accident occurred. He was buried with military honors in the Oakdale Cemetery at Dillsboro.

JAMES MOOREHEAD entered the Army in February of 1942. He would serve as a Radio Operator with the 462nd Base Unit at Drew Field, Florida. He would become a Sergeant.

LEE SIZEMORE, of Guilford, entered the U.S. Army in April of 1942. He would become a Gunner and serve in the Italian campaign.

CARL EVERETT, of Greendale, entered the U.S. Navy in 1942 and would become a Radio Technician 3rd Class.

ROY EMERY, of Aurora, entered the U.S. Army in October of 1942 and would serve in the American Theater as a Private.

HUBERT EMERY, of Aurora, was a Staff Sergeant in the U.S. Army Air Corps. He would serve as an Airplane Mechanic in 1942.

ALFRED (SQUIRE) ENNIS, of Guilford, was drafted into the Army in 1942. He would serve as a Truck Driver in France and Czechoslovakia, while earning 4 battle stars.

ERNEST HENSON, of Lawrenceburg, originally enlisted in the Army in 1938 and had duty in Panama from 1939-1941. In January of 1942, he reenlisted and in August received a commission as a Second Lieutenant. He then was assigned as Assistant Adjutant to the Signal Corps School at Camp Crowder, Missouri.

HAROLD MYER entered the U.S. Army as a Private in 1942 and took his training at Camp Swift, Texas.

WILLIAM EWBANK, of Lawrenceburg, received a Second Lieutenant's commission upon graduation from Indiana University in 1935. After a tour of duty with the 11th

Otto Boehler

Elzie Cash

Richard Ewan

Paul Sartin

Infantry at Fort Harrison, he entered business, but was called back to active duty in October of 1942. He was assigned duty with an Air Corps Base Unit in England until February 1944 when he volunteered to rejoin his original outfit who were fighting in Europe. He felt he was needed in a combat role "rather than" in a passive one of ground support for the Air Corps. As a First Lieutenant, he would be involved in the hedgerow fighting in Normandy. In July of 1944, he was killed by sniper fire in France. He was awarded the Bronze Star medal posthumously, and was buried in Arlington Cemetery at Washington, D.C.

GERALD EWBANK, brother of William, enlisted in the Navy in 1942 and would become a Lieutenant. He would participate in the battle of Palau, Philippines and the Invasion of Okinawa, serving in the Communication Department of the aircraft carrier, U.S.S. *Sitkoh Bay*. At Okinawa, his carrier would be attacked by a Japanese suicide plane which was shot down less than 100 yards from the ship.

RICHARD (DICK) EWAN, with a reserve commission in the Infantry, was called to active duty in 1942. He was assigned to the 76th Division, and later was promoted to Captain. His outfit was shipped to England and the fighting in Europe in 1944. With Patton's 3rd Army, they crossed the Rhine into Germany and were halted to avoid the Russians. As the war ended, Dick was appointed an officer in the Allies provisional government and served in Berlin when discharged.

LEE FRIEBERGER, of Lawrenceburg, enlisted in the U.S. Army in 1942, and was assigned to the Signal Corps.

CHARLES FOWLER, of Lawrenceburg, entered the Coastal Artillery in December of 1942. He would become a Cook's Helper and serve as a Private First Class.

RALPH FOLZENLOGEN entered the Marine Corps and became a Corporal in 1942, taking Glider training at Parris Island.

WILLIAM FOWLER was in the Coast Guard in 1942 and would become a Chief Quartermaster. He had been in the service prior to Pearl Harbor.

George (Pat) Harmon, wife and daughter

Gerald Ewbank and the carrier, U.S.S. *Sitkoh Bay*

James McManaman

George H. Fox

JAMES McMANAMAN, of Lawrenceburg, enlisted in the Army in July 1942. He was first stationed at the Legal Office, Second Air Force Base at Langley Field. He would then be transferred to the Counter Intelligence Corps Detachment, Tenth Army. He would serve in Hawaii, the Philippines and Okinawa where he would take the safe with the currency ashore. He would become a Technical Sergeant and serve until 1946.

RAYMOND TURNER, of Lawrenceburg, enlisted in the Army Air Force in January 1942, and was stationed at Keesler Field, Mississippi, as a Private.

JOHN NORRIS, of Lawrenceburg, entered the Army in February 1942. He was a Finance Officer in Panama. Later he became a Captain and assigned duty in Washington in the Army Postal Service.

EDGAR A. HASTINGS, of Moores Hill, enlisted in the Army Air Corps in December 1941. After basic training, he would attend radio and gunnery school, and be assigned to a combat crew as a top turret gunner on a B-24. In June 1942, he was transferred to St. Jean, Palestine. From St. Jean his crew flew combat missions curtailing supplies to General Rommel's North Africa Campaign. After about thirty missions he would return to the United States to train combat crews. He would be selected for Pilot Cadet Training at Santa Ana, California, and after completion in January 1944, would be assigned to B-17s at Kingman, Arizona. He would be called to active duty during the Korean Conflict, and continue his military career until 1970, retiring as a Lieutenant Colonel.

PARKER MILES, of Lawrenceburg, was a Ships Cook 2nd Class on a Naval Base of the Atlantic Fleet in 1941.

HARRY GILLMAN entered the Army in April 1942. He served as a Private with an Engineering Unit at Camp Sutton, North Carolina.

GEORGE HARMON, of Lawrenceburg, was an Army Military Policeman at the Army Air Force Base at Douglas, Arizona in 1942.

BERNARD FOX, of Lawrenceburg, was one of three brothers who would serve in the Army during WWII. In 1942, he was training at Leesville, Virginia.

NORVIN GRIEVE was serving in the Air Corps at Kelly Field in 1942. He would make the rank of Lieutenant and be killed in a plane crash.

JEREMY RYLE, of Aurora, was an Army Technician 5th Grade, in July 1942, with 147th Engineer Maintenance Company. He would serve as a Truck Driver in both Europe and the Pacific.

JULIUS McCOOL, of Lawrenceburg, was a Chief Boilermaker in the Navy. He had duty in Iceland in 1942 and later at the Navy Yard in Washington.

Clayton Stevens

LEO F. McCOOL entered the military in July 1942. He became a Corporal and was in the invasions of Africa and Sicily, and ended the war in the Pacific with occupational duty in Japan.

LUTHER SCHULTZ, of Moores Hill, entered the Army in February 1942. He became a Technical Sergeant, qualified as a Sharpshooter and served in the Pacific.

RALPH SHILLING, of Moores Hill, entered the Army in September 1942. As a Private First Class he would serve with the 807th Military Police in Trinidad and British West Indies.

Chester Bielby

CHESTER BIELBY, of Lawrenceburg, enlisted in the Army in July 1942. He was stationed at Langley Field in the Base Legal Office, and then was transferred to the Counter Intelligence Corps. He would serve in Australia and New Guinea, and attend Judge Advocate School at the University of Michigan.

ROBERT MATTOX entered the Army Air Force as a member of a ground crew. His unit was sent to Alaska in 1942.

ROBERT MOOREHEAD was a Corporal who received a medical discharge in 1942 after serving in the U.S. Army for 17 months.

Ralph Shilling

Oakey Draut

MARTIN HUBER, of Lawrenceburg, was a Private First Class after enlisting in the Army on December 7, 1942. He would serve as a Truck Driver in the Italian Campaign.

CARL JACOBS, of Guilford, entered the service in April 1942 with the 574th Air Service Group. He would serve as a Supply Clerk in the ETO.

MARTIN KLINKERMAN was in the U.S. Army stationed at Camp Carrabelle, Texas in 1942.

OTTO T. BOEHLER, JR. served from 1942 to 1946 in the U.S. Navy. As a Seaman First Class, he taught radar at the Navy School at Norman, Oklahoma.

EARL JACQUES, of Sawdon Ridge, served in the U.S. Army from June of 1942 to October 1945. He would become a Cook and see action in North Africa and Italy.

JOHN STANDRIFF entered the U.S. Army and was training at Camp Forrest in July of 1942.

PAUL SUTTON was in the Army Engineer Corps at Camp Shelby, Mississippi in 1942.

LINDSEY ROSSEN, of Lawrenceburg, was in the Army Infantry Band at Camp Forrest in 1942.

MAX KARR was a Corporal in the Motor Transportation Service of the Marines Corps in 1942.

LEO KANE was a First Sergeant in the Army Air Corps in 1942. He served with a ground crew.

BENJAMIN LUKE, of Dillsboro area, entered the service in August 1942. He was with a Quartermaster Company at Camp Gordon, Florida.

ALBERT HUBER was a Private First Class in the Marines. He was in training at Parris Island in 1942.

ROBERT GARDEWING, of Greendale, entered the Army Air Force in October 1942 and became a Technical Sergeant. He would serve as Engineer-Gunner on a B-24

Robert Gardewing (bottom right photo), part of his crew and bomber.

with the 14th Air Force based in China. They would fly against targets in the South China Sea, Formosa and Hong Kong, as well as doing low altitude mine-laying on the harbors of Shanghai and Hong Kong. Bob would also serve in the Korean Conflict.

JOHN GREGORY was a Seaman 2nd Class serving as an armed guard aboard a Merchant Ship. In October of 1942, when 16 vessels were lost in a convoy in the North Atlantic, he was serving on one of the ships which were sunk, and he was presumed dead.

CHESTER (PIE) GUARD, former Deputy Sheriff of Dearborn County, in 1942 was assigned to the 269th Military Police Company of the Advanced Sector Communication Force. Later they would see action in Belgium.

LLOYD D. MILLER, of Aurora, entered the Army in July 1942. He joined the 318th Infantry of the 80th Division and became a Technical Sergeant. As a Rifleman, he would see combat in France, the Ardennes and Central Europe. He would be wounded in action in 1944.

LESTER KIEFFER, of Greendale, was in the Army training at Camp Luna, New Mexico in 1942. He would be in the 58th Ferrying Squadron based in Maine and later be based in Iceland for two years.

LEO KELLNER, of Aurora, was in the band of the 10th Armored Division in 1942.

JAMES LONG was inducted into the U.S. Army in 1942. He was sent to Harrisburg, Pennsylvania for basic training.

LAWSON GRAY entered the Marine Corps in 1942. He took his basic training at the Marine Base in Oceanside, California.

RALPH CHAMBERS, a former music teacher in the Greendale School, was assigned to Army Officer Candidate School in South Carolina in 1942.

ALEX COLDWELL, of Moores Hill, was in training at St. Petersburg, Florida in 1942.

HARRY LANGON served in the Marines during WWI. He became a Private First Class in the Army in 1942.

CARL GUERMELY was a radio operator in the Second Infantry, serving overseas in 1942.

COLONEL NEAL entered the U.S. Army in April 1942. He would serve with the 963rd Field Artillery as a Private First Class.

CHARLES GROSGIA was a Private in the U.S. Army at Fort Riley, Kansas in 1942.

THOMAS GROSS, of Lawrenceburg, enlisted in the Army Air Force in 1942.

JOE TANDY entered the U.S. Navy in August 1942 and would become a Boatsman's Mate 2nd Class. He would serve on the ships: U.S.S. *Portabogo* and U.S.S. *Argonne*, earning 2 battle stars.

WILLIAM TELKER, of St. Leon, entered the Army in April 1942. He became a Mess Sergeant and a member of the 806th Tank Destroyer Battalion. He would serve in both the American and Pacific Theaters and became a Staff Sergeant.

VICTOR STENGER, of Guilford, entered the Army in March 1942. He became a Private First Class and a member

Robert Ryle

of the 174th Infantry Regiment. He would see combat in the Rhineland and Central Europe.

ALVIN DAVIS, of Guilford, served with an Army Engineering Unit in Iceland in August 1942.

HARRISON TODD, of Lawrenceburg, entered the Army in February of 1941 with the 3536th Quartermaster Training Company. He would serve as a Mechanic in New Guinea.

OMER MATTHEWS, of Aurora entered the Army in February 1942 and would become a Technician 5th Grade. He would serve in New Guinea and the Philippines as a Truck Driver.

THEODORE WATERS was a Surgical Technician in the Army, having been inducted in April 1942. He would become a Technician 3rd Grade and be discharged from Hoff General Hospital at Santa Barbara.

LEONARD SEDLER, of Lawrenceburg, a graduate of Marquette University, also graduated from Reserve Officers Training at the Naval Academy to become an Ensign in 1942. He would serve on a destroyer as the Engineering Officer.

WADE DOCTOR, of Aurora, was in the Field Artillery training at Fort Knox in 1942.

DONALD WHITE, of Aurora, entered the Army in February 1942. He served as an Upholsterer with the 328th Ordnance Company in France and the Rhineland.

RONALD WHITE, of Aurora, was a Technician 5th Grade with the 328th Ordnance Heavy Automotive Maintenance Company. He would serve in Normandy, France and the Rhineland with 3 battle stars, having entered the Army in February 1942.

ELZIE WOLKER, of Aurora, entered the Military in July 1942 and became a Private First Class. He served as a Medical Laboratory Technician in the ETO.

Paul Tittel

Lee Sizemore

ROSCOE CUMMINS, of Aurora, entered the Military in February 1942. He was a Private First Class in the 262nd Infantry, serving as a Mortarman in Sicily, Italy, Ardennes and Central Europe.

CARL WILLIAM, of Lawrenceburg, entered the Army in February 1942. He was a Private with 462nd Army Air Force Base Unit. He served as an Automotive Equipment Operator in the American Theater.

JOHN YAUGER was an Army Corporal. He served as a Truck Driver in the Pacific Theater, entering the Army in August 1942.

GEORGE WESTRICH, of Bright, was drafted into the Army in August 1942. He would serve in New Guinea, helping to build air fields. From there he would go with troops, island-hopping to the Philippines, building air strips on Leyte, Mindoro and Luzon. On Mindoro, a Jap suicide plane would land on their field, piloted by a girl. He then would go to Okinawa and Japan as a Sergeant.

BOB WELLS was in the Merchant Marines in 1942.

KENNETH WELLS, of Lawrenceburg, graduated from Officer's Candidate School as a Second Lieutenant in 1942. He was promoted to First Lieutenant at an Army Camp in Texas in 1945.

Dale Schoeff

DALE SCHOEFF enlisted in the Army in October 1942. He took Officer's Training School at Camp Davis and received a commission. He served in the Pacific Theater in New Guinea, Wakde, the Philippines and Zamboanga. He was discharged with the rank of First Lieutenant in 1945.

FRANK DOWNEY, of Aurora, was a Captain with the 40th Armored Regiment in 1942 and was soon stationed in England.

CLAYTON STEVENS, of Moores Hill, was inducted in October 1942 into the U.S. Army. In June 1944, he would enter combat in France by relieving the 101st Airborne Division. He would be wounded on July 16, 1944 in the hedgerows near St. Lo. He was hospitalized in England and the States. In 1945, he would return to duty guarding German prisoners.

RUSSELL WHITE entered the Army Air Force in November 1942. He would serve in the Pacific Theater in the Air Offensive against Japan and would receive 2 battle stars.

ALBERT AND JACOB BIHR, of the Sunman area, entered the service in 1942. Jacob was a Private First Class in the Army serving in Normandy and Central Europe. Albert was in the field Artillery as a Truck Driver. He served in the Italian Campaign.

GORDON BOCOCK, of Dillsboro, entered the Army Air Force in April 1942 and became an Airplane and Engine Mechanic. He served with the 252nd Air Fore Base Unit in Europe.

WARREN DISBRO, of Dillsboro, was a Private in the Army, training at Camp Pickett in 1942.

HARLEY DETMER entered the Army and was in training at Camp Phillips in Kansas in 1942.

DR. VIRGIL H. LONGCAMP, of Aurora, enlisted in the Navy in 1942. He was sent to the Great Lakes Training Station as a dentist. From there he was sent with the Medical Corps at Oberlin College, Oberlin, Ohio. His next assignment was to the Naval Air Station near Honolulu, Hawaii, where he remained until discharged in December 1945, having attained the rank of Lt. Commander.

IRVIN DUNN was taking Army basic training at Camp Phillips, Kansas in 1942.

JOHN BRAUN, of Lawrenceburg, entered the service in 1942. He became a Boatsman's Mate First Class with duty in the American Theater at New Orleans, Brooklyn, New York and Chicago.

WOODFORD BRIGHTWELL entered the service in June 1942. He became an Army Sergeant with the 374th Engineers Battalion, serving as a Construction Foreman.

JOHN LESTER RADSPINNER, of Aurora, was one of few WWI vets who served in WWII. He had been a Trumpeter in the Marines in France in 1917-1918. Now he enlisted in the Navy and had duty aboard the U.S.S. *Salamonia* during its invasion of North Africa.

Virgil Longcamp

John Lester Radspinner

ELMER GERKEPOTT was an Army Private First Class who entered the service in October 1942, but would serve for only some 6 months and then receive an honorable discharge.

GEORGE PRATHER, of Lawrenceburg, entered the Army in December of 1942 and became a Private First Class. He would serve with the 624th Ordnance Company as a Truck Driver in France, Ardennes and Central Europe, meriting 5 battle stars.

MANUEL SCHULENBERG, of Dillsboro, was training in the U.S. Army at Fort Custer, Wyoming in 1942.

RAY SIMMERMAN served in the Navy as an Aviation Mechanic in 1942.

OMER OHLMANSIEK, of the Farmers Retreat area, entered the Army in May of 1942. He served in the 277th Signal Pigeon Company as a Supply Clerk. He would see action in Italy, Southern France and Central Europe, earning 4 battle stars.

ELZIE CASH, of Sunman area, entered the Army in July 1942. He would serve with the 319th Infantry in France and Central Europe, earning the Bronze Star medal and 4 battle stars.

GEORGE WUNDERLICK, of Aurora, was an Army First Lieutenant. He served with the 479th Engineer Maintenance Company. He entered the service in 1942 and would see action in both the ETO and the Pacific.

LYNN ROLF entered the U.S. Navy in August 1942 and would become a Boatsman's Mate First Class. He served on the U.S.S. LST 851 and the Naval Base in Bremerton.

RAYMOND SCHAEFER, of Lawrenceburg, entered the U.S. Army in December of 1942. He was given a medical discharge in May of 1943 at Camp Carson.

RICHARD (DICK) WEAVER, of Lawrenceburg, enlisted in the Navy in 1942 and became a Torpedoman 2nd Class. He served on a submarine in the Pacific. He received a citation from Admiral Nimitz for meritorious conduct under fire.

Alfred Ennis

WILLIAM DENNIS, of Lawrenceburg, enlisted in the Paratroopers in 1942. He served first in Panama, then was sent to the ETO. He was killed in action in France August 21, 1943. He was an outstanding athlete at Lawrenceburg High School where he was honored by a Memorial Service at a basketball game by Supt. H.P. Harrison.

JOHN (NICK) PROBST, of Wilmington, entered the Navy in June 1942. He served on the *Kenmore*, a transport which hauled troops and supplies to Guadalcanal and other South Pacific ports. He would transfer to the *Henrico* which would sail on D-Day as part of the Omaha Beach Assault Force, landing troops in the first wave. Next this ship would take part in the invasion of southern France and return to the Pacific for the Philippine landings. A Jap suicide bomber crashed into her bridge at Okinawa, killing 49 of the crew. Nick survived all this and was discharged in October 1945.

FRANK COTTINGHAM was in the Navy, training at Corpus Christi in 1942.

THOMAS CHRISTIAN was in the Navy with duty at Pearl Harbor in 1942.

WILLIAM CAVENDISH was in the Navy, training at Corpus Christi in 1942.

HAROLD CARR, from Aurora, was a Private in the Army. He was in training at Camp Forrest in 1942.

RICHARD CUTTER, from Aurora, was a Technician 3rd Grade in an Army Engineer Maintenance Company in Iceland in 1942 and then England.

CHARLES BROWN entered the U.S. Navy and became a First Class Petty Officer, with duty as an instructor in 1942.

DENTON BLOOM, of Moores Hill, entered the U.S. Army Air Force. In 1942, he was serving in a ground crew.

GEORGE WORKMAN, of Lawrenceburg, entered the U.S. Navy. In 1942 he would take training at a Navy diesel school at the University of Illinois.

John Probst

ROBERT REESE served in World War I, enlisting as a Pilot in the Canadian Air Force, then joining the American forces in France and served until 1919. For WWII, he enlisted in 1942 in the U.S. Army Air Corps and served the entire war on General Patton's staff beginning in North Africa and through the entire European Campaign, and rising in rank to Colonel.

ROBERT A. RITZMANN, of Lawrenceburg, enlisted in April 1942 and was selected by Officers Candidate School in the Army Air Force. He graduated and received his wings in December at Miami Beach. He was stationed at eight Air Force bases in England, France and Belgium. He ended the war as a Captain.

ROBERT A. RYLE, of Aurora, entered the Army Air Force in December 1942 and became a Sergeant in Squadron B of the 4121st AAF Base, and was discharged in February 1946.

LESTER MESSANG, of Lawrenceburg, entered the Army in December 1942 and, as a Technician 4th Grade, became a First Cook. He served in the Army Transportation Corps in the American Theater.

PAUL TITTEL, enlisted in the Army in October 1942, and was selected to attend Officer's Candidate School. He graduated at Camp Lee as a Second Lieutenant in the Quartermaster Corps. He served in Normandy and Northern France. He was discharged as a First Lieutenant in the 537th Quartermaster Battalion.

LEO ARMBRUSTER, of Lawrenceburg, entered the U.S. Navy and took his boot training at Great Lakes Naval Base in 1942.

JAMES W. TODD, of Lawrenceburg, entered the Marine Corps in June 1942, and received his training at Parris Island as part of the 3rd Battalion, Marine Base Unit. He would become a Private First Class and would serve until December 1945.

MORTON CHAMBERS, of Aurora, was recalled in February 1942 by the U.S. Army. He was placed in an Ordnance Unit and would see action in North Africa and Italy. He was a Corporal with 2 battle stars.

James Todd (left) and Marine buddy

WAYNE HANSELL, of Bright, enlisted in the Merchant Marines and became a Fireman First Class. He served aboard a tanker and at the port of New Orleans in 1942.

HENRY HAUNTZ served in the Army Air Corps as an Engineer in the Aviation Engineering Forces in 1942.

CARL STEINER was a Private in training at Kessler Field, Army Air Corps, in 1942.

PAUL W. MILLER, of Lawrenceburg, was in the Army Parachute Battalion, serving in the Alps. He wrote home, "I regret about friend Bill Dennis' death", as he had spent the night before Bill's last jump with him at a movie.

FLOYD STEINER was a Private in the Army in the 134th Quartermaster Company in training in 1942.

PAUL SHELDON, of Dillsboro, was at an Air Station at Corpus Christi, Texas in 1942 and would later serve in battle, earning 3 battle stars by 1945.

DANA SCHWANHOLT completed his training at Scott Field and was commissioned as Second Lieutenant in the Army Air Corps in 1942.

JOE RICE, of Aurora, was an Army Private in Training at Camp Lee, Virginia in 1942.

DONALD HUFFMAN, of Moores Hill, was a Private First Class in the 19th Field Artillery in 1942.

LESTER HAAG was a Private First Class in the 141st Infantry Division at Fort Benning, Georgia in 1942.

LLOYD IRVIN, of Aurora, enlisted in the Army Air Corps in April 1942.

LLOYD INGRAM, of Greendale, was a Private in the Marines at Parris Island in 1942.

CLARE DAVIS was stationed with an Army unit in Puerto Rico in October 1942. He would serve some 20 months and became a Lieutenant Colonel.

Robert Ritzmann

Robert Reese

Murrell Weber (right) and Floyd Hornbach (Chapter 9)

FRED KORF entered the U.S. Army in 1942 and was sent to Fort Leonard Wood for training as a Private.

WILBUR MILLER, of Guilford, was an Army Technician 5th Grade. He served with the 310th Ordnance Depot Company, beginning in 1942, in New Guinea and the Philippines.

JACOB MINNEMAN, of Weisburg, was a Staff Sergeant in the Army Air Corps. He entered the Corps in October 1942 and would serve in the Air Offensive against Europe, earning 5 battle stars and a Distinguished Unit Citation with the 644th Air Material Squadron.

CHARLES GENTRUP, of Aurora, was serving at a U.S. Military Base in Ireland in 1942.

ARCH VOIT, former Deputy Sheriff of Dearborn County, had become an Army Military Policeman, but was past the upper age limit of 35, and was given an honorable discharge in September 1942.

WILLIAM RUNYAN, of Aurora, enlisted in the Marine Corps in 1942.

CLYDE TIBBETTS, of Lawrenceburg, entered the Army Air Force in August 1942, and was trained as an Airplane Mechanic at a base in Texas. He would serve in the American Theater.

HENRY PLUMMER, of Aurora, became a Seaman First Class in 1942, after attending the Navy Fire Control School in Norfolk, Virginia.

VERNON SCHWING, of Lawrenceburg, had entered the Army and was at Camp Crowder, Missouri in 1942.

RAYMOND SORTWELL was a Fireman First Class in the U.S. Navy serving in the Pacific Theater of Operations in 1942.

WILLIAM WEBER, of Lawrenceburg, served as a Private in the U.S. Army, stationed at Presque Isle, Maine in 1942.

GEORGE H. FOX, of Yorkridge, entered the Army in February 1942. He had 3 years of overseas service with an Army Air Force unit based in England. He was a Sergeant.

OAKEY DRAUT was an Army Air Force Private in a Detachment for casual patients at Jefferson Barracks, Missouri. He received an honorable discharge in November 1942 after serving some 2 months.

HOWARD MATHIAS, of Dillsboro, entered the Army Air Force in 1942 and served as a Military Policeman in the American Theater.

CARL SYKES, of Bright, entered the Army in April 1942 and become a Military Policeman at the 713th M.P. Battalion. He would help with traffic control at the Battle of the Bulge; have guard duty at the Potsdam Big Three Conference; police the American sector in Berlin; and earn 5 battle stars.

MURRELL WEBER, of Yorkville, entered the Army Air Force and was stationed at DeRidder Air Force Base in Louisiana in 1942.

Clyde Tibbetts

Carl Sykes

ALBERT OLDFIELD, of Dearborn County, took part in the famed Doolittle-Halsey raid to bomb Tokyo in April 1942. The U.S. carrier-borne bombers caught the Japs completely by surprise and was a morale-booster for pay-back for Pearl Harbor. Albert was serving in a destroyer screen, protecting two carriers, when a Jap torpedo plane came through to hit his ship. He received head wounds, shrapnel in his legs and a slashed face. He was blown into the sea and spent 52 hours in a raft. He was picked up by a cruiser and taken to a hospital ship and to the U.S. Naval Hospital at Oakland. He would receive a medical discharge as a result of his battle wounds.

ELBERT BENTLE was sent to Hawaii for his first duty station in the Army in 1942. He served as a radio operator in a tank.

CHRISTOPHER BILLUPS, of Lawrenceburg, a Major in the Army Reserve Officer Corps, was called to active duty in the spring of 1942 at the General Engineering Office in Columbus, Ohio. From Fort Hayes, he was appointed Executive Officer of Camp Perry, Ohio.

EARL STRUCKMAN, of Aurora, entered the Army in October 1942 and became a Medical Technician. He served in both the Pacific, at New Guinea, and in Europe at Normandy and France.

Elbert Bentle

FLOYD STEVENS, of Moores Hill, was a Technical Sergeant with the 319th Complement Squadron. He would serve as a Bricklayer in the ETO from January 1942 - July 1945.

RAYMOND TRABEL, of Harrison, was a Private First Class with the 162nd Field Artillery Battalion, having entered the Army in January 1942. He would serve in New Guinea and the Philippines.

LEE TODD was inducted into the U.S. Army in June 1942 and would serve for a year as a Sergeant with the 59th Ordnance Company. He was a Truck Driver.

KENNETH WELCH, of Aurora, entered the Army in October 1942. He was sent to Persia in the Mideast where he would serve for 27 months.

THOMAS NOCKS, of Aurora, entered the Army on December 23, 1941 and became a Radar Operator serving in Normandy, France, Rhineland and Ardennes, meriting 5 battle stars.

HORACE DARLING, of Guilford, entered the military in July 1942 and became a Private First Class. He would serve with the 711th Railway Operating Battalion in the African-Middle East Theater.

ROBERT PHIPPS was inducted in September 1942 and became a Private in the 763rd Military Police Battalion, but received an honorable discharge after 6 months of service.

WILLIAM H. REIF, of Lawrenceburg, enlisted in the Navy in October of 1942. He would serve as an Apprentice Seaman in the American Theater until November 1944.

PAUL HOGAN served as a Sergeant in the Marine Air Force. He was in the ground crew of the Air Engineering Force at Cherry Point, North Carolina in 1942.

C.H. MATTHEWS, of Aurora, was serving in the Army in 1942 at Almogordo, New Mexico.

PAUL E. LEIVE, of Dillsboro, Fire Control Instrument Operator, entered the Army on April 6, 1942. He saw action in Normandy, France and Germany. He was wounded in Germany in 1944. He received 3 battle stars and the Purple Heart.

LOWELL HARCOURT, of Lawrenceburg, was an Army Private stationed in St. Lucia, near Trinidad, in 1942.

CHARLES SULLIVAN entered the U.S. Navy in March 1942 and became a Gunner's Mate First Class. He served aboard the ships, U.S.S. *Breese* and U.S.S. *Downs*.

RALPH SCHULTZ, joined the U.S. Navy. He served on the cruiser, U.S.S. *Chicago*, in the Pacific in 1942.

RAYMOND RUSSELL was a Sergeant serving with the 17th Ferry Squadron in 1942.

ROGER STEIRS, of Lawrenceburg, was a First Lieutenant in the Army Air Force and was stationed at an overseas base in 1942.

Paul Leive

JOE WHITE, of Lawrenceburg, entered the Coast Guard in September 1942, and became a Gunner's Mate 3rd Class.

STANLEY MARSHALL, of Aurora, was a Seaman First Class at an Air Training Station in Corpus Christi, Texas in 1942.

EARL SOMMER, was a Private First Class, from Dillsboro, enlisted in 1942.

RICHARD SCHULZ, of Aurora, entered the Coast Guard in April 1942. He became a Machinist Mate 2nd Class and served aboard the cutters *Hydrangea* and *Mistletow*.

JOSEPH LUTHERBECK entered the Army in 1942, became a Private and trained at Camp Forrest, Mississippi. Before discharge, he completed 6 months of service.

GEORGE ROSEMEYER was a Private First Class with the Army's 23rd Armored Infantry by May 1942. He would see service in Western Europe in 1944, with engagement in a major battle.

OLIVER RIGGS, of Aurora, was a Technician 4th Grade with the 116th Signal Radio Intelligence Company in September 1942. He would see action as a Cook in France, Ardennes and Central Europe, with 4 battle stars.

ROBERT LAWSON was an Army Private First Class. He served with the 495th C.A. Battalion in New York in 1942.

DONALD YORK, of Aurora, entered the Army Air Force, and became a member of a ground crew serving at Shaw Field, South Carolina in 1942.

VINCENT YOUNG, former Athletic Director and teacher at Guilford, was an Instructor in Aviation Mechanics at Chanute Field in 1942.

ROBERT LIEBECKE, of Aurora, graduated from Officer's Candidate School in 1942 as a Second Lieutenant. He would serve first in the Quartermaster Corps and then in the Music Department of the Coast Artillery.

ALFRED ROSEMEYER, of near-Sunman, entered the Army in April 1942 and became a Private First Class. He would serve as a Cook's Helper in France and the Rhineland.

Joe White

MERLIN RUNNELS, of Harrison, entered the Army in June 1942 and would become a Technician 3rd Grade. He would serve with the 904th Field Artillery Battalion as an Aircraft Mechanic in France and Central Europe.

CHARLES RUSSELL, of near-Sunman, was an Army Private First Class. He entered the Army in May 1942 and would drive a truck in the following campaigns: Italian, Central Europe and Southern France.

RICHARD BETSCHER, of Lawrenceburg, joined the Army Air Corps in 1942. He would become a Sergeant and serve as a Ground Mechanic.

C. PAUL SARTIN, of Lawrenceburg, enlisted in the Navy in June of 1942. He was assigned to a gun crew on a merchant ship which sailed in most oceans. As a Seaman First Class, he served in the Atlantic, Pacific, Mediterranean Sea, South America at British and Dutch Guiana, and Trinidad.

RAYMOND KUHLMEIER, of Aurora, entered the Army Air Corps, and graduated from a Technical School at Sheppard Field, Texas in April of 1942 at the top of his class. He was assigned to the 571st School Squadron at the Air Base in Albuquerque, and then to Roswell Field, New Mexico.

PAUL WIEGAND served in the U.S. Navy from 1942 to 1946. He had duty on Guam and Saipan with a Combat Air Service Unit.

ALVIN FOLKE, of Lawrenceburg, served in the U.S. Army. He had duty in the Pacific Theater of Operations in New Guinea.

JAMES RAVENSCRAFT was a Corporal in the Army Air Force. He entered service in March 1942. He served in the ETO, receiving 4 battle stars.

JOHN LUHRSEN, of Mt. Tabor, was a Staff Sergeant in the Army Air Force. He served in the ETO as an Aerial Photographer. He entered the armed services in July 1942.

JOHN RIGGS, of Aurora, was a Chef in the Merchant Marines. He entered service in November 1942 and served in both the Pacific and Atlantic on the following ships: *Clara Barton, William Kent, Henry Richardson, William Rosecrans* and *Charles McCue*.

Paul Wiegand

Alvin Folke

The Andres and Henson Families' Service Records

As the war continued, there were several Dearborn County families with 5, a few with 6, members in the military service. But, the record for the most family members in the service for Dearborn County - and perhaps, Indiana - were that of the Peter Andres family of St. Leon and the Clarence Henson family of Lawrenceburg. They each had 7 members in the armed forces during World War II. Following are the data on each person in these two families:

WILLIAM ANDRES entered the military in January of 1941. He became a member of the 51st Armored Infantry, serving in Normandy and Central Europe. He became a Corporal and received the Bronze Star and Purple Heart medals, being discharged in June of 1945.

E. William Andres

PAUL ANDRES also entered the Army in 1941. He became a Technical Sergeant in the 5th Armored Division in North Africa and in Italy. He was awarded the Silver Star and the Bronze Star medals for outstanding performance of duty.

WILBER ANDRES was drafted into the Army in May of 1942. From basic training at Fort Benning, he was sent to Fort Leonard Wood where he became a Corporal, and was trained as a Mechanic in the motor pool. He received a medical discharge in 1944.

RICHARD ANDRES was drafted in 1942. He was assigned to an Infantry Division at Camp Shelby. He received a medical discharge after serving 14 months.

EDGAR ANDRES entered the Army in February of 1943. He was stationed in India with the 497th Transport Battalion which was part of the China-Burma-India operation. He was discharged as a Sergeant in March of 1946.

VICTOR ANDRES, the youngest brother, enlisted in the Navy in February of 1943. After basic training at Great Lakes Naval Station he was sent to the Atlantic Fleet Submarine Patrol as a Seaman Second Class then as a Gunner's Mate. He was honorably discharged in December of 1945.

Their sister, **ELLA FLORENCE ANDRES**, was in the Women's Army Corps (See Chapter 6).

Paul Andres

Wilber Andres

Richard Andres

Edgar Andres **Victor Andres** **Ella Florence Andres**

The Henson family service records show the following:

WILLIAM HENSON was a Staff Sergeant in the Army Amphibious Corps fighting in the Philippines.

EDWARD HENSON was a Supply Clerk with the 62nd Fighter Squadron in the ETO in November 1942. He would advance to Corporal.

ERNEST HENSON was at Camp Crowder, Missouri in 1943. In 1944 he was a Captain, Assistant Adjutant of the Signal Corps Training Center at the same camp.

ROY HENSON was a Sergeant in the 94th Infantry Division. His division received a commendation for outstanding service in Germany. Previously, he had been awarded the Bronze Star medal.

CHARLES HENSON entered the Navy in July 1945 and became a Yeoman 3rd Class. He served abroad the destroyer, U.S.S. *Hash* in the American Theater of Operations.

JOHN HENSON entered the Army in 1944 and became a Sergeant in the Infantry of the 94th Division. He served in the European Theater until 1946.

THOMAS HENSON was a Sergeant in the Army. While serving in the Philippines, he was an Engineer with the 25th Division which had been in action on Guadalcanal.

Splash One Frances! Prelude and aftermath to the crash of a Jap suicide plane which passed its target. Intent upon crashing the U.S.S. *Sitkoh Bay*, **the Frances was hit by fire from Marine planes and finally splashed by gunfire from the** *Sitkoh Bay.*

CHAPTER 4

Fighting from Africa Through Italy

Shortly after our entry into WW II, British Prime Minister Winston Churchill came to America to discuss major strategy for the Allies with President Roosevelt and his military staff. Some of the American generals wanted a European invasion in 1942, but the British quickly advised them that such a plan would be impractical because of the lack of combat experience by U. S. troops. With both partners eager to take the offensive at the earliest possible moment, they came up with a plan for attacking the Axis Armies in North Africa.

If successful, this plan would result in several benefits. One of the most important would be the squeezing of the Nazis out of Africa and the Mediterranean by a pincers movement, with General Montgomery's British Army moving against Rommel's Germans from the east, having recently driven them out of Egypt. On the other end, would be the Allied Forces which would have landed in northwestern Africa.

The African Invasion was made up of three separate landings: the Americans coming from the U.S. across the Atlantic and landing in Morocco; other Americans embarked from England to take Oran in Algeria; and a third force of Americans and British sailing from England to seize other parts of Algeria. All would be transported and protected by the U.S. and the Royal Navies. The entire force would be under the command of General Dwight D. Eisenhower.

On November 7, 1942 the largest amphibious armada the world had yet known, assembled off the coast of North Africa. It was the first Anglo-American operation of the war. Shortly after 1:00 a.m. on November 8, the fleet disgorged its landing craft and the initial stage of the invasion was on. The Axis were taken by surprise and the landings were a success.

However the winter rain bogged down the Allies advance eastward. In February of 1943, the Germans made a sudden thrust against the uncoordinated Allied advance and hurled the inexperienced Americans back in a bloody defeat at Kasserine Pass. Eisenhower replaced the field commander with General George Patton and, by March, it was apparent that the Allied Pincher movements could not be kept apart by the Germans and Italians. On May 7, Tunis and Bizerte fell and the Axis resistance was shattered.

(Opposite page) General Dwight D. Eisenhower was commander of all Allied Forces for Operation Torch, code name for the invasion of North Africa.

For the Americans, the North African victory was a breaking-in experience. No longer would the GIs and their generals be considered green troops. For the British, it was a revival of confidence for their weary soldiers. And for many French, it was the foundation of a Free French Army and government under the leadership of General Charles deGaulle.

The Next Round: Sicily

A natural stepping stone from North Africa to Italy, the island of Sicily was invaded on July 10, 1943. Although the German Panzers struck back, most of the Italian defenders offered only token resistance. They surrendered in droves, and the Sicilian civilians greeted the invaders joyfully.

Montgomery's British Army slashed up the east coast, while Patton's Army proceeded to "go like hell" up the western part of the island. Within two weeks, he drove all the way to Palermo on the northern coast. American forces took Messina on August 17 while 60,000 Germans escaped, crossing the Strait of Messina to the toe of Italy.

The loss of Sicily brought about the collapse of Mussolini's regime. The king took command, formed a new cabinet and announced that Italy was giving up. On September 8, they signed an armistice; however Hitler rushed troops into Italy as reinforcements.

Sicilian women wash GI clothes at village wells.

Slowly Up the Boot Of Italy

Early in September of 1945, General Mark Clark with his Fifth Army and some British troops landed at Salerno, Italy, some 100 miles north of the toe of Italy. Salerno was heavily defended by the Germans, unknown to the Allies; thus began one of the most bitter struggles of the war for the Americans.

It took heavy firepower from the Allied offshore naval vessels and the dropping of reinforcements by U.S. airborne units to drive the Germans away from the Salerno area. They pulled back to the Apennine Mountains and set up a defense line that reached across the whole of Italy. Due to the enemy's resistance, plus the snow, rain and a sea of mud, the Allies could make little progress during the winter. So Clark made another amphibious landing behind the German lines at Anzio. However the Germans quickly pulled in their reserves to encircle and isolate the beachhead.

Gayle Dittmer

Howard McKee

Francis Zinser

Forest Kidwell (right, 1st row)

Robert Pheister

Richard Mattingly and the plane he flew

The Allies again tried to break the main German line near the town of Cassino. However the Germans on the heights, near the ancient monastery at the Monte Cassino, which commanded the valley to Rome, maintained their defenses in the mountains. By May, the Allies received additional troops from the Free French and the Poles. The French found a weak sector in the German line and broke through with the fifth Army. About the same time, Allied troops fought their way out of Anzio, and all the Allied units were able to move northward. Clark's Army entered Rome on June 4th. The city was undefended as the Germans had withdrawn in good order.

The Germans were able to set up another defensive line across northern Italy in front of the Po Valley. During the summer, they fought numerous delaying actions against the Allies to hold the valley. With no reinforcements now available for the Germans, the Allies overcame their opponents in the spring. On April 29, 1945, the German forces in Italy surrendered unconditionally after months of skilled resistance.

HOWARD McKEE, of Greendale, had first duty in the Navy was as a Coxswain of a landing craft (LCP) on the troop transport, *Leedstown*. At the landing beaches of North Africa, Howard made his first trip with 40 soldiers aboard, but the landing craft was wrecked on the rocky beach. He caught a boat back to the *Leedstown* which then was hit by 2 torpedos from a German sub. As the ship sank, Howard swam ashore. He then had duty on the U.S.S. *Butler*, a destroyer which took part in the landings at Sicily, on D-Day at Normandy and on Southern France. At Normandy, he shot down a German plane, and recovered some 300 survivors from a U.S. ship which was sunk. In 1945 McKee went to the U.S.S. *Tularose*, a small tanker to finish the war taking high octane fuel to small islands, with air strips, in the Pacific.

HAROLD BACHELOR was an Army Private. He served in both the North African and the Italian campaigns.

JOHN BARNES fought in three major battles in North Africa and Sicily. He stepped on a land mine and seriously injured his leg which had to be amputated in a hospital in the U.S.

ELVIN BLASDEL, of Bright, had duty on the Accension Island which was a stop on the aerial crossing between the U.S. and Africa or Europe. He was an Army Sergeant.

DR. WILLIAM FAGALY, of Greendale, left his practice in Lawrenceburg to become a Captain in the Army Medical Corps. He was advanced to Major and took part in the invasion of North Africa. He was injured when a jeep in which he was riding overturned. He sustained a broken wrist, broken collar bone and three broken ribs. He was hospitalized in Africa but his arm and shoulder did not respond to treatment and he was brought back to the States, to Nicholas Hospital in Louisville where he underwent a bone grafting operation. The hospital was understaffed, and so Dr. Fagaly assisted the doctors there. Upon recovery, he was appointed to Wakeman General Hospital at Camp Atterbury.

ELMER PLATT, a Sergeant in the Service Command of the Army Air Corps, took part in the invasion of North Africa. Later he also saw action in Sicily and France.

EDWARD THEETGE was the first casualty from Lawrenceburg Township. He was an Army Private serving as a sharpshooter in the Infantry when he was killed in Africa.

ROBERT PHIESTER was a Corporal in the U.S. Army. He saw action in North Africa and the Italian campaign.

WILLIAM PHIPPS was an Army Private. He served with the Army Railroad Service in North Africa, Italy and France.

A North African bellydancer entertains the American Troops.

Dearborn Countians meet in Italy: (l. to r.) Leroy Seevers, Louis H. Taylor, Francis Zinser, Clifford Kneuven, and a friend

Wayne Seitz

Kenneth Ritter   Emmet Harry

The Fox Brothers: (left) Bernard, Charles and Robert

CHARLES RICHARDSON was a Corporal seving as a squad leader in the 351st Regiment in Italy. He helped his unit liberate Rome.

RUSSELL ROACHE was a First Lieutenant serving in a Tank Battalion in Italy where he received injuries. He became a Captain in 1945 and was awarded the Distinguished Service Cross for heroism in action.

WAYNE SEITZ, of Greendale, enlisted in the Army Air Corps in 1942 and graduated from Officer's Candidate School. He was assigned to the 1st Air Force Headquarters Air Squadron Wing in Boston and then to Mitchell Field, New York as a Squadron Officer with 1st Fighter Command. He was shipped to North Africa in January 1943 and promoted to First Lieutenant. He was then assigned to the 64th Fighter Wing. He saw action in Africa, Sicily and Italy. Promoted to Captain in September 1944, he was made Commanding Officer of a Squadron in the 64th Fighter Wing. He also served in the landings in France and on through Europe until the war's end, serving 34 months in the ETO.

LEROY SCHUMAN, of St. Leon, was a Private in the Army. He was a Cannoneer in the Field Artillery. He trained with Army mules for duty with a Mountain Battery. He served over eight months on the front lines in Italy.

ANTHONY SCHWARTZ was a U.S. Army Corporal on Sicily in 1943.

CLARENCE SMITH was a Private First Class in the Army Air Corps. He fought in Africa, Sicily and Italy. He was in seven major battles serving with the 12th Air Force.

CHARLES SMITH, of Lawrenceburg, was a member of the 68th Anti-Aircraft Gun Battalion in Italy. This unit landed at Anzio under land and air attack. They engaged the enemy in over 200 fights, repulsing German tank and aircraft assaults. General Clark cited this unit for their outstanding performance. Charles Smith also fought in Africa and Sicily.

CARL DELL was a Private in the Army Air Force serving in North Africa and Italy.

EARL DENNERLINE was a Seaman 2 Class at a Naval Base in North Africa in 1944.

Robert Kirchgassner

William Ben Gould

Elwood Houston (left) and Curtis Smith

Delmar Bennett

WILLIAM (BEN) GOULD, of Greendale, was a Sergeant serving in an Air Force ground crew of the 52nd Fighter Squadron. Enlisting in December 1941 after the Pearl Harbor attack, he served in North Africa, Corsica, Sicily and Italy.

JOHN HICKS was a Master Sergeant with the Army Air Corps. He served as a mechanic with 30 mechanics under him in North Africa and Italy.

VICTOR HOFFMEIER, of York Ridge, was missing in action at Salerno, Italy in 1943. He was a Motor Machinist Mate First Class serving aboard the Naval tug, Mauset, which was sunk by enemy action the day troops landed in Italy.

JOHN HUDSON, of Logan, was a paratrooper in the 82nd Airborne Division. His first parachute jump was in Sicily in 1943, then jumped into France in June 1944. He was awarded the Purple Heart for a broken ankle, also earned 5 battle stars for serving in Sicily, Italy, Ardennes, Rhineland and Central Europe.

BERNARD HUENEFELD, of Lawrenceburg, was a Machinists Mate 3rd Class in the Sea Bees serving for 22 months in Italian and European waters.

ROBERT JACKSON, a Coast Guard Chief Petty Officer, was on sub patrol duty in the North Atlantic in 1943.

EARL JACQUES, of Logan, entered the U.S. Army and served as a cook in Italy.

JOHN JEFFRIES, of Lawrenceburg, a First Lieutenant served as a navigator-bombardier instructor at Langley Field. He had flown 50 missions with the 15th Air Force in Italy. He was awarded the Purple Heart, Air Medal with 3 Clusters and a Presidential Citation.

JOHN JOHNSON was a Corporal in the Signal Corps in Italy in 1944.

ELMER JONES, of Greendale, was an Army Corporal who saw action in Sicily and the Italian campaign.

CARL KAISER was a Master Sergeant with the 68 Quartermaster Company of Peninsular Base Section in Italy in 1944.

RAYMOND DUNN was a Navy Yeoman having duty in the invasion of North Africa in 1943.

PHILIP EBEL was a Sergeant in the Army Air Force. He served with the Ninth Air Service Command in the Air Traffic Office at the airport in Heliopolis, Egypt.

FRANK FUCHS was a Motor Machinist Mate in the Navy, serving with the Western Naval Tank Force Salvage Group in the African and Mid-Eastern seas.

CHESTER GLENN, of Aurora, served with the Reconnaissance Company of the 66th Armored Regiment as a truck driver in Algeria, Morocco, Sicily, Normandy and Central Europe. He had 7 battle stars.

PERRY GRAVES, of Lawrenceville, was a Captain in the Army, serving on faculty of the Field Artillery School, Ft. Sill, Oklahoma. He was selected by the War Department to receive the Silver Star for gallantry in action at Tunisia. Although wounded, he continued at his post and through his effort his battalion gave effective artillery support to the 9th Infantry.

NORVIN GREIVE was a Lieutenant in the Army Air Force serving as a bombardier in Africa. He was killed in a plane crash in Algeria on December 19, 1943.

EMMETT HARRY was a Private First Class in the Army. He saw action in North Africa and France, receiving a battle star. He received a medical discharge.

ORVILLE HEATH served in the Field Artillery in North Africa in 1944.

HERSCHEL HENRY was a Private First Class in Africa in 1943 serving with 123 Signal Radio Intelligence Company.

MARTIN HUBER, former Lawrenceburg Council Member, served in the U.S. Marine Corps and took part in the North African campaign.

WILLIAM HUNTER was a Private in the Army serving overseas for 3 years. He was wounded at Kasserine Pass in Tunisia and was a prisoner of the Germans in North Africa.

Philip Ebel

Donald Landrom and bride

John Hudson

Paul Strassinger (row 2, 4th from right) and Army band in New Orleans

LAWRENCE LANG, of Dillsboro, was a Second Lieutenant with a Pack Artillery Unit which moved with mule trains for combat in mountainous territory, such as Italy.

FOREST O. KIDWELL worked on B-26 light bombers in the European-Italian Theater of Operations. He served in the Army Air Force from 1942 to 1946.

WILLIAM KLEPPER, of Greendale, was a Captain in the 52nd Ordnance Battalion in the Mediterranean War Theater. He was awarded the Legion of Merit for outstanding service during operations on Anzio beachhead.

LOUIS KREMER, of Harrison, was a Staff Sergeant with the 64th Troop Carrier Group. He entered the Army Air Force in March 1942 and would serve as a Radio Operator-Gunner in North Africa, Sicily and Italy, receiving 8 battle stars.

EDWARD KROGGELL, of Lawrenceville, was a Sergeant in the Army earning a Bronze Star for heroic achievement while serving in the First Armored Division 5th Army at the front in Italy and the drive on Rome in 1944.

STANLEY LOWER, of Lawrenceburg, was a Staff Sergeant with the 36th Depot Repair Squadron serving as a medical non-com with action in Italy near Rome and the Arno Valley, receiving a battle star.

RALPH MASON, of Guilford, served in the Army in the North Africa and Italian campaigns. He was wounded in combat in Italy. In 1945 he was also wounded in Germany.

KENNETH McADAMS was a Private First Class in the Army Air Corps. He was with the 12th Air Force, Bomber Headquarters in the Italian invasion.

VINCENT MILLICAN, of Dillsboro, was a Lieutenant, a fighter pilot in the U.S. Army Air Force. He was killed in action over Italy on August 2, 1944.

ROBERT MOORE, of Aurora, was a First Lieutenant with the Fifth Army in the Italian campaign. He was wounded in January 1944 while commanding a tank unit.

WALTER MORAND, of Aurora, entered the Army Air Corps in July of 1942, and became a Staff Sergeant.

Charles Given

Clayton Rechenbach

Loren Loftus

Walter Morand

Elvin Blasdel

FORD BAKER was an Army Private who served in the Italian campaign.

CHARLES BARROWS was an Army Private First Class. He drove an ammunition truck in Africa, Italy and France. He suffered severe leg injuries, requiring hospitalization.

JAMES CALDWELL was a Captain in the Army Air Force and in 1945 was a member of a Liberation bomber group based in Italy.

WILBUR CLARK, of Lawrenceburg, was a Technical Sergeant in the Army. He spent 18 months in North Africa and Italy. He was hospitalized with arthritis and in 1945 transferred to Aberdeen Proving Grounds.

RUSSELL CORNELIUS was a Corporal in the Army Air Force serving in the ground crew in Italy for 19 months.

CLARENCE DAVIS was a Staff Sergeant serving as a machine gunner in Italy and North Africa. He was awarded the Distinguished Unit Citation and 2 battle stars.

GAYLE DITTMER, of Aurora, was a Private First Class in the Army, assigned to 380th Medical Collecting Corps as a combat Medic and Ambulance Driver. He served in North Africa, Sicily and Italy. He earned 4 battle stars, the Combat Medic Medal and Ambulance Driver Medal.

QUENTIN ELBRECHT, of Aurora, was an Army Private First Class with the Fifth Army in Italy. He served as a Truck Driver and received 2 battle stars.

EVERETT EMERY, of Lawrenceburg, was an Army Private First Class. He served as a tank crewman with the 1st Tank Battalion in Italy, earning 4 battle stars.

OPLET FISH, of Greendale, was a Medic with the 3rd Infantry Division. As a Corporal, he served in North Africa and Italy, earning 3 battle stars.

JAMES FAIRCHILD was killed in action in Italy in November 1945. He had suffered from prior wounds both in Italy and in Sicily.

RICHARD MATTINGLY, of Aurora, was a Lieutenant in Army Air Corps, as a bomber pilot. He ferried his crew from New York to Brazil to Africa early in 1944. He then flew missions out of Africa up the boot of Italy as the Allies advanced. He flew over targets in France, Germany, Italy, Austria, Romania and Yugoslavia, including the Ploesti oil fields. As part of the 460 Bomb Group, he frequently was attacked by enemy fighter planes.

KEITH FOX, of Aurora, received a Bronze Star for heroic service in Italy. He was wounded at Cassino. He served as a Staff Sergeant.

RAYMOND FOX, of Lawrenceburg, served with the Medical Corps in Italy for 2 years and was awarded the Medical Badge for recognition of sharing the hardships of combat with an Infantry unit with the 5th Army. He also received the Bronze Star for meritorious service and the Purple Heart for being wounded in action.

ROBERT GARNIER, of Lawrenceburg, was a Staff Sergeant. He served in Africa, Corsica, Sicily and Italy, receiving 8 battle stars.

CHARLES GIVEN, of Moores Hill, was a radio operator-gunner on a B-17 Flying Fortress. This group based in Italy was awarded the Distinguished Unit Citation in recognition of outstanding bombing missions. On one mission, this group was attacked by 200 German fighter planes who knocked down some dozen bombers while the remainder flew on to the targets. During this fight, the group's gunners destroyed 65 enemy planes.

GEORGE GRAY, Private First Class, Army, served in the 337th Wolverine Regiment in the mountains on the Gothic Line in Italy in an Anti-Tank Division.

OLLIE GREEN, of Lawrenceburg, entered the service in July 1942. He became a Private First Class in the 366th Infantry and served as a Truck Driver in the Italian campaign.

LEROY GUARD, of Dillsboro, was a Sergeant in the Army Air Corps, with the 719th Bomber Squadron, 44th Bomber Group. He saw action over the Po Valley, Naples, Rome, France and the Air offense in the ETO. He received 10 battle stars.

Robert Boese

Robert Henry

ROBERT BARNES was a Private in the U.S. Army. In 1942 he had duty at Fort Bragg, North Carolina.

CARLOS BARROWS was a Corporal in the U.S. Army. In 1944 he was shipped for duty overseas from Camp Henry in Texas.

JOHN BRAUN was a Boatswains Mate First Class in the Navy, serving in the Atlantic. One of his ships was torpedoed and sunk but he survived on a raft for several hours until rescued. In 1943, he was in an Armed Guard Crew aboard a merchant ship.

LEONARD BAUER entered the U.S. Army and became a Private First Class. He served in a Tank Destroyer Battalion in 1943.

JAMES BRITTON, of Lawrenceburg, served as an Army Private in the American Theater at Camp Chaffee, Arkansas.

PHILIP BROWNING, of Aurora, was an Army Air Force Test Pilot. He had duty at a field at Macon, Georgia as a Lieutenant in 1943.

VON BURTON entered the U.S. Navy and became a Seaman 2nd Class. He was stationed in Hawaii at Pearl Harbor.

CHARLES CARR, of Lawrenceburg, was a Corporal in the Army at Camp Phillips, Kansas in 1943.

RONALD CASH was a Staff Sergeant in Hawaii in 1943 to 1945.

BERNIE CHRISTIAN, of Lawrenceburg, served in the South Pacific in communications as a switchboard operator in 1943.

CARL CHRISTIAN, of Lawrenceburg, served in the Galapagos Islands in the Pacific in 1943 in an air warning unit.

GEORGE CHASE was a Corporal in the Army's 745 Field Artillery at Ft. Leonard Wood in 1943.

HAROLD COGHILL was a Machinist Mate First Class in the Merchant Marine.

James Britton

FRED MANNING served as a Staff Sergeant at Camp Breckenridge, Kentucky in 1943.

CLIFFORD MANGOLD served with the 762d Tank Battalion as a Private First Class. He was stationed in Hawaii in 1943.

NORMAN MENDELL was in the 179th Engineers at Ft. Devers, Massachusetts in 1943.

CHARLES MENDELL was a Midshipman in the Merchant Marines at Kings Point, R.I. and later was on convoy duty in 1943.

PAUL MARKS, of Greendale, was an Army Sergeant stationed with his unit in England in 1943.

GEORGE MAXWELL served as a Corporal in Iceland in 1943.

FOSTER McADAMS was an Army Sergeant. In 1943 he was on his way to the European Theater of Operations.

LEE McADAMS was an Army Corporal. He was serving at Camp Cook, California in 1943.

FORREST WATTERS, of Aurora, entered the Army and became a Sergeant. He served with an Army Engineering Unit in England in 1943.

RAYMOND McADAMS, of Lawrenceburg, was an Army Private. After spending 3 months in a hospital for a broken hand. He re-enlisted for a year in the regular Army.

WILLIAM McCLURE, of Logan, entered the U.S. Army and graduated from Officers Training School at Ft. Bragg as a Second Lieutenant. He served in the Army Field Artillery.

HARRY (GABBY) McKAIN, of Aurora, was a B-24 bomber pilot, having received his wings at Luke Field in Arizona. After serving at 14 different fields, he was reported as missing. He was the 11th Aurora casualty since Pearl Harbor.

EDWIN McKAIN, of Aurora, was an Aviation Student in the 2538th Base Unit. He served from June 1942 - June 1945.

Victor Hoffmeier

ROBERT WUNKER, of Lawrenceburg, was a Second Lieutenant as a bombardier with the 15th Army Air Corps on a B-17 Flying Fortress based in Italy. He was awarded the Air Medal for meritorious achievement in aerial flight.

FRANCIS ZINSER, of Logan, was inducted into the Army in 1942 to serve with the 15th Army Air Force in North Africa, and Italy at Foggia Air Base. He worked on B-17 bombers and P-51 Mustang fighter planes. In May of 1945, he returned to the U.S. to receive training on the B-29 Super Fortress bomber.

HAROLD MARKLAND was the first young man to lose his life from Bright. He was killed in action in Italy on October 13, 1943. He had been wounded twice before his death, and had fought with the Infantry in Africa and Sicily.

ALVIN McMULLEN was an Army Staff Sergeant. He served a year in the Italian campaign and then received a medical discharge for illness.

ROBERT AYLOR, of Lawrenceburg, was killed in action in Italy in February of 1944. Word from his Chaplain described Robert's death as a heroic sacrifice in making a daring stand to give security for others at the Rapido River crossing.

MELVIN BADENHOP entered the U.S. Army and became a Private First Class. He served at Naples, Italy in 1944.

HAROLD BATCHELOR was a Private in the U.S. Army. He saw action in the North African and Italian campaign.

ROBERT BLACKBURN, of Greendale, enlisted in the Army Air Corps in 1942. He was sent to the Havana Statistical School and then to the 15th Air Force in Italy as Group Statistical Officer. He was part of the Second Bombardment Group, a B-17 Flying Fortress unit which flew over 300 missions in the Mediterranean Theater. Robert was promoted to Captain in 1945.

GERALD BENTLE, of Moores Hill, entered the U.S. Army and became a Military Policeman. He served in the Italian campaign.

Gerald Bentle

JOHN SCARBER, of Moores Hill, took boot training at Great Lakes Naval Base and became an Apprentice Seamen.

THEODORE WATTERS, of Aurora, was a Sergeant in the 69th Armored Regiment.

KENNETH WALSH, of Aurora, was a Private First Class who served in the Pacific and Iran.

LEROY WHITAKER was in the Anti-Aircraft Artillery at Camp Davis, North Carolina in 1943.

PAUL SUTTON was in the Army Engineers Corps for training at Camp Shelby, Mississippi.

FLOYD BURNETT, of Manchester, was an Army Private, serving at Greenwood Armory in Colombus in 1943.

HORACE HEITMEYER entered the U.S. Army and became a Sergeant. He was stationed at a base in England in 1943.

IRVIN NORRIS was in the U.S. Army Air Corps, taking training at the University of Florida in 1943.

CARL HEITMAN, of Lawrenceburg, was a Private First Class with the 472nd Field Artillery. He was stationed at Ft. Sill in 1943.

GARELD LAFOLLETTE entered the Army Air Corps. In 1943 he was serving with an AF ground crew.

ROBERT MORRELL entered the U.S. Army and became a Sergeant. He was stationed at Fort McClellan in 1942.

WILLIS MILES was a Seaman First Class on a PT boat in the Atlantic.

LLOYD MAHLER, of Guilford, graduated from the Army Air Force Technical School at Keesler Field, Mississippi in 1943, and later served in Panama.

Gareld LaFollette

Louis Taylor

JAMES CONAWAY, of Dillsboro, was a Private First Class in the Army Air Force.

CARTER CORNETT was in Basic Army Training at Camp Lee in 1943.

GEORGE COTTON was a Technical Sergeant in a Military Police unit of the U.S. Army.

FRANK COUGHLIN, of Lawrenceburg, took basic training at Camp Claibourne in 1943.

ALFORD CUTTINGHAM was in the 83 Infantry Division at Camp Atterbury in 1943.

WILBER DAVIS was a Military Police in Ft. Knox in 1943.

JAMES DAUSCH was a Corporal in the Army Engineers in 1943.

ROY DAWSON, of Guilford, enlisted in Army Air Force taking basic training at Shepherd Field, Texas.

EUGENE DETMER, of Aurora, was an Aviation Cadet in pre-flight training at Maxwell Field, Alabama in 1943.

DENNIS DIXON was an Army Private serving at Camp Breckenridge, Kentucky. He was in the Quartermaster Corps from August 1942 to March 1943.

LESLIE DOENGES, of Lawrenceburg, was a Sergeant in the Army, training at Ft. Johnston, Florida in 1943.

WILLIAM DONNELLY was a Corporal serving as a radio instructor at Ft. Meade in 1944.

JOHN DOEGNES, of Lawrenceburg, was in the ground crew of the Army Air Force as a Staff Sergeant. He served in the Dutch East Indies.

RAYMOND DOEGNES, of Lawrenceburg, a Technical Sergeant was transferred from Panama to Ecuador.

PAUL DOWNEY was a Private First Class serving in Panama in 1944.

VERNON McNAUGHTON was a Captain in the Army in England in 1943.

EUENE MEYER was in a ground crew unit of the Army Air Corps in 1943.

HARLAN MEYERS, of Aurora, was a Staff Sergeant at the Army Finance School in Wake Forest, N.C. in 1943.

JOHN MILHOLLAND was a Lieutenant in the Army Air Force serving as a Flight Instructor in Corpus Christi, Texas.

OMER MOLTER entered the U.S. Army in 1943 and served until the end of the war, he ranked as an Army Corporal.

TOM MOLTER entered the Army Air Corps and became a Corporal in 1943.

ORVILLE MOREHEAD entered the U.S. Army. He served as an Engineer of Light Equipment in 1943.

ROBERT MOODY was a Private First Class in the Army Air Corps. He served in a ground crew unit in 1943.

WARREN MORRIS was a Captain in the U.S. Army Medical Corps at a base in England in 1943.

L. H. MORRIS was a Corporal in the Army Air Corps. He served as a Radio-Mechanic.

DONALD NEAL, of Dillsboro, served in the U.S. Army as a Private First Class. He was killed in a crash at Page Field, Fort Bragg in June 1943.

ALBERT NIEMEYER, JR., of Dillsboro, was commissioned a Second Lieutenant with his R.O.T.C. training at Indiana University. He would serve in an Intelligence Unit of the Army and was promoted to First Lieutenant. His father, Albert Niemeyer, Sr., who had served in WWI, would also be called back for WWII.

LEO OBERTING served in the Merchant Marines as a Junior Engineer in 1943.

OSCAR OBERTING was a Staff Sergeant in the U.S. Army at Camp Atterbury. He served as a Chief in the Engineering Section of the base.

Oscar Oberting

John H. Leiendecker

FRED BARROTT was in the U.S. Army Signal Corps. He served at Jefferson Barracks in St. Louis in 1943.

CHARLES BANKS, of Aurora, entered the Navy and completed a training course in basic engineering at Great Lakes Naval Training Center.

RAYMOND CALDWELL, of Dillsboro, was a Private First Class in the Coastal Artillery, serving one year in India and then sent to China.

STEWARD BUCHANAN, of Aurora, served with the U.S. Army in North Africa.

ROBERT CHEEK, of Aurora, was a Radarman 2nd Class in the Navy. He served in the destroyer escort, U.S.S. *Frederick C. Davis*, taking part in the invasions of Africa, Sicily, Italy and Southern France. In 1945, Bob had just been transferred when the *Davis* was sunk by an enemy sub near Greenland. Bob was discharged in August of 1945.

Robert Cheek

ROBERT HORNBACH entered the Coast Guard in 1943. He served on a sub-chaser for two years. Then he was stationed at a light house on the coast of New Jersey.

Robert Hornbach (standing) on a 75 ft. wood patrol boat

LLOYD ANDERSON, of Moores Hill, was a Sergeant in the Army Air Corps. He served in North Africa as a Precision Measuring Instrument Specialist.

EDWARD ARMSTRONG, of Aurora, was wounded twice, once in North Africa and again in Italy. He was an Army Private First Class.

GENE KNIPPENBERG, of Lawrenceburg, was in Army Signal Corps as a Private. Served in North Africa and India.

HOWARD KNUEVEN, of New Alsace, was an Army Private First Class. He served with a Port Company in North Africa, and later in India. In his area, the men slept under mosquito netting because of the insects.

RALPH LANGE was a Private First Class serving in the Signal Corps in North Africa in 1943.

CHARLES LINDSEY, of Lawrenceburg, was a Corporal in the Army Quartermaster Corps. He served in Africa and India.

DORMAND JOHNSTON, of Aurora, was a Seaman 2nd Class serving at Casablanca in North Africa.

GEORGE MARSHALL served as a Private in an Ordnance Unit with the U.S. Army. He took part in the North African campaign.

JOHN MASSETT, of Logan, served in the North African campaign at Oran and the front lines at Tunisia.

NORMAN MARTIN, of Moores Hill, was a Sergeant in the Army Air Force North Africa Ferrying Division. He served as an Airplane and Engine Mechanic in Africa and the ETO.

JOHN MATTHEWS of the Army was wounded in late November in North Africa. He later served in the Mid-East in 1945.

PAUL McKEE served in the Army Air Force as a Staff Sergeant. He completed 50 bombing missions over Africa, Sicily and Italy. As a tail gunner on a bomber he was awarded the Air Medal with Clusters.

RALPH McMULLEN, of Lawrenceburg, was a Corporal in an Army Air Force ground crew in North Africa in 1944 and France in 1945.

Dennis Dixon

Robert G. Kennedy

Harry Nordmeyer

Robert Schneider

WALTER CORNELIUS was a Corporal in the Army Air Corps. He served as a Supply Clerk in the Italian campaign.

ESTAL CRAIG, of Guilford, was a Private First Class in the Army. He served with the 617th Field Artillery in the Po Valley engagements in Italy.

LEROY STEVENS, born in Guilford, enlisted in the Navy in 1942. He became a Motor Machinist 2nd Class and was assigned to Sub Chaser 676. In 1943 his ship crossed the Atlantic to North Africa and then took part in the Sicily campaign. At Sicily, his ship helped take in the first assault troops. In September, near the Isle of Capri, they depth bombed a German submarine. They were the first assault ship to enter Naples harbor, and also took part in the assault in the Gulf of Salerno. In January 1944, they participated in the landings at Anzio. In that summer they operated between Italy and Yugoslavia. They evacuated English and other Allied partisans in that area. They also rescued a downed B-17 crew. Next they helped with the landings in Southern France. In August 1945, Seevers spent time in a Rhode Island Naval Hospital and was discharged in August 1945.

ROBERT (SPEED) SCHNEIDER, of Lawrenceburg, went to California for primary training in the Army Air Force.

MILLARD SCHOEFF was at Brooks Field, Texas in 1943 as a Sergeant.

VIRGIL SCHOEFF was at Keesler Field, Mississippi in 1943 as a Sergeant.

CHESTER SHARP of Mt. Tabor, was in a motorized division in 1943.

RAYMOND SCHOLLE was at Camp Stewart, Georgia in 1944 as an Army Private.

CHARLES BENNETT was an Army Sergeant. He received a medical discharge in 1943.

WILLIAM SCHWING was in the Mechanized Field Artillery at Ft. Benning as a Sergeant.

JAMES SCHWING, of Harrison, received a medical discharge from the Coast Guard in 1943.

The Westrich Brothers: (l. to r.) Milburn, Walter, Mike, George, and Robert

ERNEST WEHMEYER received a medical discharge after serving 17 months at Fort Dix, N.J. He served in the Artillery in 1943.

WILFORD WELLER, of New Alsace, was a Private in the Field Artillery at St. Lewis, Washington in 1943.

LEROY WHITAKER was an Army Private. In 1943 he was in an Anti-Artillery unit at Camp Davis, North Carolina.

HERBERT WAITMAN was a Corporal in the Army Air Force. In 1943, he was training in a mechanics school for work on airplanes.

MIKE WESTRICH was a Corporal in the Army Air Corps. He got his wings for aerial gunnery at a training school in Texas.

John Renck

Edward Kaffenberger

FLOYD METTLER was in the U.S. Army invasion of North Africa. He would have duty guarding German and Italian prisoners.

HARRY NORDMEYER, of Yorkville, was a Technician 5th Grade in the Army with the 791st Railway Operating Battalion. He served as a Section Foreman in Iran and the Mid-East Theater.

DONALD PEARSON, of Aurora, enlisted in the Army Air Corp. He served with an engineering unit in the Mid-East, in Persia in 1942.

WILLIAM PHIPPS was an Army Private with the Railroad Service Battalion. He had duty in North Africa, Italy and France.

EDWIN POWELL was a Baker First Class in the U.S. Navy. He served on one of the invasion ships at North Africa and in the Mediterranean.

ROBERT RICE was a Technical Sergeant in the Medical Corps at the 93rd Stratton Hospital, serving 30 months in Africa.

DANA SCWANHOLTZ, of Aurora area, was commissioned a Second Lieutenant in the Army Air Corps in 1942 at Scott Field, Ilinois.

ROBERT ROACHE was a Private First Class in 1943, serving with the infantry in North Africa.

WILLIAM (BILLY) RUBLE was a Sergeant with the U.S. Fifth Army. He saw action in North Africa and Italy.

EDWARD RUTH was a Captain who served in the invasion of North Africa in 1942.

ANTHONY SCHWARTZ was an Army Corporal. He saw action in the North African campaign and the invasion of Sicily.

LESTER SMITH was in North Africa serving in Coastal Artillery in 1943.

CHARLES STEELE, of Aurora, was a Storekeeper 3rd Class, U.S. Navy. He participated in the Allied invasion of North Africa.

L. D. RANSOM, of Aurora, was a Cadet in the Merchant Marines at Kings Point, R.I. in 1943. Later while serving on a tanker in 1943, his tanker collided with another tanker.

CLIFFORD PERRIN was a Sergeant at the Tank Destroyer Center, Camp Hood in 1943.

ROBERT PHEISTER, of Moores Hill, was a Sergeant in the Army Air Force 5th Reconnaissance Group. He was awarded the Distinguished Unit Badge and 6 battle stars.

IRWIN PIEPER entered the Army Air Corps in 1942. He had duty at an air field in St. Petersburg, Flordia.

WOODROW POWELL entered the U.S. Army in May 1943 as a Private. He served as an Auto Mechanic in the American Theater but received his discharge in November 1943.

CHARLES PYLE enlisted in the 29th Calvary Unit at Ft. Riley in 1943.

CLAYTON RECHENBACH, of Bright, was appointed an Ensign in the Physical Education Program of the U.S. Navy. He served at the Naval Operating Base in Norfolk, Virginia where he met his wife.

JOHN REDDING, of Greendale, enlisted in the Merchant Marines in 1943.

GORDON REDWINE, of Dillsboro, was an Army First Lieutenant serving with the 410 Infantry at Camp Claiborne in 1943.

JOHN RENCK, of Bright, served in the Army Air Force. He received a medical discharge for rheumatism and then worked in a defense plant.

HAROLD RICE, of Moores Hill, was an Army Corporal in the 93rd Station Hospital Group in 1943.

EDWARD RILEY served in the U.S. Navy as an Aviation Machinist Mate First Class in South America.

KENNETH RITTER, of Aurora, entered the navy in November 1942 and became a Storekeeper 2nd Class. He served at the Naval Station in Jacksonville and aboard the U.S.S. *Patrocuc*.

Paul Woliung

Wilbert Taylor

Francis Zinser (left) and Leroy Seevers

ORVILLE SEITZ was in Army training at Camp swift, Texas in 1943.

ROBERT SHELDON, of Dillsboro, entered the U.S. Navy in 1942 and became a Seaman First Class.

CLIFFORD SHINKLE was a Private First Class serving as a Military Police Escort Guard in 1943.

GEORGE SHIPPER, of Aurora, entered the Merchant Marines and became a Seaman. He served aboard the ship *Berkshire*.

KENNETH SCHREINER was a Naval Aviation Machinist Mate Third Class who was stationed at Jacksonville, Florida.

American landing boats used for the invasion of Africa, Sicily and Italy

RAYMOND SLAYBACK, of Harrison, served in India with the 61st Transport Railway Operating Company in 1943. He was a Technician 5th Grade with 1 battle star.

CHARLES SMITH was in the Air Force in Greenwood, Mississippi in 1943.

CLIFFORD SMITH entered the U.S. Army. He was assigned to duty with the Coastal Artillery in 1943.

LOUIS SMITH entered the U.S. Army in May 1943 and served as a Private until October when he was discharged at Camp Lee, Virginia.

GENE SPECKMAN, of Aurora, was an Air Cadet in 1943 as a member of the Army Air Force.

WILBUR SPECKMAN was a Private First Class in the Army Ordnance Motor Transportation Corps in 1943.

LAWRENCE STOLL was a member of an Army Air Force Ground Crew as a Sergeant in 1943.

CHARLES STEELE entered the U.S. Navy and became a Storekeeper Third Class.

MARVIN STEELMAN, of Lawrenceburg, was a Technician 5th Grade with the Army's 300th Infantry. He served as a truck driver in the American Theater.

MELVIN P. STENGER, of St. Leon, was a Corporal in the field artillery at Camp Phillips in 1943.

PAUL STEVENS, of Dillsboro, entered the Army Air Corps and became a sergeant. He served as a Gun Sight Mechanic in a Squadron at Amarillo Air Field in 1943.

PAUL STRASSINGER, of Aurora, played in an Army Band in New Orleans, playing a saxophone and clarinet in 1943.

EARL STOREY, Technical 4th Grade, was a member of a Port Battalion which received a Unit Plaque for unloading ships in record time.

ROBERT NOWLIN, of the Guilford area, entered the Navy and became an Electrician Mate. He served for eighteen months with the amphibious force in the Mediterranean, taking part in the invasions of Africa, Sicily and Italy.

Robert Nowlin

ROBERT ROSENBAUM was a Machinist Mate 2nd Class in the U.S. Navy. He served with an armed guard crew.

DARRELL ROSS, of Aurora, was a Staff Sergeant in an Anti-Aircraft unit in 1943.

ROBERT ROPLEY was an Ensign in the Navy Sea Bees at Camp Peary, Virginia in 1943.

ROBERT RUSCHE was an Army Private who served with the 16th Armored Division at Camp Chafee, Arkansas in 1943.

Stanley Vickroy (2nd, right) and unit friends

HERSHEL STONE, while serving in the Army in Italy, a truck he was driving struck a mine. As a result he was burned severely and hospitalized in North Africa.

LOUIS H. TAYLOR, of Guilford, was inducted into the Army on July 22, 1942. He became a Staff Sergeant in the 60th Quartermaster Base Depot Company. He saw action in the Italian campaign in the Rome-Arno sector.

WILBERT TAYLOR, of Harrison, was a Sergeant and Squad Leader of an anti-tank platoon of the 34th Division which was awarded a citation for knocking out 2 enemy mortars, 2 machine guns, an anti-aircraft gun and a 75-mm gun in capturing a town on the Italian front. He served in General Mark Clark's Fifth Army.

HUBERT THOMAS, of Lawrenceburg, was an Army Private. He served in the North Africa invasion and the Italian campaign.

FRANK TUFTS, of Aurora, served 30 months with the Army's 34th Field Hospital near Naples, Italy.

STANLEY T. VICKROY, of Dearborn County, served in the Army from November 1943 until March 1946. He was a Staff Sergeant in the Army with Company B, First Armored Division. His unit was Honor Guard at General Patton's funeral. He served in Italy at Cassino, Anzio, Cisterna and the drive on Rome. As a side trip, he climbed the Tower of Pisa.

LLOYD VOGEL, of Greendale, was a Master Sergeant who participated in the campaigns in North Africa, Sicily and Italy with the Fifth Army. He was awarded the Legion of Merit from General Mark Clark for "exceptionally meritorious performance of duties… contributing to the effective operation of the entire headquarters."

OMER WEHMEYER was a Sergeant in the Army Air Corps. He served as a mechanic during the Italian campaign.

MIKE WESTRICH, of Bright, was a Turret Gunner on B-24's in the Army Air Force. He served in the air offensive in Italy, Rhineland, Central Europe and the Balkans. Once he had to parachute from his plane onto the island of Crete. He managed to escape and make his way back to the Allied lines. He became a Staff Sergeant.

DELMAR BENNETT, of Wright's Corner, was a Staff Sergeant He served as the Driver of an ammunition truck in North Africa, the Middle East and Europe in a total of 9 campaigns.

HAROLD BROWN was a Sergeant in the Army Air Corps. He served with the 307 Fighter Squadron in North Africa, Sicily and Italy.

RAYMOND THURMAN was drafted in 1943 and trained at Ft. Carson, Colorado with the 10th Mountain Division. This group prepared to fight in the Aleutians and the Italian Alps was the only group known as such in the U.S. Army. Senator Bob Dole was in this division. They fought in Italy.

RUSSELL WAFFORD, of Lawrenceburg, was private First Class, entering the Army in February 1943. He served in North Africa and Italy. He received a concussion wound in the Apenine Mountains, Italy.

SERGEANT LOUIS TAYLOR, of Guilford, was assigned to the Quartermaster Corps and served in Africa and Italy.

CLIFFORD P. KNEUVEN, of New Alsace, Tech-sergeant, stationed at Foggia, Italy, made several missions as an aerial engineer on a B-17 bomber and later handled the mail.

PHILLIP TRACY, of Greendale, served with 12th Air Force in a B-25 Bomber Group in the Mediterranean area, fighting in North Africa, Sicily, Italy and Southern France.

PRIVATE DELBERT SMITH, of Aurora, served with a radio unit attached to an Airborne outfit, and fought in Africa, Sicily, Italy, France and Germany.

ANTHONY SATCHWELL, of Lawrenceburg, was first reported missing and then declared killed in action. His duty was in Italy and his last action was with the Infantry in France.

PAUL MILLER, of Lawrenceburg, was in the Alps as he wrote his sister. He wrote he was with friend Bill Dennis the night before Bill was killed in action. They were in the same Paratrooper Division.

DONALD VINUP, of Dillsboro, was killed in action on Anzio beachhead. He was in the field artillery. He was the 35th Dearborn County casualty of the war and the first Dillsboro resident to die in action.

HUBERT THOMAS, of Lawrenceburg, was an Army Private who saw action in North Africa and during the Italian campaign.

DONALD TYLER was an Army Private First Class. He served in North Africa and India.

CHARLES WARNER, of Lawrenceburg, was an Army Private. He served two years in the Middle East Theater.

WAYNE WEIGERT, of Lawrenceburg, was a B-26 Squadron Engineering Officer in the Mediterranean Theater. He was awarded the Bronze Star Medal for Meritorious Service in support of combat operations.

OMER WEHMEYER was a Sergeant in the Army Air Force serving as a mechanic. His duty had been in Africa and Sicily and Italy in 1944.

NORBERT R. WIEDEMAN, of Yorkville, was a Technician 4th Grade with the 580th Field Artillery Battalion. He served as an Auto Mechanic in the European - African - and Mid-East Theater.

Norbert Wiedeman

An American medium tank

WILLIAM SEDLER entered the U.S. Army and became a Technical Sergeant. He served in Iceland for two years.

VINCENT SCHILSON was graduated from Army Air Force Technical Training for airplane mechanics in 1943.

CLIFFORD SCHMIDT served in the U.S. Army Coast Artillery in Delaware in 1943.

HOWARD SCHMIDT was a Second Lieutenant in the Coastal Artillery in 1943.

E. A. SCHOEPPE was in the Army Air Force, Squadron D, based at Charleston, South Carolina.

JOE SCHOOLCRAFT was in the Army Air Force. He was in the 19th Air Technical School at Jefferson Barracks, St. Louis.

JAMES SCHOOLCRAFT was in the U.S. Army Air Corps. He was in the 309th Fighter Squadron in 1943.

RAYMOND SHINKLE, of Aurora, was serving in the Army in England in 1943.

WAYNE SHOOK was a Corporal in the Army, serving in the 65th Chemical Depot in Alabama in 1943.

WILLIS SCHULER was in the Navy. He served with 5th Amphibious Group and the 2nd Marine Division. He contracted malaria while serving.

LUTHER TODD, of Lawrenceburg, was at Ft. McClellan, Oklahoma for basic training in 1943.

LOUIS TURNER, of the Moores Hill area, was in the Transportation Corps of the U.S. Army. He received a disability discharge while at Camp Claiborne, Louisiana.

LOUIS TURNER, of Lawrenceburg, was a Private. He took basic training at a camp in New Orleans in 1943.

MARION VAN WINKLE, of Bright, received radio training at the University of Wisconsin for the Navy. He became a Seaman First Class.

JAMES VAN WINKLE, of Bright, received engineering training for the Army at the Texas School of Mines. Later, as a Private First Class, he would be hospitalized in England.

WILFORD VASTINE, of Mt. Tabor, entered the U.S. Army and became a Private First Class. He served in a Tank Destroyer Battalion at Camp Young, California in 1942.

VIRGIL ULMANSIEK, of Dillsboro, was a Private First Class in the Army in 1943.

JAMES WALLACE was a Radioman First Class in the U.S. Navy. Due to a shoulder injury, he received a medical discharge at Camp Blanding, Florida.

ARTHUR WALLACE entered U.S. Army and took his basic training at Camp Steward, Georgia in 1943.

CHESTER WALKER entered the U.S. Army in November 1943. As a Private, he had duty at a convalescent hospital as a Laundry Machine Operator.

EARL WARBURTON, of Lawrenceburg, served briefly in the Army as a Private. He entered the Army in April 1943 and was discharged in October 1943.

JOHN WEBER was a Private at Camp Livingston, Louisiana in 1943. He had been at Camp Shelby in 1942.

O. P. WEBSTER, of Mt. Sinai, an Aviation Ordinanceman First Class served in the navy for more than 4 years. He had duty at a Naval Base in Florida in 1943.

A Nazi fighter plane down in Italy

ELTON SCHILSON, of Aurora, was a Corporal in the Army Air Force who served in India in 1943.

FRANK SIEMANTEL was a private in the Army who trained as a radio operator at Ft. Knox.

CHAUNCEY SLACK was a Sergeant stationed in Puerto Rico in 1943.

NORMAN WILDRIDGE, of Lawrenceburg, was a Seaman First Class in the Merchant Marines serving in Egypt, West Indies and European waters.

EDGAR ABDON, of Lawrenceburg, was a Sergeant in the Army Air Corps. He served as a truck driver in North Africa and Italy.

FRANK ABDON, of Aurora, was an Army Private First Class. He served as a truck driver in the Infantry in the Italian campaign.

HARRY WILSON, of Moores Hill, was in the 171 Engineers Battalion in 1943.

JESSE WILLIAMSON served in the U.S. Army as a Doctor's Aide in Philadelphia in 1943.

LES WORKMAN was in the U.S. Army, attending Diesel School at the University of Illinois in 1942. He was then a Lieutenant.

CLARENCE WULLENWEBER was a Private in the U.S. Army. He attended Vehicle Maintenance and Repair school at Fort Knox, Kentucky.

WILLIAM WUNKER, of Lawrenceburg, served at Kerns, Utah where he was attached to the medical division of the Army Air Force. He achieved the rating of Corporal.

NORMAN ARMSTRONG enlisted in the Merchant Marines and was assigned to Officer's Training and graduated as an Ensign. He sailed on a tanker which was torpedoed by an enemy submarine, but Norman was one of the survivors.

Modern conquerors visit Caesar's statue in Rome.

Beth Elliott Taylor and baby near her husband's photo. He was away flying planes in the CBI Theater.

CHAPTER 5

On the Home Front

Unlike any other time, life at home was severely affected by WWII. American civilians, of course, were more fortunate than those in England, Europe and Asia where combat and bombings occurred in their cities, towns and villages. Nevertheless all Americans were caught up in the war effort and life became radically different. Now there were blackouts, rationing, women doing men's work in factories, blood donations, production schedules with little time for leisure, scrap drives, bond drives, and the absence of husbands, fathers and sweethearts, and at times, mourning over the loss of loved ones in battles in foreign lands. Dearborn County had never experienced this kind of life before; but they adapted well.

Most civilians "made do." They shared rides and patched up old cars. Housewives used saccharin instead of sugar. Smokers revived the practice of 'roll-your-own' cigarettes, and coffee drinkers rebrewed grounds. Many women painted their legs to look like they wore hose, for all the silk was being used in parachute production. Banners with stars, to indicate the number of sons and daughters in the armed forces, were placed in the windows of most homes. Flags flew everywhere. In general, spirits remained high and very productive on the home front.

Civilian Defense

One of the first concerns of the home front was for Civilian Defense, a term used for the protection of civilian lives and property from enemy saboteurs and air raids.

Elmer Harry, Lawrenceburg business and civic leader, was appointed Dearborn County's first Civil Defense Director by Governor Schricker and Indiana Defense Director C.A. Jackson. Mr. Jackson stated that civil defense in Indiana would have two major thrusts: protection and civilian participation programs. The second one would include activities in the fields of health, education and recreation. It would involve such programs as the Red Cross and the U.S.O. (United Service Organization). Mr. Harry stated that he would organize the county by towns and communities for civil defense as quickly as possible. Meanwhile Miss Anna Belle O'Brien, Greendale, volunteered to assist Mr. Harry.

"Blackouts" were one of the main defense measures taken. When the signal for blackouts were given, all lights in homes and communities were to be turned off or eliminated by special shades. This action was to protect against presenting targets during enemy air raids. To enforce blackout rules, each community had a group of air raid wardens. The first Dearborn County blackout took place on Sunday evening, May 23, 1942.

Here's the way Tom Ward remembers blackouts in Aurora: "Each street had one or two wardens, equipped with helmets, gas masks and whistles. During air raid drills, the wardens walked the neighborhoods looking for any signs of lights from the darkened homes. If a room had a light on - the shades had to be solid, not translucent - the warden would blow his whistle, or knock on the door, with a friendly reminder that the home was to be blacked out. Once in Aurora, Tom Dartnell was walking his end of Fifth Street when he heard signing and saw a bright light shining from his own home. His daughter, Carol, was taking a bath, signing at the top of her lungs, while the rest of the family sat on the porch in the dark. She later responded, "I just knew that the enemy was over 3,000 miles away."

Another civilian defense measure taken was the formation of a Coast Guard Auxiliary Flotilla, based in Aurora.

E.G. Harry
Director of Civil Defense

William E. Barrott, Sr. was appointed Commander. The Flotilla's purpose was to relieve the regular Coast Guard on the Ohio River of some routine duties and to guard against any disruptions on the river in Dearborn County.

Members of the Flotilla included: James Schuyler, H.T. Johnson, Harold Poellman, William Siebert, W.C. Scripture, Lance Booher, Joe Grenat, Curtis Lischkge, A.E. Abshire, Edward Fehling, Frederick Parker, Robert Simmerman, Rev. Morris, Gale Banta, Leslie Weaver and Daniel Nields.

Women's Roles

One of the biggest changes on the home front that would have far reaching effects in the post-war era was the roles women performed. Up until 1940, not much had changed in the roles women had played in America. The norm was, "The woman's place is in the home". Those who had outside positions were restricted to such careers as teaching, nursing, clerical and librarian.

With the absence of men, it was soon apparent that women would be needed as substitutions in the nation's factories, offices and on the farms. The change took place with not only single women but also many married females. Although they did the work once limited to men, they were not treated equally when it cane to pay which averaged about 60% less.

In Dearborn County, it was not so radical for women to work in industry, for the local distilleries had been employing women on their bottling lines since production began in the 1930s. And once the war started, the Seagram Distillery was a national leader in using women in supervisory positions.

In addition to civilian work, hundreds of thousands of women answered the call to serve in the armed forces. They served not only in the nursing corps, but in other positions to relieve men for front-line duty. (See chapter on Women in the Military.)

**William Barrott, Sr.
Commander of the Coast
Guard Auxiliary**

The Role of Black Americans

Jim Crowism still prevailed for most black Americans during WWII. There were still separate facilities, such as restaurants and restrooms, for white and blacks. Segregation continued to be a stain on America's record during the Second World War.

Black Americans, however, were allowed to work at jobs not previously open to them, because of the great need for manpower. Most of the jobs were in war plants in the North, and southern blacks began the greatest migration in U.S. history to secure jobs that paid considerably more than any employment available to them in the South.

In the military, blacks were drafted but put in positions of supply or service, truck driving or material handling. In the beginning, the Navy was worse in this respect, for until the war was underway, black sailors could only serve as mess-boys. It was almost impossible, but not quite, for a black soldier to get a commission. White officers continued to command black troops in the Army for the most part. However, this situation would change.

During the Battle of the Bulge in Europe, blacks received their big opportunity to serve in combat on a non-segregated basis. The emergency need for more troops in this battle, forced Eisenhower to take the position of using black soldiers on the firing lines. Overall they performed well and started the Army to review its policy on use of blacks. Within a decade, the U.S. Military would change from being one of the most segregated organizations to being the most successfully integrated.

As for Dearborn County, our black population during WWII was limited to a section of Lawrenceburg. Such families as the Todds, Brightwells and Parkers served their country well in the armed forces.

Dining rooms continued to be segregated for black Americans.

Aerial view of the A.D. Cook and Schenley plants

Industrial Miracles

At the Big Three (Roosevelt, Churchill, Stalin) Conference held in Teheran in 1943, Premier Josef Stalin made the following toast, "To American production, without which this war could have been lost." What an apt statement.

America not only performed production miracles to make her own tools of war, but she also helped supply the needs of her allies. Under the direction of Production Board Director Donald Nelson, industrial production definitely became a vital factor in the Allies victory.

It all began on the home front a year before Pearl Harbor when F.D.R. urged America to become "an arsenal of democracy". Factories then began producing war machinery and materials in addition to their normal products, which were decreased. For instance, automobile manufacturers were heavily involved in the making of tanks and airplanes.

The Ford Motor Company in Detroit built a new factory for the production of aircraft. Called Willow Run, it was the largest aircraft plant in the world. The building was

An emergency delivery of penicillin from Schenley's plant to a Buffalo, New York hospital, carried by George Horn of Lawrenceburg

nearly a quarter of a mile wide and a half a mile long, designed to produce bombers at the rate of one every hour. Counting other plants, before the war ended, American industry built 296,430 airplanes, 102,350 tanks and 87,620 warships.

In shipbuilding, Henry Kaiser revitalized this production by prefabricating sections of ships and then welding them together. At the peak of the war, he built a ship in only 80 hours and 30 minutes. He built one third of America's 2,700 Liberty Ships. Another outstanding person in this kind of business was Andrew Higgins whose yards in New Orleans mass produced the landing craft, known as Higgin's boats, which were used on D-Day and for other invasions.

In all, some 200,000 home front companies - large, medium and small - successfully converted to war production. Operating at full production schedule, industry had to use new sources of manpower. The most significant addition to the work force, of course, was the more than 6 million women, who were nicknamed "Rosie the Riveter", whether they were in the airplane business or other war production jobs.

In addition to women, factories also hired black Americans in jobs hitherto closed to them. Also teenagers, convicts, the handicapped and aged were utilized. Unemployment disappeared totally.

Some of Dearborn County's civilians took jobs in war plants and offices in Cincinnati at the Wright Aeronautical plant, forerunner of the G.E. plant, and elsewhere. Carolyn Elliott McManaman, Guilford, and Flo Hill Abdon, Aurora, among others, were employees in the Army's Ordnance District Office in Cincinnati. They worked in the Personnel Department processing Civil Service paper for employees, from clerks to inspectors in the Cincinnati and Indianapolis areas. John Taylor, Guilford, and Justin Murtaugh, Dover, were young chemists who worked at the Du Pont Powder Plant in Charlestown, Indiana.

Without a doubt, the best known war production performed in Dearborn County was for penicillin at the Schenley Distillers, Inc., plant in Greendale. Schenley was a leader nationally in the development of this miracle drug which saved the lives of many wounded and sick servicemen.

The first operation in Greendale was a research laboratory and a pilot plant, where women, dressed in surgically white uniforms, performed as technicians and helpers. By 1942-1943, production of penicillin began in earnest, and the War Production Board approved the construction of a new penicillin plant scheduled for operation in 1944.

In addition to penicillin, Schenley also began to produce commercial alcohol for the armed forces a month before Pearl Harbor, and completely did away with their whiskey production in October, 1942. War products used alcohol in the manufacture of smokeless powder, synthetic rubber and anti-freeze for tanks and planes. By 1944, the Greendale plant of Schenley had made a total of 24 million gallons of alcohol for government usage.

The local Seagram distillery also began in 1941 to convert production of whiskey to commercial alcohol for war-time needs. Ordinarily commercial alcohol was distilled from the by-products of sugar cane, but a shortage of tankers drastically reduced this supply from the Caribbean nations. This was the first time that grain alcohol in large quantities was used in the production of munitions, announced Fred Wilkey, Seagram Vice President in charge of plant operations.

The A.D. Cook Company, neighbor of Schenley in Greendale, was another local well-known company to devote production time to the war effort. In Cook's machine shop, the machining on a variety of parts was performed. Some of these were gun openings to be fitted onto tanks and also wheels were made for tanks. A.D. Cook shipped some of its pumps to Russia for war-time service.

Stedman Foundry and Machine Works in Aurora made parts for the U.S. Navy and Merchant Marine ships laid up in Pacific shipyards awaiting repairs. Mr. Noble Pfeiffer of the U.S. Employment Service ran a special campaign to recruit employees for Stedman. He said the war effort with Japan would be delayed if this work were not completed. Stedman also did some work for the Navy on gun turrets.

It was reported that the Wooden Shoe factory in Aurora, which had been involved in furniture production, made ammunition boxes for the Army during World War II.

Seagram Distillery office and warehouse

Agricultural Production

Farm production too had to be increased during WWII to feed not only our fighting forces, but also many of our allies, and with less manpower, machinery and fertilizers. To help farmers on the home front cope with this problem, the Farm Security Administration was organized by the federal government. This organization provided training and other incentives for farm laborers.

Early in the war, fifteen families in Dearborn County gave up living in town or on small, unproductive farms to work as year-round laborers on some of the larger, more productive farms. Women, too, were encouraged and used to do farm work.

President Roosevelt declared January 12, 1943 as Farm Mobilization Day. The Lawrenceburg Kiwanis Club held a special farmers meeting with Harry Jackson, State Agriculture Fieldman, as guest speaker.

Dearborn County farm families who took part in the huge 1944 Food Production Program, sponsored by the government, were awarded a Certificate of Farm Work Service in recognition of their vital work in the war effort. The certificates were signed by the Secretary of Agriculture Claude Wickard. They made handsome displays in many farm homes in Dearborn County.

Farmers were also asked to keep close track of their farm machinery as to replacement parts needed. These items were to be reported early to their dealers so that procurement could be prioritized and secured when needed. Committees to supervise this type of action were set up in each township of Dearborn County.

Louella Brooker did farm work during WWII.

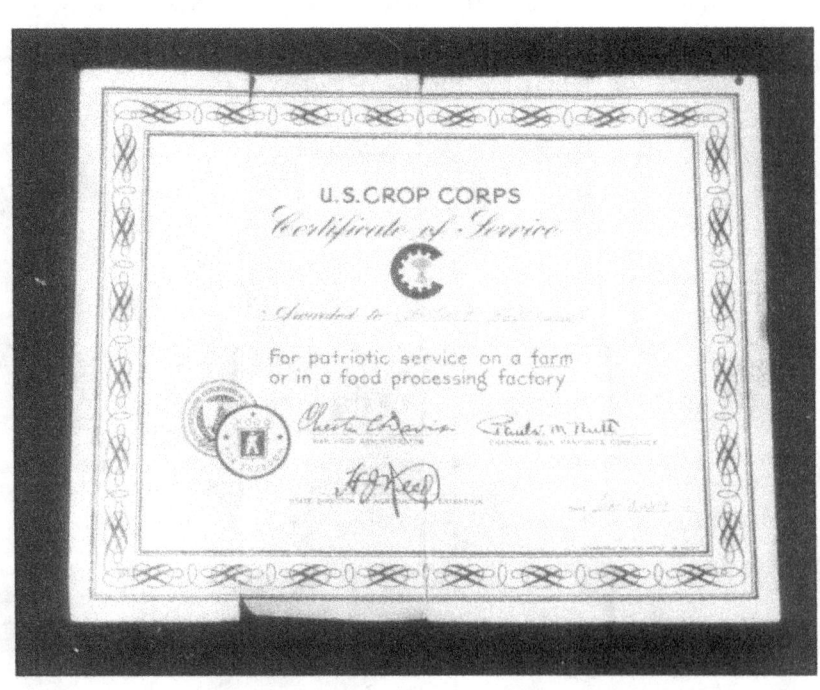

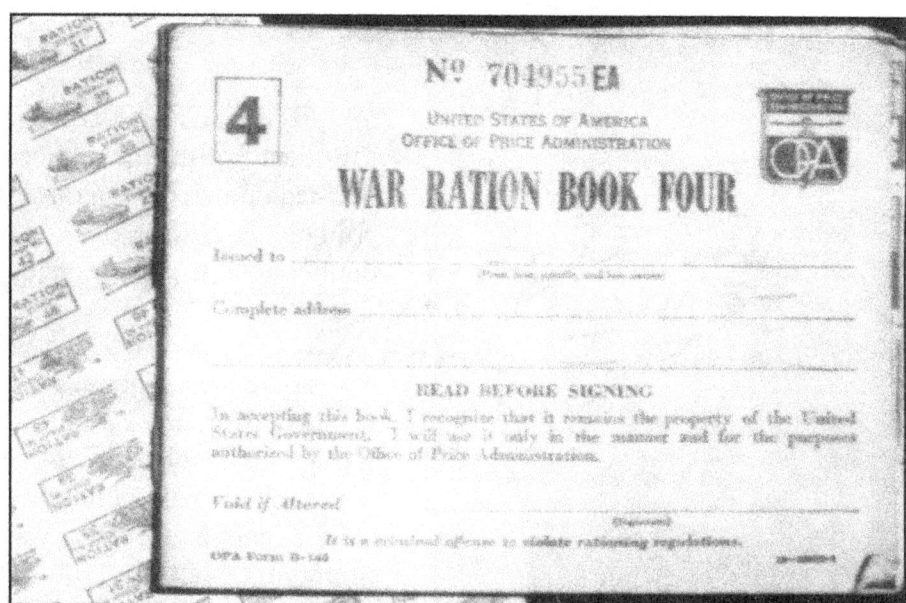

War Ration book and stamps

Rationing

War demands meant shortages on the home front. To deal with this emergency, the President used a rationing program to distribute scarce items on a fair basis. Rationing began shortly after Pearl Harbor when F.D.R. froze the sale of new automobiles and tires, which were doled out to physicians and other civilians with essential work.

In May of 1942, War Ration Book No. 1, the sugar book, was issued. On November 12, gas rationing began in Dearborn County. Gas was rationed with the aid of "A," "B" and "C" cards, placed prominently in the windshield of every auto. The only people who rated an "A" card were those working at essential jobs in defense plants, such as the Jefferson Proving Ground or the Charlestown Powder Plant. Drivers to these kinds of plants received the highest allotment of gasoline but not enough for any side trips. "B" cards went to those who needed autos in their business but not in essential war jobs. "C" cards were for drivers who made non-essential trips.

Meat began to disappear in late 1942 and rationing was imposed in March of 1943. Also in that month, rationing was used on more than 200 items of canned, dried and frozen fruits and vegetables. War Ration Book No. 2 was inaugurated for this food rationing system. Other rationing programs limited Americans as to coffee, shoes and fuel oil. By late 1944, most stores would frequently post a "no cigarettes" sign.

The OPA (Office of Price Administration) issued books of rationing stamps, administered by local Rationing Boards. In Dearborn County the various Board Chairmen were: Frank Barnes (Aurora), E.G. Harry (Lawrenceburg), Anthony Hassmer (Lawrenceburg) and John T. Martin (Aurora).

War Bonds

To finance the war would take more than federal taxes, so President Roosevelt and Secretary of the Treasury Morgenthau decided upon a continuous effort to get Americans to buy government defense or war bonds. It was another way that people on the home front were encouraged to give sacrificially to the war effort.

Cornelius O'Brien, head of the A.D. Cook Company in Greendale, was appointed Executive Chairman of the Dearborn County's Defense Savings Staff for the sale of war bonds and stamps. In October of 1941, he had solicited committee members from all parts of the county (at this time "war" bonds were called "defense" bonds) and began planning for the work of promoting and selling these bonds from the Treasury Department.

The first campaign for the sale of war bonds took place in April and May of 1942, with a quota of $80,600 for Dearborn County. Solicitations were made in public gatherings, door-by-door, and by payroll deductions for industrial employees.

Although home front people were expected to buy war bonds continuously, there were occasional drives to stimulate sales. In October of 1942, there was a special program held at the Liberty Theater in Lawrenceburg, with a preview of the movie, "Wake Island". The price of admission was a signed pledge to buy at least one war bond by November 1. This rally was in charge of the Women's Division, chaired by Mrs. Earnest Oertling of Lawrenceburg.

Marie Edwards Seitz was a Red Cross Nurse Aide.

The Red Cross

As in World War I, the Red Cross was active on both the home front and overseas. Colonel Robert H. Nanz, head of Schenley Distillery in Greendale, was chairman of the local chapter of the Red Cross.

In peace time, Dearborn County had experienced the relief work performed by the Red Cross during the 1937 flood. Now in war time, the organization would provide such services as canteens for service men, blood banks for both the military and civilian populations, first aid training, volunteer nursing aides, as well as being of service to traveling service people.

As an example of the work performed by the Red Cross, the Aurora Chapter on RC Relief Projects, sent a total of 650 male garments made by local women, for hospital use, to the Red Cross distribution center in St. Louis. Mrs. William Stedman, Chairman of the Aurora Chapter, was in charge of the project.

Beyond a doubt, one of the most valuable services performed by the Red Cross was the collecting of blood and making it available to the armed service. Many lives were saved by blood available to wounded men on the battlefield from blood collected on the home front.

Township Red Cross chairmen were: Frank Hutchinson (Lawrenceburg), Robert Sykes (Miller), Bernard Losekamp (Harrison), Shirley McClure (Logan), Stella Stiegler (Kelso), George Gutzweiler (Jackson), Richard Collier (York), and Ray Kyle (Manchester).

Robert Nanz
Schenley Manager and
Chairman of the local Red Cross

Victory Gardens

Dearborn County's home front participated in the Victory Garden program, which was an effort to encourage civilians to produce their own food to ease the demand created by the war effort. These gardens ranged from several acres to a tiny plot in the town's backyards and the vacant lots. Joseph E. Seagram & Son., Inc. provided 25 plots of their land in Lawrenceburg for employees' gardens. By 1943, it was estimated that in the U.S. there were 20 million Victory Gardens producing 8 million tons of food.

The Dearborn County Farm Agent, C.A. Alcorn, promoted Victory Gardens. His office was available to help any one with plans and information on how to plant and take care of gardens.

There was also a canning center at the old shoe factory in Newtown, installed by the Lawrenceburg High School to help individuals can the produce from their Victory Gardens. Costs to individuals was only for the cans used. This operation was under the direction of Mr. Bruce Miller, Director of the high school Vocational Education program.

Elmer Davis, formerly of Aurora, headed the Office of War Information.

Recruiting poster: Air Corps

Communications

President Roosevelt established the Office of War Information in June of 1942. The mission of OWI was not only to coordinate and distribute news of the war, but also to sell the objectives of the war and to present America to the world with a strong, positive emphasis. In addition to printed messages, OWI ran 18 radio stations beaming "Voice of America" broadcasts overseas in 40 languages.

To head OWI, the President selected Elmer Davis, a native of Aurora. Davis possibly served in the highest civilian position of anyone from Dearborn County during WWII. Elmer had been a writer and a newscaster in New York for some years before his new position took him to the nation's capital for the remainder of the war.

Another WWII communication effort was the encouragement by the Dearborn County Commissioners to erect a Service Honor Roll in a public place in every community. These Honor Rolls would give the names of all the men and women in the county in the armed forces and date of entry. Sally Ritzmann Polk, Lawrenceburg, was placed in charge of that community's Honor Roll which stood in Newtown Park. Sally was also appointed by the Indiana Historical Bureau to keep the record of Dearborn County boys who lost their lives in WWII. In addition to community Honor Rolls, many industries followed suit and posted a list of employees who entered the military during WWII.

The federal government also made use of posters to communicate to the home front. The best-known one had a white-bearded old man dressed in red, white and blue pointing a finger and declaring: "Uncle Sam Needs YOU". Each branch of the military had their own version of recruiting posters, which were widely displayed, especially in the early days of the war. There were other government posters to improve the war effort. For example, there was one cautioning people not to allow certain information to reach the enemy, with the slogan, "Loose Lips Sink Ships."

The Lawrenceburg Consolidated High School had a display of its graduates in the military. It was a beautiful silken flag, having blue and gold (deceased members) stars on a white field. It was presented with an appropriate ceremony for the public at the school on February 1, 1943. Superintendent Harrison read the names of the graduates whose stars appeared on the flag. With the house lights darkened and only a spot light showing, the stage curtains were parted to reveal the new flag. The school band then played the national anthem followed by taps. Another feature of the program was a solo by Richard Horn of Lawrenceburg.

In the same vein as the school program, many churches in Dearborn County would hold services during the war to honor their members who were serving in the armed forces.

The communications which involved most people during the war was that of writing and receiving letters to and from loved ones in the military. To accommodate this exchange, which was a morale booster for men far away from home as well as the home folks, the government gave free postage to service people and instituted the idea of V-mail, which was a photographically reduced version of one's letter written on light-weight stationary. V-mail was less bulky and easier to transport.

Mail call was definitely an important time for the home front people as well as the military. However, there were pieces of mail or telegrams which were dreaded on the home front. These were the ones which informed the family of the death or the wounding of a loved one in combat. For example, the following excerpts are taken from a letter written by First Lieutenant William Ewbank of Lawrenceburg to his wife, just before his death and given to a friend to send to her in case of his demise. (William Ewbank was killed by a German sniper in France in 1944...see Chapter 8.)

Recruiting poster: Marines

Lt. William (Bill) Ewbank

Dearest Wife,

I am sending this letter to Gus to keep and forward if anything should ever happen that I shouldn't get to come back to you and our darling children...There isn't any way I can tell you how much I love you now that I haven't done before and I hope my actions have spoken louder than my words...don't grieve too long and I do earnestly hope that you will marry again if you find some one worthy of you. If you do, remember he's human too, and don't keep my picture on the piano...You are so wonderful that I know you will raise a fine son and daughter I will be proud of...Always remember I love you.

Bill

Pelgen's Tavern in Aurora during WWII, notice war posters on wall

Scrap and Other Collections

Boy Scouts and others were involved in many scrap drives to conserve war materials on the home front. In 1943, Governor Schricker proclaimed October 1 - November 15 as a Hoosier Victory Scrap Bank Campaign. He urged every citizen to do his utmost to help the state surpass its quota of 150,000 tons of general scrap metal.

In July of 1942, there was a scrap rubber drive held in Dearborn County. James Welch, Aurora, was chairman. He stated that 219,560 pounds of scrap rubber had been collected. The county quota was set at 12 pounds per person.

The War Production Board requested the home front to conduct a collection of old clothing in December, 1943. Such items were needed to clothe refugees in liberated countries. Chairman Givan Heller arranged for the campaign to be conducted through the churches in the county.

The most unusual collection was the gathering of milk weed pods. The floss was used for the making of life jackets; since kapok was no longer available as it comes from the South Pacific islands. The first farmer to report a collection of milk weed pods was Charles Emery of Washington Township. He picked four bags on his farm.

Other Actions

Due to the sudden decrease in the number of practicing physicians in Lawrenceburg, Dr. J.C. Elliott, Guilford, made arrangements to have office hours in Lawrenceburg three days a week, using the office of Dr. William Fagaly, who was serving in the Army Medical Corps.

Believing that every prospective serviceman should understand the nature of military life before entry, Superintendent of Lawrenceburg High School instituted a course entitled, "Preparing to Enter the Armed Forces." The course was taught by George Bateman, boys counselor at the school.

Sally Ritzmann, Lawrenceburg, ran a classified ad in the local newspaper for "four tires with a car attached." She said it wouldn't be any trouble to sell the tires and she would throw in the car as a bargain. For transportation to her job at Seagram, she would use a bicycle.

Sparta Township's Service Roll

CHAPTER 6

Women in the Military

Following the example of other involved nations, the U.S. opened up her military service to women, besides nurses, during World War II. But unlike Russia, they could take no part in combat. This move by America was advantageous in relieving many men in the armed forces for combat duty instead of doing behind-the-lines support jobs. Moreover it would pave the way for the widespread acceptance of women in many positions in the American military today.

The Army with its Women's Army Auxiliary Corps (WAAC) was the first branch of service to open its ranks to women. They did so in May of 1942 under the leadership of Oveta Culp Hobby. They soon shortened their name to WAC (Women's Army Corps), and grew to some 5,750 officers and 93,550 enlisted females. They served in the U.S. and some 10,000 were sent overseas to England, France, Italy, North Africa, Australia, New Guinea and India.

The Navy was next to take in women with its WAVES (Women Accepted for Volunteer Emergency Service). Captain Jean Palmer was Commandant. When the war ended, there were 86,000 gals in the U.S. Navy. (Incidentally, the Navy had recruited women "Yeomanettes" in WWI.)

The Coast Guard called their women SPARS, taken from the Coast Guard motto, "Semper Paratus," Always Ready. By the war's end, there were 10,000 SPARS performing duties in the U.S., Alaska, and Hawaii. Commanding Officer was Captain Dorothy Stratton. (The Coast Guard had recruited women during WWI.)

The Marine Women Reserves was organized last on February 13, 1943, with just a plain name. They served in administrative, supply, training, mechanic, driving, photography and in control towers. Ruth Streeter, as Colonel, headed the program, which reached a peak of 18,500.

WASP (Women's Airforce Service Pilots) served with the A.A.F. Their mission was to fly aircraft from factories to designated military bases. They also towed targets and ferried weapons and personnel.

The women in Dearborn County who served in the Armed Forces during World War II are noted in the following paragraphs.

(opposite page) Recruiting poster for WAVES. Each branch of the military services used attractive posters for recruiting. Awanda Calver of Lawrenceburg was photographed for a WAC poster.

MILDRED HILKER CORNS, of Aurora, was the first woman from Dearborn County to enlist in the WAACS on August 8, 1942. She reported for training at Ft. Des Moines, Iowa and graduated from Motor Transport School. Duties included inspection, maintenance and operation of Army motor vehicles. Transferring to Ft. Hood, Texas, she was promoted to Auxiliary First Class rating.

MARY FOX ANDERSON, of Lawrenceburg, was in the Cadet Nurses Corps at Christ Hospital, Cincinnati, Ohio from 1942-1945. She worked in a Veteran's hospital on graduation as a Registered Nurse.

ELLA F. ANDRES, of St. Leon, served in the WACS from 1944 to 1945. She was overseas in Berlin as a Clerk Typist.

ARMADA FISCHER BAKER, of Aurora, a former Public Health Nurse in Ohio County before her marriage to Lester Baker in 1940, enlisted in the Army Nurse Corps in 1945. She served at a hospital in Galesburg, Illinois caring for wounded troops from the Pacific Area.

GRETNA BARKER, of Greendale, enlisted in the Women's Reserve of U.S. Marine Corps. She had her basic training at New River, North Carolina, and received a rating of Private First Class at Camp Pendleton, California.

MARY JANE BIRMINGHAM, a Dearborn County Health Nurse, entered the Navy Nurse Corps and was commissioned an Ensign in June of 1991.

MARTHA BLOCK had WAC training at Fort Des Moines, Iowa.

MARGARET SCHNEIDER BRANDEL of Lawrenceburg entered the WAVES, completed training at Hunter College, N.Y. and was sent to Medical Department, Naval Hospital, Bethesda, Maryland. She was Master-of-Arms of WAVES quarters and was promoted to Pharmacist 1st Class and put in charge of the records office at Bethesda. As a supervisor, she had 200 WAVES reporting to her.

MARY JANE BYRANT, of Lawrenceburg, a WAC at Ephrate, Washington Army Air Base, had one of the principal roles in a theatrical production "Yours For Victory" for the base personnel in November 1994.

Nurse Rosemary Witt

WAVE Anna Probst Warren

WAC Virginia Hess   Marine Gretna Barker   Army Medic Edith Rullman Callon

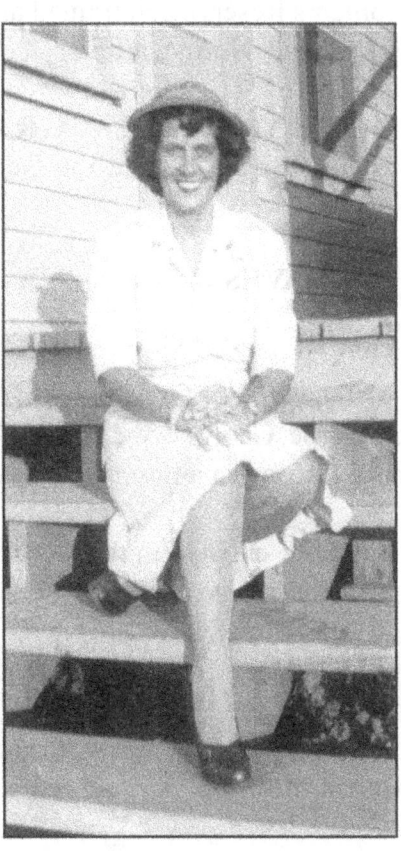

GRACE FOLSOM, of Lawrenceburg, was as a Yeoman 3rd class in the WAVES. She was in the Communications Department in Washington, D.C. She was also an attendant at Franklin D. Rossevelt's funeral in 1945.

DELLA GILLUM, of Greendale, trained with the WAVES at Hunter College, Bronx, New York. She had worked as a dental assistant and laboratory technician prior to enlistment.

KATHLEEN GOOD, of Aurora, enlisted in the WAACS. She had attended Indiana University and became a First Lieutenant and was sent to the Dutch East Indies. Her work was that of a Public Relations Officer.

AWANDA CALVERT GOODMAN, of Lawrenceburg, initially trained in WAACS at Camp Crowder. She was awarded the Good Conduct Medal for serving a year with exemplary behavior, efficiency and fidelity. Serving in Central Signal Corps, she was promoted to Corporal, then Sergeant Technician 5th grade. Being a very attractive girl, she was chosen to be on a WAAC recruiting poster. While in the service, she married Sergeant Walter Goodman of New York.

ELVA B. GOODPASTER, of Moores Hill, enlisted in the Marine Corps Women's Reserve and trained at New River Marine Base, Camp LeJuene, North Carolina.

MARGARET HARTWELL GRANATIR, of Lawrenceburg, was a Cadet Nurse at the General hospital in Louisville in 1944.

DOROTHY GRAVES, of Aurora, served in the Army WACS.

MARY HAMILTON, of Greendale, took training in the WACS at Ft. Oglethorpe, Georgia. She entered Photo Lab Training at March Field, California and served there.

VIRGINIA HESS, enlisted in the WACS on February 1, 1944. Her husband had already left for the Army, so she decided to go in the Army, too. Her basic training was at Ft. Des Moines, Iowa, followed by 22 months at Great Falls, Montana. She worked by assisting the Chaplain and in the Post Office. She attained the rank of Staff Sergeant working as a WAC Clerk Typist in Stockton, California. She served 22 months in the WACS.

DOROTHY BURTON, of Wilmington, enlisted in the WACS in 1945 getting her basic training at Ft. Worth, Texas.

EDITH RULLMAN CALLON, of Aurora, was a Medic in the Army, gaining the rank of Staff Sergeant. She served as a scrub nurse in operating rooms in hospitals in Clinton, Iowa; Denver, Colorado and San Francisco. She also worked with paraplegics in the patient wards.

EVELYN CARTER had her basic training in the WACS at Ft. Des Moines, Iowa. She served overseas in England as an ambulance driver with the European Wing of the Air Transport Command. She also delivered supplies to the forward areas. As an ambulance driver, she met planes and brought wounded soldiers from the invasion centers to hospitals.

ESTER CLARK, of Lawrenceburg, had basic training in the WACS at Ft. Oglethorpe, Georgia. On graduation as a Medical Technician, she was assigned to Harmon General Hospital, Long View, Texas.

HARRIET MATTOX COCHRAN was a Pharmacist Mate 3rd Class in the WAVES. She was married while in the WAVES to Crawford Cochran, Seaman 2nd Class.

EMILY BAKER CONWAY, of Aurora, was a Cadet Nurse in the training at Christ Hospital, Cincinnati, Ohio from 1942 to 1945. On graduation as a Registered Nurse, she was assigned to duty at a government hospital in Fort Defiance, Arizona.

VIRGINIA DOERR, of Aurora, took her training in the WAVES at Indiana University to become a Storekeeper. With further training, she was assigned to a Naval disbursing, supply and commissary office. After WWII, she continued in the Navy and retired after 24 years of service.

LEONA EDRINGTON, joined the WACS in January of 1943.

ROBERTA SCHILLER ENGLISH, of Aurora, served in the Coast Guard Spars from 1944-1946. She was a Storekeeper 2nd class.

SPAR Roberta Schiller English

Nurse Armada Fisher Baker

Nurse Margaret Hartwell Granatir

Margaret Schneider Brandel

WAVE Virginia Doerr

WAC Margaret Todd

WAVE Eloise Busse Lambert

Judy McKain Hughes (1st r.) and Margaret Schneider Brandel (2nd l.) celebrate VJ Day with friends.

MARY SWIFT HUBBEL, of Aurora, enlisted in the Women's Auxiliary Air Corps in March 1943. As a Sergeant, she served in the office of Embarkation at Ft. Lawton, Washington.

JUDY McKAIN HUGHES, of Lawrenceburg, was in Washington following basic training at Hunter College as a WAVE. She was assigned to Communications Department and was promoted to Petty Officer and assigned to Arlington, Virginia.

KATHRYN JOHNSON, of Aurora, trained with the WAVES at Hunter College, N.Y.

MARGIE CARTER JOHNSON wife of John Johnson who was serving in the Pacific, enlisted in the Hospital Corps and was sent to McGuire General Hospital Richmond, Virginia.

HAZEL KARST, of Aurora, Airman First Class, completed a six weeks course at the Army Administration School WAAC Branch No. 4, located at Texas State College for Women at Denton, Texas.

ALLEAN KLINE, a Registered Nurse of Dillsboro, enlisted March 19, 1945 in the Army Nurse Corps. She took her basic training at Ft. Benjamin Harrison.

ADA KOONS, of Lawrenceburg, completed her basic training at Ft. Oglethorpe, Georgia. Then she was transferred to McClain, Mississippi.

MARGIE KREINHOP, of Lawrenceburg, a graduate of St. Elizabeth Hospital, Covington, Kentucky, enlisted in the Army Nurse Corps and was assigned to an Army hospital for six months duty.

ELOISE BUSSE LAMBERT, of Aurora, served as a Corpsman in the WAVES entering in December 1944. She was assigned to the Naval Hospital at Great Lakes.

FREDA LANGE, a graduate of Bethesda Hospital, Cincinnati, Ohio, reported for duty at the Naval Hospital, Philadelphia, Pennsylvania.

MILDRED CORNS LEIDOLF, of Lawrenceburg, was one of the first 10 WACS in the ETO to receive her wings as a flight traffic clerk. She was a member of the European Division, USAAF Air Transport Command. Her organization was the Trans-Atlantic Aerial supply line between United States and Europe operating passenger and cargo planes.

EL JEAN McCRIGHT, was sworn into the SPARS in January 1944. Her training was in Miami, Florida.

MARY CATHERINE McCRIGHT, was sworn into the SPARS, U.S. Coast Guard, in Cincinnati in January 1944. She trained in Miami, Florida.

MAJORIE KURTZMAN McDOUGAL, of Lawrenceburg, was in the WAVES, getting basic training at Hunter College then serving in Seattle, Washington.

GRACE McMULLEN, of Homestead, entered the WACS training at the First Women's Army Training Center at Fort Des Moines, Iowa. She served in the Florida-Caribbean Wing of the Army.

TOMMY LOU STRACK McMULLEN, of Lawrenceburg, took WAVE training at Hunter College. She was one of the 24 chosen to pass an exam for the Singing Platoon who appeared regularly in NYC for broadcasting. She also played cymbals in the drum and bugle corps. Her assignment was the Receiving Station, Washington Naval Yard and she was Seaman First Class.

EDITH MORLING was a Cadet Nurse and was commissioned a Second Lieutenant in the Army Nurse Corps. She was stationed at Newton Baker General Hospital, Martinsburg, West Virginia.

DOROTHY WAFFORD NOCKS, of Lawrenceburg, was a Corporal in the WACS. She was stationed at Harmon Hospital, Longview, Texas. Her husband Harry Nocks was also serving in the Navy.

BETTY POWELL, of Lawrenceburg, entered the WAVES and was trained at Hunter College.

OLLIE LAMBERT POWELL, enlisted in the WACS in 1943 and was the first Aurora woman assigned overseas, going to New Guinea in August 1944. Her later assignments earned her the Asiatic Pacific Ribbon with three battle stars and the Philippine Ribbon with one star.

MARGARET REES, of Aurora-Lawrenceburg Road, enrolled in the Cadet Nurse Corps at Christ Hospital, January 1945. She had two brothers in the service: Ellis Rees who enlisted in the Navy in 1940 and Ralph Reese who enlisted in the Army Air Force in 1943.

ALICE RUHLMAN, of Aurora, a registered nurse, left for active duty in the Army Nurse Corps at Oliver General Hospital, Augusta, Georgia in March 1943. Her husband, Hal, was a Captain in the U.S. Army Engineering Corps.

HELEN SNYDER, of Greendale, trained with the WAVES at Hunter College, N.Y.

WANETA SPECKMAN, of Aurora, was sworn into the Army Air Force Division of the WACS in Cincinnati, November 18, 1944. She had her basic training at Ft. Des Moines, Iowa.

MARGARET TODD, of Lawrenceburg, was a WAC in the U.S. Army.

EULALIE TRESTER, of Aurora, was sworn into the WAVES in May of 1943. She became a Pharmacist 3rd class at Bainbridge, Maryland.

ANNA PROBST WARREN, of Wilmington, entered the WAVES in 1943. Her rating was Seaman First Class and she was stationed in Washington, D.C.

GERTRUDE WELLS, of Aurora, was assigned to Company 4, 3rd Regiment at Ft. Des Moines, Iowa for basic training. She became a member of the Air Transport Command, Ferrying Division.

ROSE MARIE WIDOLFF, of Yorkville, enlisted in the WAVES taking basic training at Hunter College, N.Y. She took more training at Milledge, Georgia and graduated as a Petty Officer, Storekeeper 3rd Class and was stationed in New York.

AURELIA WILLERS, of Greendale, was a member of the Army Nurses Corps serving in Normandy, France, Ardennes, and the Rhineland. She was awarded the Bronze Star and had 4 battle stars. She attained the rank of Major and was in charge of Nursing for the 32nd Division.

NAOMI WINE, of Aurora, was the first woman of Aurora to join the Women's Reserve of the Coast Guard, known as the SPARS. She trained in Palm Beach, Florida.

ROSEMARY WITT joined the Army Nurse Corps as a 2nd Lieutenant, July of 1945. She retired from the Corps in July of 1965 as a Major. She served in WWII and the Korean Conflict at the Tokyo General Hospital.

RUBY WOODFILL resigned as a Registered Nurse at Seagram's Distillery to enlist in the Nurse's Corps of the U.S. Navy. She had duty at Great Lakes Naval Base.

JEAN YANDLES enlisted in the Marine Corps Reserve in July of 1944.

ROSE MARY YOUNG, of Lawrenceburg, entered the WAVES getting basic training at Hunter College, N.Y.

General MacArthur wades ashore as he returns to the Philippines

CHAPTER 7

On the Offensive in the Pacific

In the Aleutians

From March to August of 1943, there were operations in the Aleutian Islands in the North Pacific. President Roosevelt had set a priority to take back these islands so close to the continental U.S. An amphibious force was formed to recover Attu. The battleships *Pennsylvania*, *Nevada* and *Idaho*, with a covering force of cruisers and destroyers acted as the fire support group for the landings there. On May 11, Marines and the 7th Infantry Division invaded Attu, and after two weeks of heavy fighting, drove the Japanese off the island. On Kiska, a large U.S. force landed unopposed to discover the Japanese had evacuated this island.

During the remainder of the war, except for some feeble Japanese raid attempts, there was little further combat activity in the Aleutian Islands.

Taking New Guinea and the Solomons

With the Japanese drive halted on the Owen Stanley Mountains and the Coral Sea and Guadalcanal secured, the Allies could begin their major Pacific offensive. The Joint Chiefs decided upon a two-pronged strategy. MacArthur and Halsey would drive up through New Guinea and the remainder of the Solomons; while Nimitz with his Navy and Marines would strike Japanese bases in the Central Pacific.

The Japanese tried to save their forces on New Guinea by reinforcing bases at Lae and Salamaua. On March 1, U.S. reconnaissance planes spotted this convoy and two days later the Fifth Air Force, operating from southern New Guinea, attacked and destroyed the convoy and the Japanese plans for holding this large island.

At the same time, MacArthur's forces were moving forward along the northern coast of New Guinea, Halsey's forces went up the ladder of the Solomon Islands at the Russels, New Georgia and Bougainville. Within a little more than a year, MacArthur's army had reached far up New Guinea. By mid-1944, the final landings were made on the neighboring islands. With the great help of the Sea Bees, advance U.S. bases and airfields were built there for the invasion of the Philippines.

Offensive in the Mid-Pacific

Moving westward in the Central Pacific, Admiral Nimitz pushed his amphibious forces across Japanese-held islands, including the Gilberts, Marshalls, Marianas, Kwajalein, Eniwetok and Tarawa. On November 20, Makin in the Gilberts was taken. But Tarawa was another story. It was one of the bloodiest battles in the Pacific. Tarawa was an atoll of islets linked by coral reefs. The place had been bombed for a full week. No one knew that the Japanese were protected by reinforced concrete bunkers with steel beams and coconut logs. Landing boats got caught on the coral reefs and the Marines had to wade ashore for hundreds of yards under murderous fire. About half of them made it safely. It took four days to overcome the enemy, and the cost was terribly high.

On each island, the Japanese fought savagely from debris of American bombings. The U.S. advance was sure but slow; as each fortification on each atoll had to be taken or burned out with flame-throwers. With the Marshall and Gilbert groups taken, Nimitz headed for Saipan in the Marianas and made an initial landing on June 15, 1944. The Japanese fleet steamed into the area four days later and the most intensive carrier battle of the war took place. The Japanese thought they were undetected, but a U.S. submarine sighted them as they left their base in the Philippines and radioed the news to the U.S. fleet which was able to pick up the enemy ships on its radar, and then launch planes to intercept it. U.S. bombers and fighters caught the Japanese completely by surprise. The aerial battle was so one-sided, it was referred to as the "Great Mariana Turkey Shoot." In a few hours, the Japanese had lost 350 planes and 2 aircraft carriers. By August, the Marianas were completely in American hands.

Retaking of the Philippines

Conditions were now right for MacArthur to act out his promise, "I shall return." Plans called for both his forces and Nimitz's forces to converge on the Philippine Islands.

In October of 1944, MacArthur made the initial landing in retaking the Philippines at Leyte. This brought out the Japanese fleet to oppose U.S. naval units there, Halsey with the Third Fleet and Admiral Kincaid with the Seventh Fleet. The final result was the greatest naval battle of all time, the Battle of Leyte Gulf. The Japanese divided their forces into three units: the northern one to lure Halsey away from the main fighting-and he did take the bait-and the central unit to converge on the Leyte landings, and the third unit to come up from the south. Kincaids's ships were able to repulse the enemy central force and he figured the enemy force would come through the Suriagao Strait to reach Leyte Gulf. He ordered Rear Admiral Oldendorf with the fire support unit of six battleships, eight cruisers and some destroyers, to block the Strait from the enemy. Oldendorf was able to pull off the classic naval maneuver of "crossing the enemy's T" with his battleships and cruisers and some destroyers, when the Jap ships attempted, in a line, to enter Surigao Strait. American gunfire on the opening salvo landed squarely on the Japanese leading battleship. In the final tally, two Japanese battleships and three destroyers were sunk and other ships were badly damaged. The enemy was forced to retreat from the scene. Meantime, Halsey had sunk four carriers in the decoy force. In this series of naval battles off Leyte, the Japanese suffered immense losses which crushed their naval effectiveness.

The appearance of Japanese kamikazes, or suicide planes, came in this engagement. One U.S. carrier was sunk and two others were damaged by kamikazes which would be a terrible weapon as the position of the Japanese's position grew more desparate.

The liberation of the Philippines was well begun at Leyte. By early November, U.S. forces had drawn the enemy from the southern and northeastern sectors; and the Philippine guerrilla movement was giving aid to the invasion on most islands. The Japanese tried to bring in reinforcements, but the U.S. Navy and Air Force prevented that; and so the enemy's position became hopeless. In February of 1945, Manila and Corregidor fell. After that it was a matter of overcoming pockets of resistance in the mountains and jungle. Actually this mopping up action would continue until the war was over.

James Sedler   **Joseph Tanner**

Larry Steigerwald (left) and crew members on New Guinea

ROBERT LEASURE was a Mess Sergeant in the Marines in the Pacific. He fought in New Guinea and the Philippines, receiving three battle stars.

JACK SNIDER, of Lawrenceburg, was a Private who served in Italy with the Fifth Army.

JAMES R. SEDLER, of Lawrenceburg, a Marine Corporal, was killed in action in June 1944 in the South Pacific. He was survived by his wife and son not yet a year old. James took part in the battle of the Marshall Islands soon after going overseas. Later, he was returned to Hawaii where he was stationed at a rest camp. After a short rest, he was returned to battle. Then tragically he lost his life in combat, and was buried on the Island of Saipan.

HAROLD RUDOLPH, from Lawrenceburg, was with the 32nd Infantry Division, serving in the Philippines.

THOMAS JACKSON served with the Army Air Force at Keesler Field in Mississippi in 1943.

CARL HART, of Sawdon Ridge, trained at Tennessee Poltytehnic Institute for instruction before appointment as a Cadet in the Army Air Force.

VIRGIL LACEY, Radioman third Class, in the Navy, served in the Pacific Theater. He entered service in September 1943 and took part in the invasion of Okinawa, serving aboard LCI694.

RICHARD LACEY, Seaman First Class in the Navy, served on the U.S.S. *Oklahoma* in the Pacific. Helped sink a Japanese destroyer, transport and 12 planes. He also fought at the invasion of Truk, Saipan and the Philippines.

WILLIAM W. LYONS, a Sergeant in the Army, participated in the jump on Corregidor with the 503 Paratroop Division in the retaking of the Philippines in 1945.

DONALD LAWRENCE, Corporal with the Artillery served in Manila, Philippines Islands 1943.

TOM MURRAY, of Bright, served in an Ordinance Repair Company in the Army. He served in the Pacific Theater, the Philippines, and other island bases.

Harold Rudolph

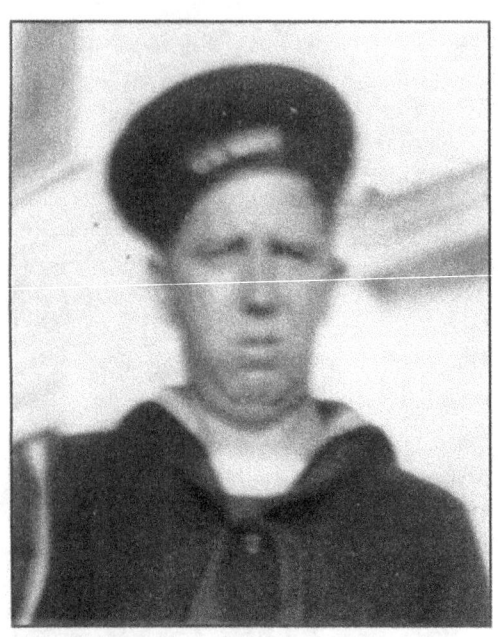
Sylvester Vogelsang

Edward Terrill

JIM JACOBS, from Greendale, was a Sergeant Major working with cinema photography at Culver City, California.

LOUIS STRUCKMAN was in the Navy. He was a Seaman First Class. He was an Aerial Gunner on a Navy Patrol Bomber. On one mission he faced intense anti-aircraft fire which repeatedly hit his plane. As a Gunner, he assisted in the destruction of two enemy aircraft. His plane also did extensive damage to enemy installations on the ground. Louis received the Distinguished Flying Cross.

WILLIAM LOVE, a Private in the Army Air Force, was in gunnery training in New Mexico in 1943.

ARTHUR RUMP, of Farmer's Retreat was a Sergeant with the 338th Bomber Squadron and trained at Page Field, Florida.

HOBART WALSER served with an Airborne Engineer Battalion. He received his training at Ft. Bragg.

JAMES BARBER, of Lawrenceburg, had duty in Australia and on to New Guinea and the Philippines.

SYLVESTER VOLGELSANG, Third Class Petty Officer, was on Saipan with the Sea Bees in 1943.

EDWARD TERRILL was a Captain in the Army Dental Corps. He was stationed at Camp Chaffee.

ROY MASON, of York Ridge, was in the Merchant Marines.

JAMES BARNES served in the Army in Panama in 1945.

JOSEPH C. KNUEVEN, of New Alsace, as a Corporal was a maintenance engineer at Fort Lewis, Washington.

JOSEPH TANNER, of Wrights Corner, served in the Pacific Theater as an Infantryman in New Guinea, South Philippines and Luzon.

FRANK SAVAGE, of Lawrenceburg, was called into active service in 1942. He was a Second Lieutenant, having completed 3 years of Citizens Military Training. He was assigned to the 31st Division as a Special Platoon Leader for landings in New Guinea and Morotai Islands. While he was Cargo Control Officer at a port in Morotai, the Navy brought in a captured Jap hospital ship which was carrying their troops, not sick and wounded personnel. Before they were taken to the Philippines, Frank had to arrange for the unloading and assigning of temporary quarters for these prisoners. Later he moved up to the Philippines where he became an Executive Officer, as a Captain, of the 93rd Infantry Division. For meritorious service in these campaigns, Frank was awarded the Bronze Star and an Army Commendation.

JOHN ULLRICH, of Aurora, served in the Navy on LST (Landing Ship Tanks) 919, in the Pacific theater. He spent much time transporting troops and supplies between New Guinea and making landing on the Philippines. In September 1945, the ship sailed to Okinawa, Korea and in November went to China and Japan.

PAUL TIBBETS, of Dillsboro, was in Naval supply with duty on New Caledonia.

JAMES SMITH was in the Coast Guard for a time and then received a medical discharge in 1943.

NOBLE LIGGETT, of Lawrenceburg, a Corporal in the Cavalry Division, died in March 1943 of wounds he received in the Southwest Pacific. He was one of the first selectees in service from Dearborn County and had been in the service three years.

WILLIAM LAND was a Water Tender First Class in the Sea Bees in 1943.

OMER VINUP, of Dillsboro, was a Motor Mechanic and served with the Army in Hawaii for a year. He died of a gunshot wound to his head which occurred in his barracks, cause unknown.

CHARLES WEAVER, of Lawrenceburg, a Torpedoman 3rd Class in the Navy, served in the South Pacific aboard a submarine.

WILLIS THOMPSON, was a Water Tender First Class in the Navy serving in the Philippines.

Frank Savage

John Ullrich

Robert Miller

Robert Stadlander and wife

ROBERT MILLER, served in the Alaska Division of the Air Transport Command. He was a Personnel Sergeant Major for the base at Ladd Field with the rating of Master Sergeant. In July 1944, he was assigned to the Air Inspector General's Office at Wing Headquarters in Edmonton, Canada. This group inspected air bases spread across Canada and Alaska with Bob as Chief Administration Inspector.

HAROLD (HAL) RUHLMAN, of Aurora, served as a Lieutenant (j.g.) in the Navy where he had duty in the Pacific. He was with the Sea Bees on Guam. He contracted undulant fever and after a ten month stay in a Naval hospital he was discharged from the service.

LARRY STEIGERWALD, of Lawrenceburg, was a Private First Class in the Army Air Force, stationed in New Guinea.

CHARLES TEANEY, of Aurora, was a Hospital Apprentice 1st Class during 1944-1946.

PAUL WARE served in the Marines. He entered the service in 1943.

LOUIS WHITAKER was a Private in the Army at Fort Wood in 1943.

ROBERT STADTLANDER was trained in mechanical repair. His unit kept jeeps operating during the campaigns.

EARL SUMMER, of Dillsboro, was a Private First Class who served with the Army in India in 1944.

HARRY SCHAEFER, of the Sunman area, was a corporal in the Army with duty in the Philippines in 1945.

BERNARD TEANEY, of Aurora, served as a Sergeant in the Army Transportation Corps in 1943.

ALBERT SEILER graduated from Naval Air Training School at Norman, Oklahoma as an Aviation Ordnance Man 3rd Class.

ALBERT SELLERS served as a turret Gunner on a Carrier. He participated in strikes on Guam, Saipan, Philippines and China. He received the Purple Heart for being wounded.

PAUL M. GREIVE, of Dillsboro, served 29 months overseas as a Corporal on a Cavalry Reconnaissance Team of the 37th Infantry Division. He was a Machine gunner on armored half tracks traveling into Japanese held jungles gathering enemy information and traveling to front lines with supplies. He was presented the Distinguished Unit Badge, and Presidential Citation. He served in New Zealand, Guadacanal, Fiji Islands and New Georgia Island.

ALLEN GRELLE, of Dillsboro, served with the Army Field Artillery in Alaska in 1943, transferring to Italy in 1944.

LEROY GULLEY entered the Army and became a Private First Class. He was wounded for the second time in Attu of the Aleutian Islands.

CLARENCE HEATH was a Technician 4th Grade with the 596 Signal Air Warning Battalion. He served in the Philippines as a Cook.

EUGENE HIGGINS was a Staff Sergeant in a Maintenance Engineering Division. He served in North Africia, Sicily, France and Italy.

LUTHER HUGHES, of Dillsboro, was a Private First Class with the 33rd Infantry Division. He was killed in action on Luzon in June 1945.

CLYDE HYMAN was with the 85th Sea Bees. He served in the Aleutian Islands for 17 months and at Pearl Harbor in 1945.

CECIL KEITH was playing a saxophone in a Navy band in 1944.

CLIFFORD KERR served as a Corporal in the Army in the Aleutians in 1944.

THOMAS KIDD was an Army Cook with the 1919 Ordnance Anti-Aircraft Artillery in the Pacific Theater of Operations.

IRWIN KINNETT served in the Marines as a Machine Gunner on Guam in 1944.

Paul Greive

Warren Kemper

RAYMOND STONE was burned in a mine explosion and sent to a Canadian hospital to recover.

FREDERICK BAKER, of Greendale, was killed in action on Leyte in the Philippines. He had been involved in the conquest of New Guinea.

WARREN A. KEMPER enlisted in the Army in 1941. After basic training at Ft. Hood, Texas he became a First Lieutenant. At Fort Benning, Georgia, he trained to be a paratrooper but injured his knee while parachuting. He was then sent to the Island of Attu for duty.

GEORGE WOLKING, of Aurora, served at the Key West Naval Station. He entered the Navy in December 1943 and was a Sonarman 2nd Class.

WILLIAM BUCHANAN, Private First Class in the Army served in the South Pacific in 1943.

LEROY BULTHAUP served in the Army at Camp Meade, Maryland in 1943.

ROBERT (MUSH) HUBER, of Lawrenceburg, served on the ship, U.S.S. *Puget Sound*, as a Seaman First Class.

HERMAN TRANSIER, of Dillsboro, served in the Navy.

CHARLES BRUCE, of Lawrenceburg, was a Gunners Mate 3rd Class in the Navy in 1942. He received the Purple Heart for wounds during landing operations at Rendova in the New Georgia Islands. He was returned to the States and his wounded leg amputated in the Naval Hospital at San Diego.

RALPH RUMP was in the Army Air Force with the 1103 Bomber Squadron having trained at Morrison Field, Florida.

LELAND TEANEY, of Aurora, served as a Pharmacist Mate 1st Class at Quantico in 1942 and then the Pacific Theater.

CARL LOMMEL, of Lawrenceburg, was a Yeoman 3rd Class in the Naval Dental Corps in 1943.

U.S. troops landing on a South Pacific Island

FLOYD MONTGOMERY was a Private in the Army and had service in New Guinea in 1944.

LAWRENCE STEVENS was a Sergeant in the Army serving in gliders in 1943.

NORBERT STEELE was a Sergeant in the Army Air Force. He was a Crew Chief.

JAMES SCHNETZER, of Lawrenceburg, was a Radioman 3rd Class who spent 16 months in the Aleutians.

WILLIAM STEDMAN, of Aurora, was in the Army Air Force as an Air Cadet in 1943.

JOHN MORROW was a Staff Sergeant with the Marines. He served 20 months in the Solomon Islands.

PAUL RUTENKROGER was an Aviation Cadet in the Army Air Force in 1944.

EDWARD SCHAEFER served as a Gunners Mate 3rd Class in the Navy operating in the Pacific in 1945.

THOMAS STAHL became a Radio Technician 3rd Class and served in the South Pacific for 26 months in the Navy.

WILLIAM NORMAN, of Wilimington, was stationed on Guam in 1944.

EUGENE (DUKE) RUNYAN was a radio operator with a Signal Company that served on Guam, in the Philippines and in Japan.

CHARLES SHELDON, of Aurora, was a Seaman First Class in the Navy. Entered service in June 1943 and served in the Pacific Theater of Operations.

OTIS TANNER, of Wright's Corner, served in Australia and New Guinea. He was awarded the Bronze Star.

RALPH EDWARDS, of Aurora, served in the 145th Infantry and received the Bronze Star and Distinguished Unit Citation for service in the Northern Solomons and the Philippines.

(l. to r.) **Leland Teaney, Courtney Dicken and Bob Robinson in Guam**

Bill Brandt and the Great Lakes baseball team

WILLIAM (BILL) BRANDT, of Wright's Corner, was a professional baseball player with the Pittsburgh Pirates when he enlisted in the Navy in November 1943. He was stationed at Great Lakes, Illinois for almost a year and played on the Great Lakes baseball team with other professional players. They would travel to other bases and entertain the troops. Later, he would be sent to a small island in the Philippines. There he played ball and worked in the ship's service. He was separated from the Navy in December 1945.

DONALD ERNEST, of Lawrenceburg, served as a Rifleman with the 1467th Infantry in the Philippines, earning 3 battle stars. He was a Private First Class.

ROBERT LEISURE was in the Army Engineers. He served in New Guinea in 1944.

DAN STERLING, of Aurora, was a Staff Sergeant in a Chemical Service Company. He took part in 3 major battles in the South Pacific.

ALFRED (WICK) SCHNEIDER, of Lawrenceburg, trained at Drew Field, Florida and became a Private First Class. He served as a Radarman with the Army Air Force in the South Pacific.

CHARLES MARSH, of Aurora, served in the Pacific Theater of war. He was a Pharmacist Mate Third Class.

VICTOR MONDARY was a Private First Class who served 18 months in the Pacific Islands. He was with the 168th Infantry Divison.

CLARENCE (DENNY) MORAND, of Lawrenceburg, was a Sergeant in the Army Air Corps serving at the Air Base in St. Petersburg and Lakeland, Florida.

MICHEL MOLTER was an Army Private assigned to a training school in Abilene, Texas in 1943.

DICK STACY, of Moores Hill, made the landing on Eniwetok Island on the first wave in an advanced machine gun position. He was an Army Technician 5th Grade.

TOM WELDON served as an Army Captain in the Second Airborne Artillery Unit in 1943.

JOSEPH STEPHENSON, of Lawrenceburg, served with the Marines at the battle of Cape Gloucester and other islands in the Pacific Theater. He was a Private First Class.

WILLIAM GLENN was a Fireman First Class who served on a ship which ran supplies from Hawaii to the Pacific Fleet in 1943.

ARTHUR TUCKER was with a Signal Radio Intelligence Company at Camp Custer in 1942 and later was in the South Pacific as a Master Sergeant.

CLYDE SKIDMORE served in the South Pacific and the Philippine invasion.

EARL SCHOLLE was in the Army Air Force in 1944 serving as a Corporal.

EARL FERDON, of Aurora, was a Motor Machinist Mate 3rd Class with the Sea Bees in the South Pacific, participating in the taking of the Mariannas.

GEORGE STALKER, of Lawrenceburg, served in an Army motor pool as a Corporal at the South Pacific Headquarters in New Caledonia.

Alfred Schneider

Earl Scholle

Charles Lambert

Carl Harmeyer

CHARLES LAMBERT, of Aurora, an Aviation Ordnanceman in the Navy was injured in a plane crash in 1944. He was the plane's tail gunner.

ENYARD SMITH served in the Army Air Force as a Staff Sergeant and engineer on a B-29 bomber in the Pacific Theater.

FLOYD GERKIN, of Lawrenceburg, was a Chief Boatswain Mate with the Sea Bees and was in the Pacific Theater for 2 plus years. He was Chief Master at Arms of the battalion that built a massive air installation on Tinian Island.

RUSSELL BAKER was in the Navy as a Machinist Mate First Class serving aboard a ship in the Pacific.

EDMUND RUSSELL graduated from the Army Air Force Navigator School at Hondo, Texas and was assigned to the transport Command in Florida in 1943.

LESLIE WEAVER, of Lawrenceburg, was a Radioman 2nd Class on a landing ship in New Guinea and the Philippines in 1945.

CARL HARMEYER, of Dillsboro, was severely wounded and would spend two years in hospitals for treatment and partial surgery. To understand something of the pain and trauma of a service combat wound, read his description in the following: "In March 1945, I was wounded for the first time on the Island of Mindanao. Later, I was sent back to the same outfit and company. Four weeks later, I was hit the second time. The Japs fired two 80MM. The second round landed by me. It almost blew my left arm off; there was very little left to hold it on. I could not hear out of my left ear. The tip of my nose was shot off. My face was cut from shrapnel. I somehow managed not to black out. I used a tourniquet to keep from bleeding to death. I was hospitalized on Mindanao. The doctors said I had very little blood left. They used an arm bone from the bone bank. It got infected and they had to replace it. I was shipped to Leyte. I was there for four weeks. They put maggots inside an upper torso body cast. When they removed this cast my body weight was down from 180 pounds to 92 pounds. They put on a 45 pound shipping cast before I left Leyte. We flew from island to island until we landed on Honolulu and then returned to a hospital in the states."

RAY STUARD was a Corporal in the Army Air Force. He served with the 5th Ferrying Group in 1943.

W. LEE CROUCH, of Lawrenceburg, had been an officer in the Marine Corps since 1936 (see Chapter 1). He was with the Second Marine Division on Guadalcanal, Tulagi and the Solomon Islands. As Admiral Nimitz advanced his forces across the Central Pacific, Lee and the Second Marine Division next saw action at Tarawa, for which they were awarded the Presidential Unit Citation. At the invasion of Saipan, he, now a Major, was Commanding Officer of the Third Battalion, Tenth Marines. During this battle, Lee was killed in action on July 7, 1944. He was awarded the Navy Cross medal, one of the highest medals to be received by a Dearborn County military man, posthumously in ceremonies at Camp Lejeune, North Carolina, attended by his wife and three year old son. The Navy Cross citation, signed by Secretary of the Navy, read in part: "For extraordinary heroism in action against the enemy Japanese at Saipan on 7 July 1944. When Japanese launched a fanatical 'Bonzai' attack, completely surrounding his position, Major Crouch valiantly fought on in face of insuperable odds and held his position for a grueling 12 hour period until relieved by infantry reserves. With his command post especially hard hit when an enemy tank penetrated the area, Major Crouch led the battery in fighting off the vicious onslaught. Realizing the urgent need for tank support after communication lines had been severed, he fearlessly braved the withering barrage to cross an open field in an effort to secure aid, but was fatally struck down by hostile fire. His inspiring leadership and great personal valor in the face of tremendous odds reflect the highest credit upon Major Crouch and the United States Naval Service. He gallantly gave his life for his country."

WILLIAM (BILL) ABDON completed training at Midshipman's School at Notre Dame University and was commissioned an Ensign in the Navy. He served in the Pacific Theater and in Alaska in 1944.

JOHN AIKMAN was a Seaman 2nd Class in the Navy. He was a Physical Education Instructor at a Naval base on the East Coast.

EARL LEFFLER was an Army corporal in the 398th Field Artillery, serving as a Carpenter in 1944.

FRANK LONGCAMP, of Aurora, was a Second Lieutenant serving in the Army Medical corps in 1943.

CHARLES STEUVER was a Sergeant in the Army. He was trained as a Radio Technician. He served with the 285th Field Artillery.

A native of New Guinea

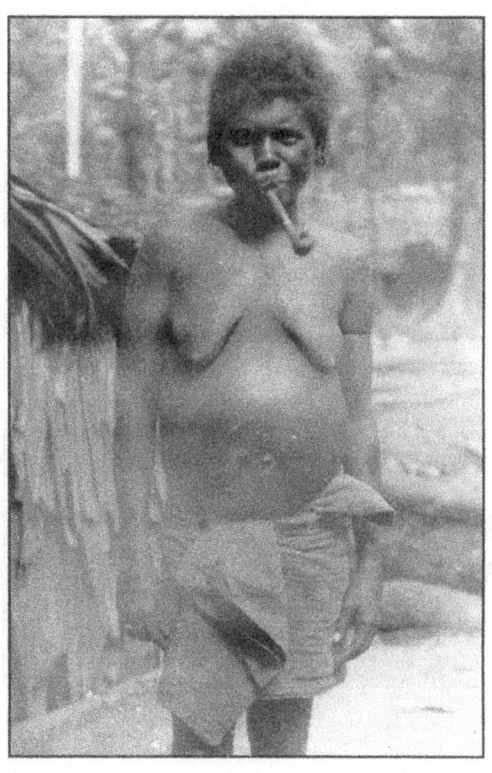

Herbert Aust

Willard Aust

WILLIAM ALBRIGHT, of Lawrenceburg, was an Army Staff Sergeant. He served as a Payroll Specialist in the Personnel Unit at VanNuys Air Field, California.

GEORGE (HONK) ALBRIGHT was in the Marines on a cruiser in the Aleutians.

CARL ANDREWS, of Milan, was a Staff Sergeant in the Army Air corps. He served as a Mechanic on P-38 fighter planes.

HERBERT AUST was killed in action on February 16, 1945 near Manila in the Philippines. He was a Private serving with the 511 Parachute Infantry Regiment. They were engaged in a battle with the Japanese when enemy shrapnel fragments struck him in the chest.

WILLIARD AUST was inducted into the Army in March 1943 and became a Technician 5th Grade. He served as a Cargo Checker in Bombay, India.

HOUSTON COLE was a Motor Machinist Mate Third Class who served 19 months in the South Pacific.

ERWIN FISCHER was in the U.S. Navy. He served on a Landing Ship for Tanks in the Pacific Theater.

CLIFFORD COLEN, of Lawrenceburg, entered the U.S. Navy in 1945 and took his basic training at the Great Lakes Naval Station.

BEN FRYER, of Bright, was a Private First Class in the Army serving in Hawaii and in the Fiji Islands from March 1943 to November 1945.

LOREN GILMORE was a Private First Class in the Philippines in 1945. He was wounded on Luzon Island.

CLAYTON GOODPASTER was in the Army and was stationed at Ft. Leonard Wood, Missouri in 1943.

GLENN GREIVE was a Carpenters Mate 3rd Class on the U.S.S. *Avery Island*, a new auxiliary ship. He was in the Philippines in 1945.

KENNETH KITTENBRINK was a Private First Class in the Marines in 1944.

CALVIN H. KLINGELHOFFER, of Aurora, served in the U.S. Army Engineers from Sept. 1942 to Jan. 1946. He graduated from Engineering Officer Candidate School in Jan. 1943. He left for Scoffield Barracks, Hawaii, where he joined the 34th engineers Regiment in April 1943. He participated in four major battles: Kwajalein, Saipan, Tinian, and Okinawa. He received the Navy Presidential Unit Citation. He attained the rank of Captain.

GENE KLOPP was a Corporal in the Marine Corps. He participated in the invasion of several Pacific Islands, including the Marshalls and Saipan.

JOSEPH KLOPP, of Lawrenceburg, was a Gunner in a Tank Destroyer unit in the Marines. He fought in Saipan in 1945.

RAYMOND LEONARD entered the Marine Corps in April 1943. As a Private First Class in New Britian in the Pacific Theater.

GEORGE LINGG was a Radioman 2nd Class in the Navy from November 1943 to April 1946. He served aboard the carrier, U.S.S. *Solamana*.

ARTHUR E. LIPSCOMB entered the U.S. Navy in 1944 and served until 1946 with duty at Pear Harbor, Hawaii and at Leyte in the Philippine Islands.

HOWARD MENDELL was in Army Ordnance. He was a Sergeant in New Guinea in 1944.

EUGENE MICKENS was a Navy Gunnery Instructor in Florida in 1943.

HERBERT MILES served as a Staff Sergeant in the Infantry, 38th Cyclone Division 6th Army and was wounded in Luzon.

EDWARD D. MILLER of Greendale, was an infantryman in the Army, he was a Private. He was awarded a Purple Heart for wounds suffered in the right shoulder during combat in the Philippines in 1945.

Calvin Klingelhoffer (l.) and Don Ritter

Arthur Lipscomb

Edward Miller (l.) and comrades

Cornelius Widolff

Walter Nelson

GILBERT MILLER, of Mt. Tabor, served in the U.S. Army briefly in the American Theater, and received a medical discharge in August 1945.

JAMES LOUIS MILLER served in the U.S. Navy as a Coxswain, principally in the Asiatic Pacific Theater. He served on the U.S.S. *Wolverine* and U.S.S. YMS65.

RAYMOND MILLIGAN was a Staff Sergeant in the Field Artillery 38th Division in 1943.

WILMER MOLTER was serving as a Corporal in the Army in 1943.

EARL MURPHY was an Air Cadet in Kansas in 1944.

EARL MURRAY, of Moores Hill, was in the Navy at Flight School Ohio, Weslyan University in 1943.

EDWIN MORRIS enlisted in the U.S. Navy in June of 1944 as an Apprentice Seaman. He received an honorable discharge at Great Lakes in July of 1944.

CARL NAEGELE, of Dillsboro, entered the U.S. Navy in 1943 and served aboard LCI (L) 462 in the Philippines, receiving 4 battle stars.

WILLIARD NEFF entered the U.S. Navy in June of 1941 and became a Seaman 2nd Class. He served briefly and was discharged from Great Lakes U.S. Naval Hospital in October of 1944.

WALTER NELSON, of Aurora, was an Aviation Machinist Mate in the U.S. Navy. He served twenty-five months in the South Pacific Theater.

RALPH EDWARDS, of Aurora, served in the 145th Infantry and received the Bronze Star and Distinquished Unit Citation for service in the Northern Solomons and the Philippines.

ROBERT OCHS, of Aurora, entered the U.S. Army in December 1943 and became a Technician 4th Grade. He served as a Marine Engineman in New Guinea, Solomons, and the Philippines.

JOSEPH STEINMETZ, of Guilford, was an Army Technician 5th Grade. He served as a Warehouseman in the Pacific Theater with the 199th Ordinance Depot.

DONALD STOOPS was a Seaman 3rd Class who operated a blinker signal at a Marine base in Oregon in 1944.

LESTER STOVER, of Friendship, was a member of the 15th Field Artillery of the 35th Infantry Division who fought in New Guinea and the Philippines.

JAMES SYKES, of Bright, was a Technical Sergeant who served with Army Quartermaster Corps in the Pacific Theater stationed in and Mid-Pacific Islands.

LEE TRANSIER, of Aurora, entered the U.S. Marine Corps and was in active service in 1943.

ROBERT WALKER, Seaman First Class, was aboard the carrier, U.S.S. *Princeton*, when it was sunk in the Philippines. He received the Purple Heart for wounds and 4 battle stars for battles in the Pacific.

HARRY WATTS, of Aurora, was a Technician 4th Grade with the Headquarters Detachment of the Xth Corps. He served as a Clerk-Typist and had duty in the Philippines.

THOMAS WATTS, of Aurora, was in the Finance Section of the X Corps of the U.S. Army. He served in New Guinea, the Philippines Islands and Japan. He served from January 1943-January 1946.

CORNELIUS (DUTCH) WIDOLFF, of Yorkville, entered the Marines in August 1942 and was placed in the 21st Marines, 3rd Battalion. He served at Guadalcanal in 1943 and next at Bougainville. He was promoted to Corporal and then First Sergeant. In 1944, he went to Guam and in 1945 landed in Iwo Jima and saw the raising of the American flag on Suribachi.

PAUL WIEDEMAN, of Guilford, served in the Marine Corps as a Corporal. He saw action in the Pacific Theater of Operations.

James Sykes

Robert (Bob) Walker

Ben Fryer

Lester Baker

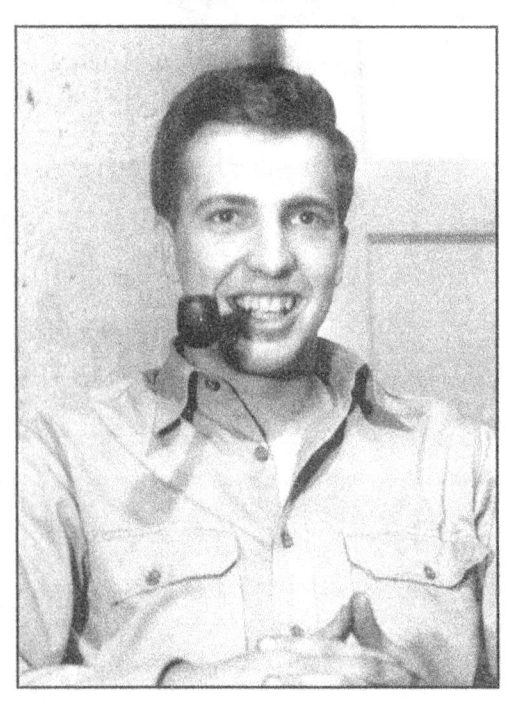
William Barrott

HARRY MCKINNEY was a Military Policeman in the Army in 1943.

RAYMOND MCELFRESH was a Technical Sergeant with a Harbor Craft Detachment serving in the Aleutian Islands. Also served on a Sea Bees ship in Seattle.

WILBUR MCMULLEN, of Lawrenceburg, was a Seaman 1st Class with the Sea Bees in the Marianas in 1945. He advanced to Sea Bees Ship Fitter and served on Saipan and Manus.

LESTER BAKER, Prosecuting Attorney for Dearborn and Ohio Counties, resigned that office and was inducted into the Army in September 1943. He was assigned to the South Pacific Joint Purchasing Board in New Zealand. Four months later, he was appointed to the rank of Warrant Officer and to duty in the office of U.S. Attaché to New Zealand.

WILLARD BAKER, of the Sunman area, was a Private First Class, he served with the 451st Bomber Group in the Air Offensive in Europe and the Balkans, in the Po Valley, Naples, Rome and Normandy. He had 10 battle stars and won a Distinguished Unit Citation.

GALE BANTA, of Aurora, was graduated from Basic Engineering at Great Lakes.

WILLIAM BARROTT II, of Aurora, enlisted in the Army Air Force and served in the Pacific Theater. He was in the Philippines preparing for the invasion of Japan when the war ended.

ALGER BASCOM, of Aurora, was a Private First Class with the 130th Engineering Construction Battalion as a Carpenter in the Pacific Theater.

PAUL BENNETT was a doctor from Dillsboro who was in the military service and stationed overseas.

RUSSELL BENNING, of Lawrenceburg, was an Army Technical Sergeant. He served as a Radar Repairman in the American Theater.

G. WILSON BENTLE, of Bright, served in New Guinea with the U.S. Army in 1944.

WILLIS BENTLE enlisted in the Navy in July 1942 and was assigned duty on the U.S.S. *Alcor* (AD34) which operated in the Pacific Theater and took part in the Philippine Liberation.

RUSSELL BOURQUEIN entered the U.S. Army as a Private and was sent to Texas A&M University for special training in 1943.

GEORGE BENTLE entered the U.S. Army and became a Sergeant. He had desert training in Goffs, California.

NORBERT BOEHLER served two years in the Aleutian Islands with the Mechanized Artillery. He was a Private.

HAROLD BOSSONG was a Corporal serving in the 22nd Fighter Squadron stationed in Puerto Rico.

STOWE BOVARD was a Storekeeper Second Class in the Navy. He served in the Philippines and received 2 battle stars.

ROBERT BRAUN was a Motor Machinist Mate 2nd Class. He served on a LCT in the landings on Leyte and Bataan in the Philippines in 1944.

EUGENE BROOKS entered the U.S. Army as a Private. He served at the Chanute Field and then was shipped overseas in 1944.

RAYMOND BROWN entered the U.S. Navy and became a Seaman First Class. He had duty with an Armed Guard crew on a tanker in the Mediterranean Sea.

GLENN BUTLER, of Lawrenceburg, entered the Navy in August 1943 but was given a disability discharge in November 1943.

ROBERT BUTTERLY was in the Navy V12 training program at Purdue University in 1944.

AMOS CHARLTON, of Aurora, was a Boatswain Mate Second Class in the Navy Sea Bees in 1944.

G. Wilson Bentle

Willis Bentle

WILLIAM CAIN, a dentist from Dillsboro, joined the Army Dental Corps and became a Major serving in New Guinea and the Philippines.

RUSSELL CALVERT was training in the Army at Camp Barkley, Texas in 1944.

WILLIAM COLLINS, of Lawrenceburg, was a Coxswain in the Navy participating in the invasion of the Gilbert and Marshall Islands in 1945.

HAROLD COLE entered the U.S. Navy in 1944 and served aboard the U.S.S. *Columbia* in Lingayen Gulf in the Pacific where he lost his life in January 1945.

JEROME COSBY, of Aurora, was a Technical Sergeant in the Army Air Force serving as an Aerial Gunner. He spent two and a half years in South Pacific. He was with the first U.S. Convoy to land in New Guinea. He earned a commendation for "Victory of the Fifth Air Force against enemy in recent destruction of convoy off shores of New Guinea"

THOMAS COOK, of Lawrenceburg, was an Army Private in engineering training at Oklahoma A&M University in Stillwater, Oklahoma in 1943.

CARROLL COLE, of Dillsboro, served at Dutch Harbor, Alaska in 1943.

WILLIAM COOK, of Greendale, was in the Navy. He was a Fire Controlman 2nd Class, serving on a destroyer in the South Pacific in 1943.

ALFRED COTTINGHAM, of Moores Hill, enlisted in the Army Air Force and became a Radio and Radar Repairman.

STANLEY CARLSON, of Wilmington, was a Sergeant in the Marines receiving the Bronze Star for leading an Amphibious Battalion while landing on Iwo Jima. He also fought in campaigns on Guadacanal, Saipan and the Marshall Islands.

WILLIAM CARTER, was a Gunners Mate in the Navy on the U.S.S. *Abner Doubleday* during the Philippine invasion. He was made an honorary member of Philippine government

Thomas Cook

for obtaining information on the Japanese. His ship was bombed in the Philippines in 1944.

RAYMOND CHEEK was a Corporal with the Anti-Aerial Artillery Division in 1944.

RALPH CHANDLER was a Corporal in the Army Air Force serving as assistant to a Chaplain in Alaska.

MALCOM CRAIGMILE, of Lawrenceburg, was a Seaman Second Class on the cruiser *Savannah*, LSD20 and APA36.

CHESTER CLARK, of Dillsboro, was an Army Sergeant serving in the Pacific Theater. He saw action in New Guinea, Philippine Islands and Bismarck receiving 4 battle stars.

EARL CLARK was a Private First Class in the Parachute Infantry and was wounded on Leyte in the Philippines in 1943.

GERALD CRIDER, of Lawrenceburg, became a Master Sergeant in the Army Air Force and served as a Line Chief for a bomber squadron in the Pacific Theater.

OAKEY CRIDER was a Sergeant in the Army Air Force. He was a Tower Operator in the Philippines in 1944.

ROBERT CURTIS was a Technical Sergeant in the Army Air Force in the South Pacific. He served as a radio operator-gunner on a bomber in New Guinea and the Philippines. He received the Air Medal for outstanding service.

JOE DAVID was a Technical Sergeant in the Army and served in the Aleutians.

KENNETH DARLING was a Technician 4th Grade with the 5th Air Force. He saw action in New Guinea and other parts of the Pacific Theater.

JOHNSON DIBBLE was a Corporal in the Army with a railway operating battalion in Alaska. He received a commendation for outstanding leadership during a destructive flood, restoring the White Pass and Yukon Route to normal operation.

Amos Charlton

Thomas Watts

Three brothers and a brother-in-law (l. to r.) Alford, Frank, Harry Cottingham and Lawrence Stevens

WILFRED WEILER, of Guilford, was a Private First Class with the 204th Field Artillery. He served in the European and Mideastern Theater of Operations as a Canoneer.

EVERETT WESTMEYER, of Dillsboro, was a Private First Class in the 544th Engineer Boat and Shore Regiment. He served as a Seaman, Landing Craft. He had duty in New Guinea and the Philippines.

KENNETH WILLIAMS, of Lawrenceburg, while serving as a Sergeant in the Marianas Island, had the task, with a Lieutenant, of crawling to the top of Bloody Ridge on Saipan and rescuing his wounded Captain, and dragging him back to the rear line. He served 3 years in the Pacific Theater.

JACK WILLKIE was a Private First Class serving on the Marshall Islands, Saipan and Tinian. He was wounded on Iwo Jima in 1945.

JAMES WILLOUGHBY joined the U.S. Navy and became a Sonarman 3rd Class. He served aboard the ship, U.S.S. *Sheldrake*.

FILMORE WINGATE entered the U.S. Navy and was promoted to Electrician Mate Third Class. He was serving in 1944.

HUBERT OLDFIELD, of Aurora, was a Technician 3rd Grade with the 692nd Engineer Specialist Shop Battalion. He served as a Stock Clerk with duty in New Guinea and the Philippines.

FREDERICK PARKER, of Lawrenceburg, was an Army Staff Sergeant with the 573rd Quartermaster Company. He served as a Labor Foreman and a Clerk. He saw action in France, Ardennes and the Rhineland until discharged in December 1945.

VERNON RANSOM was a Corporal in the 71st Tank Battalion in the Philippines.

CHARLES RILEY was a Corporal in the Marines 4th Division serving in Saipan and the Marshall Islands.

FREDERICK RODENBURG, of Lawrenceburg, was a Technical Sergeant in the Philippines with the Combat Engineers Division. He was in the Leyte invasion. He had four battle stars.

ROBERT ROSEBURROUGH was a Fireman 2nd Class in the U.S. Navy. He was training for amphibious duty in 1943.

FRED ROWE entered the U.S. Army in 1943. As a Private he took basic training at St. Petersburg, Florida.

DELMAR RUMSEY entered the U.S. Navy and became a Seaman 2nd Class, but was discharged because of a physical disability after serving some 5 months in 1943.

WALTER STADLER, of Dillsboro, was a Truck Driver. As a Private First Class, he served in the Pacific on the Islands of Tinian, Marianna and Ryukyus as well as the occupation of Japan.

GEORGE STALKER, of Lawrenceburg, was a Corporal at New Caledonia. He maintained schedules for a transportation pool at SOPAC Command Headquarters in 1944.

JAMES MCCARTY was an Army Staff Sergeant. He served with the 24th Anti-Aircraft Artillery in the Philippines in 1945.

JOHN MCKEE, of Greendale, was in the Merchant Marines in 1944 serving in the Engineers Department on a merchant ship.

Floyd Gerkin (l.) and Gerald Crider

Kenneth Darling

EDWARD DROSGIA, of Lawrenceburg, was a Private at Brooklyn Army Base in 1944.

MELVIN DUNN, of Lawrenceburg, was a Captain in the Eighth Army Air Force stationed in England. He was flying as a Combat Wing Navigator in a B-17 group during heavy assaults on targets in Belgium, France and Holland. Veteran of 30 bombing missions, he earned the Distinguished Flying Cross and the Air Medal with 3 clusters. Dunn was an alumnus of Father Flanagan's Boys Town.

DENZIL EAGLIN was a Corporal in the Army Air Force stationed in New Guinea in 1944. He had been trained in the Army's Aircraft Sheet Metal School.

CLETUS ENGLER was a Pharmacist Mate First Class who served with the U.S. Navy Sea Bees.

NORMAN ENT, Ship's Cook 2nd Class, was killed when his ship, LST 577, was lost in action in the Philippines. The LST took a fatal torpedo shot from a Jap submarine, and quickly sank.

LEO T. FAHEY, of Aurora, served in the U.S. Army from June of 1941 to November 1945. He served at Milne Bay, New Guinea, Toem-Wakde and Sansapor. He received the Bronze Star at Toem-Wadke and New Guinea. He landed at Lingayan Gulf, Luzon, Philippine Islands on D-Day. He was made a First Sergeant after declining a field commission.

HAROLD FEHRMAN was a Chief Petty Officer in the U.S. Navy. He led a Navy Commando Unit in the Pacific in 1943.

WALTER FITZPATRICK was a First Lieutenant in the Army's Coastal Artillery. He was stationed off the coast of Venezuela, South America.

JAMES FOWLER was a Technical Sergeant serving in the Pacific Theater. He was a member of the 16th Signal Battalion. He saw action in New Guinea and the Philippines.

LELAND WOODWARD, of Aurora, served with the 331st Engineering Construction Company as a Construction Foreman in the Pacific Theater. His unit earned a Distinguished Unit Badge for unusual performance of duty. He was a Staff Sergeant in 1944.

Melvin Dunn

WILLIAM FULTON was in the Army Corps of Engineers. He served in the Pacific Theater of Operations, in the Philippine Islands.

GLENN GILLESPIE, of Aurora, enlisted in the Coast Guard in July 1942. He was stationed on the East Coast until 1943 when he was sent to the South Pacific for duty on the U.S.S. *Centaurs*.

JACK GILLESPIE, of Aurora, enlisted in the Navy in July 1945. He served aboard the cruiser *Phoenix* in the Pacific and received 7 battle stars. He received a medical discharge after being hospitalized in Australia and the States.

PAUL GILLMAN, of Logan, was an Army veteran of fighting on New Guinea. He was hospitalized stateside for serious wounds inflicted on New Guinea in 1942.

PHILIP (ZEKE) GIVAN, of Moores Hill, was a Corporal in the Marines, serving as an Automatic Rifleman. He regretted shooting no more than four Japs on Kwajalain. He was wounded and hospitalized on Saipan in 1944.

PHILIP GIVEN, of Lawrenceburg, a Marine Corporal fought to retake the Philippines, then on to Iwo Jima and Okinawa. The Indiana Governor named a day in his honor for a War Bond drive.

KENNETH GOMPF, a Seaman 2nd Class, served two months in the Navy and then was released because of a physical disability.

BERNARD GAYNOR was a Seaman First Class in the Navy. He served in gun crews on the following merchant ships: *Joseph Carey*, *Ivan VanZahot*, *Alcor Polaski*, *John Rawling*, and then aboard the Naval transport U.S.S. *Dickens*.

CLAYTON GIFFIN, of Aurora, was a Private First Class serving as a Radio Technician in the Army Air Force.

RALPH L. GILMORE, a Private, served at Ft. Mason, California but was released for essential civilian employment.

REUEL FUGITT, of Aurora, was a Sergeant with the Army. He served 2 years on Hawaii, working in the Adjutants office and also with the Ordinance Battalion.

Paul Wiedeman

Reuel Fugitt

Richard Horn

Joseph Hornbach

FRANK L. HILL was a Sergeant in the Marine Corps. He took part in the Marshall Island invasion, acting as the Sergeant Major of a dive-bombing squadron.

ALFRED HOFF, of the Sunman area, served in the Army as a Technician 5th Grade. He served as a Diesel Mechanic with the 347th Harbor Craft Company in the New Guinea and Philippines Campaigns.

JAMES HODGES, of Dillsboro, served as a Highway Construction Machine Operator with the 968th Engineering Maintenance Unit in the Ryukyus Islands in 1943. He was a Technical Sergeant.

RICHARD HORN, of Lawrenceburg, entered the Navy and became a Radioman 2nd Class. He served aboard the U.S.S. *Montauk*.

JOSEPH HORNBACH, of Guilford, served in the U.S. Army in the South Pacific.

WILLIAM (BILL) HUMBLE, of Lawrenceburg, was with the 1st Infantry of the Army 6th Division. He served in the liberation of the Philippines.

LEONARD HONCHELL was an Army Private in the 35th Cyclone Division on Luzon near Manila in the Philippines.

ROBERT HONCHELL was an Aerial Gunner in the Naval Air Force. He saw action in New Guinea and the Philippines, receiving 2 battle stars.

GEORGE HONCHELL was a Corporal in the Army Air Corps. He served as a Cryptographer in the Aleutians and Alaska.

VIRGIL HOFF served in the 268th Army Air Force Base Unit at Peterson Field, Colorado in 1943.

PAUL HOWARD was stationed at the Lincoln Army Air Force Base at Lincoln, Nebraska in 1942.

HOWARD HUDSON, of Dillsboro, was a Technician 5th Grade with the 339th Engineering Construction Battalion as a Truck Driver in New Guinea and the Philippines, with 3 battle stars.

GROVER GILLAND was a Machinist Mate 3rd Class in the U.S. Navy. He served aboard the U.S.S. *Coluse* and at the Navy Yard in the Philippines.

HOWARD GORDON entered the U.S. Navy and became an Electrician Mate First Class. He served on the repair ship, U.S.S. *Ajax* in the Pacific.

EARL GREEN was in basic training at Greensboro, N.C. in 1943.

JAMES GRIMSLEY, Private First Class, was a Truck Driver with the 1514th Service Unit at a P.O.W. camp in the U.S. He served from January 1941 to December 1944.

PAUL GRIEVE was a Technician 4th Grade in the Army serving as a Cook and Baker in Bougainville in the Solomon Islands in 1944. He received a commendation for volunteering to take an infantryman's place and do patrol duty and to operate a machine gun on a half track personnel carrier.

KENNETH HARNEY was a member of the Marine Corps. He served in the Pacific Theater of Operations where he was wounded.

ALTON HELLER, of Moores Hill, was a Seaman First Class who served on LST (Landing Ship Tanks) 947 in the Pacific.

HENRY HEMPLING served as a Seaman First Class on the following transports in the Pacific: *Cresent City* and *Blue Ridge*, plus the destroyer *Tausig*.

RALPH HENRY was a Seaman 2nd Class at Naval Air Station in Norman, Oklahoma.

RUSSELL HENRY was a Sergeant in the Army Coastal Artillery.

CARL HERZOG served as a Corporal in the Army in the Aleutian Islands.

LEONARD HILL served in the Marines Corps as a Supply Sergeant. He was wounded in action in July 1941 in a battle with the Japanese in the South Pacific.

Alfred Hoff

William (Bill) Humble

William Fulton

John Klump

HERBERT KENNEDY was at army Camp Wallace, Texas in 1943.

JERALD KERR, of Aurora, was killed in action in the South Pacific in 1944 while serving with a Marine Signal Corps Unit. The news was received locally on his Mother's birthday. Mrs. Kerr told friends she had had a dream in which she saw Jerry lying in a heap on a battlefield. "He looked up at me and smiled," she said.

GEORGE KIDDER was a Fireman 2nd Class in the South Pacific in 1944.

LAWRENCE KIENINGER served in the 152nd Infantry in the Philippines.

LEO KITTLE, of Aurora, was an Army Sergeant serving as a Warehouse Foreman in the Pacific Theater.

VERNON KITTLE entered the U.S. Navy and became a Coxswain. He served on LCI 4436 and LSA 151 in the Pacific Theater of Operations.

BERNARD KLEIN, of Dillsboro, entered the Marine Corps in 1943 and served until an honorable discharge in 1946.

EUGENE KLEIN, of Lawrenceburg, was a Private in the U.S. Army entering in March 1944. He served in the American Theater.

JOHN KLUMP entered the Army and served in the 34th Infantry Regiment as a Technical Sergeant. He was wounded by a Japanese hand grenade in Mindanao. He fought during various invasions in retaking the Philippine Islands and later with the occupation troops in Japan.

ROBERT KNIPPENBERG, of Aurora, was a Staff Sergeant in the Army, serving in Philippines in 1945.

EDWARD KNUE had his infantry training at Fort McCellan and then served with the Army on Luzon. He is one of five brothers serving in the Armed forces. He earned a Bronze Star and a Meritorious Unit Award.

COURTNEY DICKEN, JR., of Aurora, was a Corporal in the Marine Corps who served in the Pacific Theater of Leyte in the Philippines and on Guam as a Field Telephoneman from August 1943 to 1946.

CHARLES DILS, of Manchester, was a Coast Guard Specialist 2nd Class.

HOWARD DILS was a Chief Yeoman on a minesweeper in the South Pacific. He received wounds and earned four battle stars.

KENNETH DAUGHERTY, of Aurora, was a Private First Class in the Marines having fought on Tarawa in 1943.

RICHARD DAWSON was a Seaman First Class seeing action at Tarawa, Marshalls and Guam in 1943.

JAMES DAY was a Staff Sergeant in the Air Services Commands in 1943.

DONALD DARLING, of Lawrenceburg, was a Staff Sergeant in the Army Air Force receiving an Air Medal for flying in the South Pacific. He helped evacuate casualties and dropped supplies to the guerrilla forces in the Philippines in 1945. He traveled in an unarmed transport plane.

FORREST DENNERLINE was serving as a Corporal in the Marines in the Pacific Theater in 1944.

JACK DENNERLINE, of Aurora, was an Electrician Mate 2nd Class on a Navy submarine in the Pacific in 1943.

ERNEST DECK was an Electrician Mate First Class in the Navy serving in North Africa and 27 months in the South Pacific. He took part in the invasion of Saipan.

WALTER DECKER, former manager of the Lawrenceburg Utilities Department, joined the Army Corps of Engineers and served at the Blue Grass Ordinance Depot and the Liberation of the Philippines with the rank of Lieutenant Colonel.

NORBERT DRAPER, of Aurora, was a Private First Class with a Marine Corps unit serving on Kodiak Island.

Walter Decker

Jack Gillespie

Harvey Poshard and bride

HARVEY POSHARD, of Aurora, completed officers training at Ft. Sill and was commissioned a Second Lieutenant. In New Guinea, he was made Liaison Officer for his battalion to direct artillery fire from aircraft and forward observation posts to support ground troops. For combat in the Philippines, as a Captain, he received the Bronze Star medal and Purple Heart for being wounded in action. He was separated from the Army in late 1945.

NORMAN PRUSS, of Farmers Retreat, was a Sergeant in the 12th Cavalry of the Army. He was a Section Leader and served in the Philippines with 3 battle stars.

EARL REED, of Lawrenceburg, was a Seaman 2nd Class in the Pacific in 1943. He served on the LST (Landing Ship Tank) 638.

CARL SCHWING, of Lawrenceburg, became a Staff Sergeant with the Army's 127th Infantry Regiment. He served as a Mess Sergeant in New Guinea and the Philippines. He was in 5 major battles in these islands.

GEORGE SIZEMORE, of Guilford, was a Marine Sergeant taking part in the invasion of Pelelieu. He had a skirmish with the Japs at a cave and was able to demolish it.

AUBREY SMASHEY was a Private First Class in the Army Air Force. He served on the Island of Guam in the Pacific in 1945.

F. L. SMITH was a Motor Machinist Mate in the South Pacific for 17 months earning 3 battle stars.

LLOYD SMITH was a Private First Class in the Marines serving on Guam as part of a B-29 crew.

LOWELL SMITH entered the U.S. Army. He saw action in the jungle combat on the island of New Guinea.

WILLIARD SNYDER, of Dillsboro, was a Radio Operator, serving as an Army Private First Class in New Guinea and the Philippines, earning 3 battle stars.

DALE SPLANGLER, of Dillsboro, was an Army Sergeant with an Ordinance Battalion. He was a Message Center Chief in the Philippines, with 2 battle stars.

WILLIARD STEUVER, of Dillsboro, was a Technical Sergeant in the Army Field Artillery. He served in the Pacific Theater on New Guinea, Leyte and Luzon.

JOHN SWINFORD was a Corporal in a ground crew for the Army Air Force. He served in Santa Ana, California in 1943.

RALPH TEKE served as the pilot of a landing craft in New Guinea where he was wounded in 1944. He was a Sergeant.

VERN TEKE was a Corporal in an Armored Artillery unit at Camp Chaffee in Arkansas.

JAMES TAYLOR was a Seaman First Class serving in the Pacific in 1944 in the Navy.

Norbert Draper

SAMUEL ROHRER was a Second Lieutenant in the Army Air Force who received his wings at Randolph Field, Texas. Later he attended Instructors School at Randolph.

L. EUGENE ROSS, of Aurora, served in the U.S. Army at Attu and Kodiak, Alaska in 1944-45.

HARVEY ROSS, of Aurora, was a Fireman First Class in the Navy. He served aboard the escort aircraft carrier, U.S.S. *Ormany Bay* which was hit by a Jap suicide plane and sank with the loss of 100 men. This action took place during the invasion of the Philippines in 1944.

ROBERT ROSS, of Manchester, graduated from Machinist School at the Navy training station at Great Lakes in 1944.

NORMAN RULLMAN was an Army Corporal with the Field Artillery. He served in New Guinea in 1944.

THEODORE RUPP was in the Merchant Marines. He had duty as a First Assistant Engineer on an Army Transport serving the New Guinea area in 1944. He was in the Pacific Theater for 21 months.

LLOYD RUSH was a Sergeant with a ground crew with the Army Air Force in 1944.

DENVER SCHMIDT, of Lawrenceburg, was a Navy Specialist Third Class, serving in a Navy Post Office on Samoa in 1943.

PAUL SCHMIDT, of Lawrenceburg, graduated from Navy Radio School at Northwestern University. He was a Navy Seaman Second Class.

RONALD SCHMIDT was a Private First Class in the Marines. He served in the Solomons, Guam and the Marianas.

WILLIAM KAISER was a Sergeant in the 5th Army Air Force as Crew Chief on a B-24 bomber in New Guinea and the Philippines.

IRVIN HUESMAN was a Boat and Shore Engineer in the Army in 1944.

Eugene Ross

ROBERT HUNEFIELD was a Seaman 2nd Class in the Navy serving aboard a Landing Craft as Coxswain in the South Pacific.

DORANCE HUFFMAN, of Dillsboro, was a Second Lieutenant in the Army Air Corps with the 91st Air Force in the South Pacific in 1945. He was wounded while serving in the Philippines.

FLOYD HUNTER, of Lawrenceburg, served as a Pharmacist Mate 3rd Class at the Naval Operating Base on Guam in the Pacific.

ROBERT CLARK enlisted in the Army in 1943 and volunteered for Paratroops. He became part of the 511th Parachute Infantry Regiment of the 11th Airborne Division. In New Guinea, he served as a Company Scout. He was wounded in the Philippines in 1944. After being hospitalized for 6 months, he returned to his unit.

STANLEY HADDEN was at the Naval Air Station in Kodiak, Alaska serving in the Chaplain's Office in 1942.

FLOYD HELLER, of Moores Hill, was a Radarman 2nd Class serving on the LST (Landing Ship Tanks) 947 in the Pacific.

RUSSEL JACKSON, of Bright, served with the Army in New Guinea in 1944.

JOSEPH JEHN was in the Coastal Artillery in California in 1943.

JOHN JERGER, of Lawrenceburg, was a Naval-Aviation Ordinanceman 3rd Class and graduated from air gunnery school in Miami.

MERVIN JOHNSON was awarded the Distinguished Flying Cross for courageous service in long range bombing missions over enemy territory in the South Pacific from August 1943.

NATHAN KABAKOFF, of Aurora, served in one of General MacArthur's Armies as a Supply Sergeant, with duty in New Guinea and the Philippines.

Robert Clark

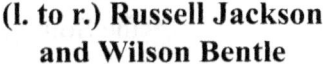

(l. to r.) Russell Jackson and Wilson Bentle

GENE KITTENBRINK served as a Private First Class in the Army Signal Corps in 1943.

JOHN KOONS, of Aurora, was an Army Corporal serving as a Rifleman with a Battalion Headquarters Group in the Pacific Theater of Operations in 1945.

JOHN (JACK) KRAUS, of Lawrenceburg, was a Storekeeper 3rd Class in the Sea Bees and served 18 months in the Pacific Theater.

JOSEPH LAKE, of the Sunman area, was a Private First Class in the Signal Headquarters of the 13th Fighter Command serving in China, East Indies, New Guinea, Philippines and western Pacific. He was a Truck Driver with 2 battle stars.

WILLIAM LAKE, of the Sunman area, was a Technician 5th Grade with the Headquarters Troop, 7th Cavalry. He served as a Field Lineman in the Philippines.

ROBERT LEWIS was a Seaman First Class in the U.S. Navy. He served aboard the LST 1089 in the Pacific Theater from September 1944 to March 1946.

BOBBY LICKING, of Aurora, was a Corporal with the 37th Infantry. He served as a Truck Driver in the American Theater from 1943-1946.

ROBERT LUTZ, of Sawdon Ridge, was a Radio Technician in the Navy aboard a repair ship, the U.S.S. *Prometheus*, in the South Pacific.

BENNIE LYNN, of Aurora, served in the U.S. Navy aboard the U.S.S. *Broadwater* in the Pacific Theater of Operations.

ORVILLE MARKSBERRY, of Moores Hill, was an Army Private in the 385th Infantry Regiment at Camp McCoy, Wisconsin. He served as a Rifleman in the American Theater in 1944-45.

HAROLD MARTIN, of Manchester, was an Aviation Ordinanceman First Class serving on the destroyer *Cabot* in a carrier task force in the Pacific. He was wounded in enemy action in November 1944.

LESTER OCHS, from Dillsboro, was an Army Private First Class in 1944.

JOHN MARTIN was a Seaman First Class in the U.S. Navy at an Amphibious Operating Base in the Pacific Theater, having enlisted in the service in 1943.

GEORGE MOODY, of Aurora, was an Army Private First Class. He served as a Medical Technician in New Guinea, receiving a battle star for major combat.

DOUGLAS MCCRORY, of Aurora, was a Carpenter's Mate 3rd Class in the U.S. Navy. He served aboard the U.S.S. *Samuel Chase* in the Pacific Theater of Operations.

WALTER MENDEL was a Corporal in the Army Services of Supply in the South Pacific in 1944.

HENRY MILLER, of the Sunman area, was a Private First Class in the 369th Engineering Combat Battalion. He was a Section Hand with duty in many combat areas such as Algiers, Morcco, Tunisia, Sicily, Italy, France, Rhineland and Central Europe. He earned 8 battle stars.

ARTHUR MEYER, of Moores Hill, was a Hospital Apprentice Second Class in the Navy serving with a Marine Unit in 1944.

FRANCIS MEYER, of Aurora, was a Staff Sergeant in the 123rd Infantry of the Army. He earned the Silver Star while serving in the Philippines and the South Pacific.

THOMAS H. MILLER was a First Lieutenant in the Army Air Force. He entered the service in October 1943 and would serve as a fighter pilot in New Guinea.

JULIAN OBERT, of St. Leon, was a Seaman First Class in the Naval Air Transport Squadron based at Oakland, California. He served as a Radio Maintenanceman.

ROBERT OBERTING entered the U.S. Navy and became a Cook on a ship serving in the Pacific Theater of Operations.

ROBERT OELKER served aboard the battleship U.S.S. *New Jersey*, which was one of the newly-built naval combat ships during WWII. She was commissioned in 1943 and sailed to take part in the Pacific Fleet. She took part in the Kwajalein invasion and most Pacific naval actions thereafter.

Frank L. Taylor

Ray Tettenhorst

RAY TETTENHORST was a Staff Sergeant in the 6th Combat Engineers Battalion. He was stationed in the Philippine Islands and Korea. Korea was then used as a training base for the planned invasion of Japan.

FINLEY THOMPSON was a Private First Class in the Marines. He had service in New Britain and elsewhere in the South Pacific.

FRANK L. TAYLOR served in the U.S. Army from March 27, 1943 until December 13, 1945. He saw action in Italy and the European Theater of Operations as a Corporal.

WILLIE TRENNEPOHL was in the Navy in 1944. He served in the Pacific Theater of Operations aboard the ship, U.S.S. *Montgue*, as a Baker.

CHARLES TSCHAENN, of Lawrenceburg, entered the U.S. Army as a Private in February 1944 and served briefly as a Utility Repairman at Camp Swift. He was discharged in February 1945.

FLOYD ZIMMERMAN entered the U.S. Navy in March 1944 and became an Electricians Mate 2nd Class. He served in the Philippines liberation campaign.

U.S troops fighting in the jungles of the Pacific

ROBERT (BOB) OHLER, of Lawrenceburg, entered the U.S. Army as part of the 24th Medical Battalion. He served in the Philippines, with 4 battle stars, and in the Occupation Army of Japan.

WALTER (BUD) PALMER, of Guilford, entered the Army and was placed in the Infantry. He served in the Liberation of the Philippine Islands.

ERNEST PALMER, of Aurora, was part of the 9314 Engineering Construction Company as a Technician 5th Grade. He served as a Truck Driver in New Guinea and the Philippine Islands, with 4 battle stars.

DELMAR PERKINS, of Moores Hill, was a Staff Sergeant. He had training at Ft. Knox in armored radio and was sent to England.

JAMES PETTIT, of Lawrenceburg, entered the Navy in December 1943 and became a Seaman First Class. He received a medical discharge from a Naval Hospital in California in July 1944.

WILBUR WINGATE, of Dillsboro, was a Technician 5th Grade, in the 129th Base Unit. He served as an Airplane Mechanic in New Guinea, the Solomons and the Western Pacific with 6 battle stars.

ARTHUR EARL WERNER, of Aurora, entered the Army in February of 1945, he had his basic training at Fort Meade, Maryland and was a Private First Class in the Army Medical Corps.

DELBERT BAKER, of Lawrenceburg, served in the Army from 1941-1945. He had his basic training at Fort Bragg, North Carolina. He was with the 233rd Re-enforcement Battalion. He saw action in Germany during the European Theatre and became a Sergeant before leaving the service.

Ernest (l.) and Walter Palmer

American troops leave thier landing craft and wade ashore at a Normandy Beach on D-Day, 6 June 1944, as the Allies begin assaulting Europe

CHAPTER 8

Assaulting Europe

D-Day

With the successes in Africa, Sicily and Southwestern Italy, the Allies accelerated the planning of the cross-channel invasion of Europe. By May 1943, the Anglo-American Navies had gained superiority in the Atlantic struggle with the German submarines. By then, the U.S. could move its armed forces and equipment safely by convoy to invasion bases in the British Isles. In Scotland, Ireland and Wales, as well as England, the Yanks came to encamp, train and to wait for the invasion.

By early 1944, the German General Staff recognized that such an invasion would take place soon, and so they undertook a massive construction program for defending the French coast. They sowed millions of mines, built thousands of bunkers with gun emplacements, and installed anti-landing-boat obstacles along the beaches. However, they miscalculated the landing site. They estimated it to be in the Calais area instead of Normandy, and the Allies added to the miscalculation by faking maneuvers to make it appear as though Calais would be the invasion site.

After months of bombing Germany by the U.S. Army Air Corps and the R.A.F., the Allies had virtually destroyed the Luftwaffe (the Nazi Air Force). In the spring of 1944, the Allies could control the air spaces over the invasion beaches, which was a major factor for the Allied success.

Once the Allied troops and equipment were in place and organized, the major problem facing the Allies was selecting the landing date. To pull the attack off at dawn and at low tide (to avoid the peril of the anti-boat obstacles) limited them to just a few dates a month. And, of course, the weather needed to be favorable during the selected dates for air, ship and personnel movement.

Taking the tides into account, the Allied General Staff scheduled the landing to take place between June 4 and 6. The weather on June 5, 1944, however, turned out to be the worst in years. General Eisenhower had to postpone the landing for June 5, but the weather forecasters predicted a short break in the weather for the 6th, and Eisenhower decided to land on that date rather than waiting for several more weeks.

The first Allied soldiers to invade Normandy began in the dark. Shortly after midnight, British gliders landed in the field on the eastern flank of the invasion beaches. Within an hour, they stopped a German counterattack. At about the same time on the western flank, paratroopers from the American 101st and the 82nd Airborne Division dropped behind the German defenses.

At 5:20 a.m. on June 6, 1944, the mighty invasion fleet of the Allies appeared on the horizon off the Normandy beaches. More than 5,000 ships and craft were getting ready to land 175,000 men and 50,000 vehicles. Within 15 minutes, an air force of 11,000 planes began bombing and strafing German positions on the beaches and coastal areas. More fire support would be delivered from ships of the U.S. and British Navies. Operation Overlord was poised to strike Fortress Europe.

On Utah Beach, the westernmost landing, strong currents pushed the landing craft 2,000 yards off their target. However, that accident enabled the troops of the 4th Division to outflank the Germans and get beyond the beach.

As for the British and Canadians, landing on the easternmost beaches, they were able to gain control by mid-day. It was on Omaha Beach, in the middle section, that the invasion almost floundered. Nearly all the artillery pieces sunk, and the artillery support that the other beaches had, did not make it to Omaha. However, the Navy began beaching their Landing Craft Tanks to get the tanks ashore. U.S. destroyers began coming in close to the beach, so their 5-inch guns could lend support in lieu of artillery.

American survivors barely made it to the dunes below the cliffs. Although the cost was high with 2,500 Americans killed, the GIs gradually fought their way up draws that led to the areas on top of the cliffs. By afternoon, they had established the foothold needed to drive the Germans back.

By sunset on June 6, the Allies on all beach sectors had secured a successful lodgment on the coast of western Europe from which to drive the Germans inland.

Breakout

While the Germans had trouble bringing in reinforcements into western Normandy due to the Allies bombing the French rail system, the Allied breakout took more time than anticipated. The Germans had the terrain in their favor, especially considering the hedgerows. These objects were ancient mounds of earth, stones and hedges, used by the French to divide their fields. They averaged 4 feet thick at the bases and grew 8 to 10 feet high, encompassing areas varying in size from one to three football fields. Germans sited hidden tanks or anti-tank guns in the fields and protected strong points with machine guns. Finally, GIs designed steel beams, cut with jagged teeth and welded them to the front of their tanks to smash through the hedgerows.

By early July, the Allies had put a million men ashore in Normandy, but still the Germans were able to keep them from breaking out of that part of the country. However, German General Rommel recognized that Allied superiority on the ground and in the air was wearing his forces down. At the end of July, General Omar Bradley unleashed the decisive offensive. Allied bombers were used in preparation, even though bad weather interfered and many bombs fell short onto American troops, however, the bombs also hit the German lines and hurt them significantly, creating holes through which American infantry and tanks could pass. The situation was exploited and the collapse of German positions made possible a complete breakout of U.S. forces. The German line which had stretched from the western beaches of Normandy to the English Channel near Caen, had been penetrated.

General Omar Bradley

Invasion of Southern France

On August 15, 1944, the Americans, along with some Free French forces, made an invasion landing in Southern France on the Mediterranean Sea. The purpose was to drive north and link up with the Allied force from Normandy, and to capture the ports of Marsailles and Toulon since additional ports were needed to handle American supplies bound for Europe. Even though the Americans needed to pull much of the Army's strength out of Italy, to make the invasion, the decision proved right.

On September 11, French patrols from the invasion made contact with Patton's third Army. The Allies now had an unbroken front that ran from the Channel to Switzerland.

For a Dearborn Countian's first-hand observations on the invasion of Southern France, see the following excerpts from a letter written by Harold Clements, Turret Captain on a Navy battleship during the invasion to this parents.

"The Allies struck a heavy blow in the invasion of Southern France several days ago, and the American war ships, as in the Normandy invasion, were present at the initial assault helping to blast a path for the landings. During the night many transports were overtaken and left behind in the darkness as we moved into our forward position. Angry rumblings of bomb bursts and fire flashes came from the distant area as bombers unloaded their deadly cargo...When the skies began to glow just before dawn, we found ourselves surrounded with other ships and landing craft while the shores of France loomed surprisingly near, shrouded with a haze of smoke and dust from the bombing attack. We were then well within range of coastal batteries, and I, for one, hoped we would not delay our opening fire. Our main guns were trained on an enemy installation of casemated guns when the buzzer sounded to standby for the opening salvo. With a deafening roar, we sent our salutation to Hitler's crowd on the beach. We fired salvo after salvo while hundreds of landing craft moved to shore. ..As you know, the Army took the beach in stride.. We had a number of German prisoners on board for a while. They didn't have the tough, superman appearance the German propaganda experts would have you believe...We are getting worried that the war might be over for the Navy. Anticipating this possibility, our gunners are having our engineers install wheels on our ships so we can catch up with the Army and help chase the Heines through the streets of Berlin.

Yours,
Harold"

Battle of the Bulge

The last great German offensive of WWII in the West began on December 16, 1944. It took place on a 60-mile front in the region where the Belgium, Luxembourg and German borders come together. Here, Hitler planned a massive drive in front of the Ardennes Forest, the one area where the Allies were not attacking at the time.

Due to extending their lines and incurring heavy casualties in November, the Americans had by mid-December, a 3 to 1 disadvantage in manpower to the Germans. The Nazis had filled up their ranks with young conscripts, convalescent soldiers and civil prisoners. The one place they had a decided disadvantage was in air power. To offset that factor, Hitler launched his attack after ten consecutive days of snow, rain and fog which allowed his forces to move undetected.

The German offensive began with a pre-dawn, forty-five minute artillery barrage, which struck U.S. positions throughout the Ardennes. This was followed by attacking armor and infantry out of the fog and night to take the Americans by surprise. On the northern shoulder of the German breakthrough, the Bulge, the Americans waould hold during the remainder of the battle. Farther south, the German Panzers were more successful. The next day, the American front in this sector collapsed with between 7 and 8 thousand Americans capitulating, which was the low point of the U.S. fighting in Europe.

Further south, U.S. defenses were more tenaciously holding the roads leading into Bastogne until late on the 17th. Meanwhile, Eisenhower ordered in his reserves. He also ordered the 82nd and the 101st Airborne Divisions to move up. Embarking by truck, the 82nd was sent to the north end of the bulge and the 101st moved to Bastogne to help defend the crucial crossroads that ran through the town. Eisenhower then had Patton change the direction of the Third Army to move toward Bastogne.

Patton, under dreadful winter conditions, immediately sprang into action and sent a relief column to the besieged town of Bastogne by December 26th. In the meantime, the weather cleared over the battlefield, allowing U.S. Air Forces to smash the Germans across the whole front at Bastogne.

With the defeat of the German counteroffensive from the Ardennes, it meant the complete loss of their reserves, in both men and tanks, west of the Rhine River. They could never make up these incredible losses.

Edward Aust

Marvin Beckmeyer

Carl Bocock

EDWARD AUST served as an Army Medic and fought in the Battle of the Bulge in the European Theater.

EDWARD BUDUNNAH entered the U.S. Army and became a Sergeant at Camp Hood, Texas in 1944.

JOHN BARRY, of New Alsace, was an Army Private with the Seventh Army. While serving in the ETO, he was presented with the Bronze Star medal and a Presidential Citation.

EARL BAKER, of Aurora, was a Navy Seaman First Class. He was attached to the Navy Amphibious Headquarters in England.

WALTER BAKER was a Private in the Army Air Corp. He had duty at an Air Force Field in Lincoln, Nebraska in 1944.

FLOYD BAKER was an Army Private with the 61st Training Battalion at Camp Fannin, Texas in 1944.

MARVIN BECKEMEYER was a member of a Tank Destroyer Battalion, U.S. Army. He saw action in France, Luxembourg and Germany.

NORMAN BERNING, a pastor from Lawrenceburg, served as a Chaplin in an Army Engineer Unit with the rank of Captain in Reims, France.

ELMER BISCHOFF, of Harrison, was a Staff Sergeant, serving in the Army in the European Theater of Operations.

CARL BOCOCK, of Dillsboro, was a Surgical Technician with the 410 Infantry. He saw action in the Rhineland and Central Europe, receiving 5 battle stars.

DAVID BOWLING, of Moores Hill, was an Army Staff Sergeant, serving with a Headdquarters Company in the Intelligence Corps as an Administrator.

VICTOR BROOKBANK, of Lawrenceburg, fought in the Normandy Invasion on D-Day. His tank sank in the Channel and many men were drowned. As a result of this accident, he spent 6 months in a hospital in France. As a Private First Class, he went on to fight in Europe until October 1945.

EARL BROWNING was in an army Specialist program in engineering at Pennsylvania State in 1944.

CHARLES BROSSART was an Army Private. He fought in North Africa, Italy, France, Rhineland and Central Europe, earning 3 battle stars.

ROBERT BROOKBANK was an Army Private. In 1944 he was assigned to a Medical Training Battalion.

J.W. BROOKS entered the U.S. Army Air Force and became a Private First Class. He served as an Engineer on a B-24 bomber.

LOUIS BRYANT entered the U.S. Army in 1944. He was a Private training in the Infantry at Camp Carson, Colorado.

WATSON BROWN entered the U.S. Army as a Private. He saw action in France in 1944.

CLIFFORD CHASE was a Sergeant in the Army Air Force. He served in a ground crew in both Alaska and the ETO.

FRANCIS A. CHAMBERS was a Corporal in the Army serving with the 62nd Armament Maintenance Battalion. His unit received a meritorious plaque for their participation in landings in Southern France.

DALLAS CHATHAM was a Technician Fifth Class in the Army 749th Tank Battalion. His unit landed on Utah Beach on June 29, 1944 and fought their way through France, Belgium and Germany. He wears 4 battle stars.

RUDOLPH COLEN was a Corporal in the Army Airborne Engineers in North Africa, India and Burma in 1944.

HAROLD CRAIG, of Guilford, was a Private First Class who served as a Military Policeman with the 456 M.P. Escort Guards in the Rhineland part of the ETO.

ROBERT CRANDALL was a Second Lieutenant in a tank destroyer unit in 1945.

ARTHUR CRONTZ was a Radioman 3rd Class in the Navy. He served in the Atlantic and Mediteranean on the destroyer escort, U.S.S. *Otter*, which destroyed a German submarine.

LEONARD CROUCH, of Moores Hill, was a Sergeant in the Army Air Force. He served as a mechanic on a B-24 bomber.

Elmer Bischoff

Victor Brookbank

Dallas Chatham

CHARLES CHEEK, of Aurora, was a Technician Fifth Class with the 204th Armored Division in France, Belgium, Austria and Germany.

CLYDE CHEEK, of Lawrenceburg, was a Private in the Army Air Force with the 61st Fighter Squadron serving as a mechanic.

JOHN COLLIER, of Guilford, was inducted in the V7Navy program in November 1944.

RALPH COLLIER, of Guilford, was a Radioman First Class, U.S. Navy. He served in the Pacific, earning 5 battle stars.

HAROLD CONRAD, of Aurora, was a Sergeant in the Army with the 35th Tank Battalion serving as tank commander fighting in Normandy, France and the Rhineland.

EUGENE CASH was a Private First Class with the Air Service Command in England. His unit repaired and overhauled engines to return them to planes for air service over Europe.

Ralph Collier and the ship (LCI 624) he served on during the Philippine invasion.

E. FORD CONNELLY, of Lawrenceburg, was a Corporal in the Army. Served with the First Army in France and Luxembourg as a Mail Clerk.

HAROLD CONNELLY, of Moores Hill, was a Sergeant in the Army Air Force as a Radio Technician. He was in the fighter group of the 15th Air Force. Awarded a Distinguished Unit Citation and wore 12 battle stars.

STANLEY COTTINGHAM, of Harrison, entered the military in April 1942. He would serve as a Clerk with the 212th Reinforcement Company in the Ardennes and Rhineland in the ETO.

ROBERT COTTON was a Private First Class taking basic training in the Army Air Force in 1945.

RUSSELL CUTTER, of Dillsboro, was an Army Corporal with an Anti-Aircraft Artillery Unit in 1944.

LESTER CUTTER, from Dillsboro, was in the Army Air Force in 1942.

CHARLES CUTTER was a Sergeant with the 3rd Army in France and Germany. He was a tank mechanic, and was awarded the Bronze Star medal.

MICHAEL CUSICK was an Army Staff Sergeant who was killed in action in France. He served as a Supply Sergeant with a Mechanized Cavalry Unit.

LEONARD CZARNIECKI was a Captain in the Army at Portland, Maine in 1944.

EDWARD (BUD) CHRISTIAN, of Lawrenceburg, was a Corporal in the Army Infantry, serving and being wounded in Luxembourg in January 1945.

ALBERT DIEZMAN, former assistant pastor at St. Lawrence Church, Lawrenceburg, was a Lieutenant, serving as Chaplain with the infantry in western France.

DONALD CASEY was a Sergeant in the Army Air Force serving in England in 1944.

E. Ford Connolly

Edward Christian

Three Dearborn sailors in 1944 (l. to r.) Bill Christian, Fred Banshbach, Tom Collier

FRANK DIESELBERG, of Weisburg, a Private First Class was a messenger with the 914th Infantry in central Europe where he was awarded the Bronze Star.

JOHN DENT was a Private First Class in the Army. He was wounded in the Normandy invasion and was killed in action in Germany, October 4, 1944.

HARVEY DERON, of Aurora, served in the Infantry as a Surgical Technician 5th Grade in Rhineland and central Europe. He received two battle stars.

ROBERT DEWERS, of Aurora, graduated from Officer's Training School at Ft. Knox with a commission of Second Lieutenant. He was sent to the 4th Armored Division in eastern France as an assault gun platoon leader in the 37th Tank Battalion 4th Armored Division under Colonel Creighton Abrams for whom the Abrams tank was named. As the war progressed he was promoted to First Lieutenant.

DALE DARLING, of Lawrenceburg, was a Technical Sergeant in the Army Air Force. He was awarded a third Oak Leaf Cluster to his Air Medal for participating in bomber operations over Germany. He was a Radio Operator-Gunner on a B-17 of the 91st Bombardment Group.

ARTHUR DARLING, of Guilford, served in the European Theater of war, earning the Bronze Star, 4 battle stars, the Cross of Lorain and a Presidential Unit Citation.

DENVER DAVIES, of Dillsboro, landed in France on D-Day and was wounded. Later he was awarded a Bronze Star for his service as a Medic with the Infantry.

ROBERT DAWSON, of Lawenceburg, a Private First Class in the Army served with an Anti-Aircraft unit in France and Germany. He earned 5 battle stars.

CHARLES DENNIS was a Sergeant in the Army and was wounded three times while fighting in France in 1944.

DAVID DENNIS was a Private First Class. He was wounded in France in 1944.

RUDOLPH DENNIS was an Army Private. He was wounded in Germany in 1944.

Robert Dewers

JOHN DENNIS was a Sergeant and was wounded while serving in France in 1944.

HARRY DERON was in the Medical Detail of an Infantry unit in 1944.

CLAYTON DENMURE was a Master Sergeant on a B-24 bomber squad in England in 1944.

HARRY DICKERSON, of Aurora, was a Technician 5th grade in the Army at Camp Atterbury, Corpus Christi and Seattle, Washington.

WORTHINGTON DAVIES, of Dillsboro, served with the 1918 Service Command Unit as a Military Policeman. He entered the Army in 1944.

A.H. DOGGETT was a Corporal in the Army Ordnance Division in France in 1944.

TOM DONNELLY completed Air Cadet course at Yale, and as a Lieutenant served in the 561st Army Air Force base unit at St. Joseph in 1944.

ROBERT DOWDEE was wounded in France in 1944.

EDWARD DRIVER, of Aurora, was a Lieutenant (i.g.) at the Naval Base in Portland, teaching anti-submarine warfare.

BUFORD DUNCAN, of Greendale, served with the Army's 114th Infantry Regiment in the Rhineland part of the European Theatre of Operations.

THOMAS DUNN, of Aurora, had 26 months service in Ireland and England prior to the invasion of France in 1944. He was a Corporal and was killed in combat in France.

CLARENCE ECKLER served with the 605th Field Artillery Battalion. He cared for the horses and mules used as carriers of supplies in the mountains. In 1944 he was in a mechanized cavalry unit.

FREDRICK ECKLER was a Staff Sergeant. He served with a combat engineering unit who took part in the Leyte invasion in 1944.

HUGH EDWARDS, of Manchester, was Staff Sergeant in the Army Air Force in 1944.

Ep Fehling (bottom row, second from right) and his bomber crew

WILLARD EHLERS served in the Air Service Command in England in 1944.

ROBERT EISENSHANK, of Lawrenceburg, served in the U.S. Army Infantry in Germany and the European Theatre of Operations.

ALBERT EMERY, of Aurora, served as a Field Lineman in the 357th Infantry in Normandy and Central Europe. He earned 5 battle stars and a Purple Heart for being wounded in action.

JAMES EWBANK, of Lawrenceburg, was a Staff Sergeant in the Army's 33rd Depot Repair Squadron. He was an Aircraft Welder serving in the Rhineland.

PAUL FACKLER was a Private First Class with an Army Quartermaster Truck Company. He served in Rome, Southern France and Central Europe as a Tractor Truck Driver.

LOUIS FAHEY, of Aurora, served with the 379th Infantry Regiment as a Supply Sergeant in Northern France and the Rhineland, earning 2 battle stars. He was wounded in France in November 1944.

James Fairfield

JAMES FAIRFIELD, of Aurora, landed in Normandy 2 weeks after D-Day with a unit in relief of the 101st Airborne Paratroops and fighting from hedgerow to hedgerow before his division could break out. That December, he was engaged in the Battle of the Bulge, and in January he was wounded by a hit in his shoulder. For recovery, he was sent to a hospital in Paris, but was back on the front lines within two weeks. His division, the Thunderbolt, was now with General Patton's Army pushing toward Berlin. However, they were ordered to halt at the Elbe River to wait for the Russians. He returned to the states in November, 1945, after he received a Bronze Star for outstanding performance of duty in action against the Nazis.

EDWARD F. FEHLING, of Aurora, served in the Army Air Force from January 1944 to January 1946 when he was honorably discharged as a Sergeant, a Finance Technician Clerk. He was a gunner on a B-17 bomber. He was stationed at Las Vegas Army Air Force base at the Third Air Force Flexible Gunnery School.

C.E. FELLER was a Staff Sergeant in the Army Field Artillery. He served in the European Theater of Operations, receiving 3 major battle stars.

ROBERT FOX, of Lawrenceburg, served 16 months in the ETO, as a tank gunner, with 5 battle stars. His unit was awarded a Certificate of Merit for outstanding performance of duty.

MADISON FRAKES was a Private First Class in the Army Air Force. He was stationed in England in 1943.

CHARLES FUERNSTEIN served with the Infantry in the 7th Army in North Africa and Italy. Later, he was reported missing in action in France.

ROBERT FUGATE, of Greendale, served as a turret gunner and engineer on the "Nevada Avenger," one of the oldest flying fortress bomber groups in England. He was awarded the Flying Cross and the Air Medal with 3 clusters. Robert also flew on several other bombers in many missions over Europe.

RICHARD GIBLIN of Moores Hill, was a messenger in the Army in 1945. He was wounded in France and taken to an army hospital for treatment.

EDWIN GOMPF, of Greendale, served as a Supply Sergeant with the 48th Armored Infantry Battalion in Normandy. He received the Bronze Star award and 5 battle stars.

EARL GODFREY, of Aurora, was a Private in the 501st Parachute Infantry. He was a Machine Gunner in the Ardennes.

FRANK GOODPASTER, of Aurora, served in the 8th Signal Company as a Field Lineman in the Ardennes and Central Europe.

ELMER GOODPASTER, of Aurora, served as a Cannoneer with the 736th Field Artillery Battalion in the European Theater. He was a Private First Class.

ROBERT GLENN was wounded three times in combat in Europe. He was a Private First Class with an Infantry unit. The last time wounded, it happened in Germany.

WILBUR GRAF, of Guilford, was an Army Private First Class with the 550th Field Artillery Battalion. He went into the service in November 1942. He would see action in Normandy, France, Andennes and the Rhineland.

Robert Eisenshank

Louis Fahey

Roger Grubbs

Alvin Hartman

HAROLD GRANARD served as an Army Warrant Officer for six months in Greenland in 1944.

ROBERT L. GREEN, Sergeant, of Moores Hill, served in the 264th Infantry Regiment as a rifleman in Northern France, receiving 1 battle star.

FERNINAND GREEN, of Aurora, was a Private in the army. He was wounded in Germany in 1945 and returned to U.S.

CHARLES GRIFFIN, of Lawrenceburg, was a Private in basic training in 1944.

FRANK GRIMSLEY, Staff Sergeant with the 123rd Army Air Force base unit, served as an Airplane Armourer in the European Air Offensive. He received 4 battle stars.

FRANK GILLESPIE was in the Coast Guard in both the Atlantic and the Pacific in 1945. He served as a Motor Machinist Mate 3rd class.

DELMAR GILMORE was a Second Lieutenant with the Artillery in the European Theatre of Operations in 1945.

ROGER GRUBBS was a Corporal with the 453rd Anti-Aircraft Battalion. He was in the 83rd Infantry Division as a radio operator, spending 20 months overseas. He entered France on D+3 Day, fought in the Battle of the Bulge and had face wounds there. Also he saw action in Northern France, Ardennes, Rhineland and Central Europe. At the end of the war, he had earned 5 battle stars.

ORVILLE GUARD, of Lawrenceburg, was an Army Corporal with the 997th Field Artillery Battalion. He served as a Field Lineman in Normandy, France, Rhineland and the Ardennes, receiving 5 battle stars.

MELVIN GULLEY, of Lawrenceburg, was a Technician 5th grade with the 54th Armored Infantry Battalion. He served as a Tank Driver in the Ardennes, Rhineland and Central Europe.

HUBERT HAMILTON, of Dillsboro, was a Waist Gunner on a Flying Fortress. He received the Air Medal for meritorious achievement in destroying enemy airplanes while on a bombing mission over Europe.

ALVIN HARTMAN was inducted into the U.S. Army on June 8, 1942. He became a Technician 5th grade, served with the 79th Quartermaster Company, and was discharged in April of 1944.

HUBERT HARPER, of Lawrenceburg, was a Corporal in the 319th Infantry Regiment serving as a Truck Driver in the Rhineland with 1 battle star.

BEN HOLDEN JR., of Lawrenceburg, was an Army Private in France and Germany. He was returned to the states for treatment of trench foot.

LESTER HOLZBACHER was a Captain in the War Finance Department. He had a year of duty in France and Germany in an Infantry division in 1945.

ELLIS HOUZE, Private in the U.S. Army, served as a Laborer in 1944-1945 at Camp Stewart, Georgia.

GEORGE HORNBACH, of Yorkville, was a Private First Class, U.S. Army with the 331st Infantry, 83rd Division. He was wounded in action on July 4, 1944 in Europe and was hospitalized in a hospital in England.

FRED HOUZE, of Aurora, was a Staff Sergeant in France in 1944.

JAMES HOWARD, of the Marine Corps, received an Honorable Discharge after 5 years of service in Europe, Africa, Sicily and Italy.

WALTER HOWARD, a Private serving with the Paratroopers of the 307th Engineers Battalion of the 82nd Airborne Division, took part in the Normandy invasion, Sicily, Italy and Holland. Earned a silver star, 2 battle stars, the Purple Heart, Legion of Merit and a Presidential Citation.

EDWARD HUGHES, of Moores Hill, was an Army Technician 5th Grade with the 818th Engineers Aviation Battalion. He saw action in Normandy, France, Rhineland and Central Europe, receiving 5 battle stars.

MORRIS HUNTER, of Lawrenceburg, was a Corporal with the 110th Infantry Regiment. He served as a Guard Patrolman in Central Europe.

FRANK HUNTER was a Private First Class in the Army serving in Belgium in 1943.

LOUIS HYDE, of Moores Hill, was a First Lieutenant in the Army Air Force serving as a navigator over France, Germany and the Ardennes, with 3 battle stars. He was awarded the Air medal with an Oak Leaf Cluster.

Lester Holzbacher

EDWARD INMAN entered the Army and became a Technical Sergeant. He had duty in General Eisenhower's Supreme Headquarters of the Allied Expeditionary Forces in Paris.

LEROY JEFFERIES, of Logan, served in the U.S. Army with a Military Police unit in Germany. He was in the Army from 1942 to 1945.

HAROLD JAMESON, of Aurora, enlisted in the Army Air Force and became a Sergeant. He was in the 343rd Squadron of the 98th Bomber Group as a Radio Operator.

EDWARD AND ERNEST HARTWELL, of Lawrenceburg, twin brothers entered the Army Air Force and both received their pilot wings and commissions as Second Lieutenants. They flew B-17s through transition as pilot and co-pilot on the same crew in the American Theater.

ERNEST HAWKINS, of Lawrenceburg, was a Seaman 2nd Class in 1945 at Camp Parks, California.

DALE HENRY, a Sergeant in the Army Air Force, attended mechanics school in 1944 and served in a ground crew.

RAYMOND HIGHAM, of Aurora, served in the 10th Armored Infantry Battalion as an automotive mechanic in Central Europe, receiving 1 battle star. He was a Technician 5th Grade.

EDWARD HILL was a Corporal in an Army Air Corps Engineering unit. He served for two years at an AAC base in England.

ELMER JACKSON was a Sergeant in the Army. He was reported missing in action. His last letter was from Luxembourg.

DONALD JOHNSON was a Corporal in the Army Air Force at Lincoln, Nebraska in 1944.

GLENN JOHNSON, of Wilmington, was a Corporal in a ground crew of the Army Air Corps. He served as a Radio Mechanic.

HERMAN JOBE, of Lawrenceburg, was in the 141st Infantry Unit of the Army. He was a Technical Sergeant serving in Aftica, Italy, France and Germany. He was awarded the Purple Heart and 5 battle stars. His unit was the first to reach German soil in 1945.

Edward (l.) and Wally Inman in Paris

The Hartwell Twins, Edward and Ernest, in the cockpit of a B-17 bomber.

Harold Jameson

Leroy Jeffries

Raymond Kaffenberger

Paul Knue

BURL KARR, of Aurora, was a Private First Class in the 263rd Infantry in Normandy, France and Central Europe. He had 5 battle stars.

HOWARD KAISER was a Sergeant in the Army Air Corps. He served for 26 months in England and France, receiving a battle star. He was with the 8th AAF Service Command in 1944.

RAYMOND (RAY) KAFFENBERGER, of Lawrenceburg, entered the Army Air Force to become a Sergeant with the Troop Carrier Command in the ETO. He had 7 battle stars.

IRVAN KAMMEYER, of near Sunman, was an Army Sergeant with the 4th Armored Division. He served as a Supply Clerk in the Ardennes and Central Europe, earning 3 battle stars.

LEROY KARRER was an Army Sergeant. He served in France as an M.P. on a prison transport, escorting German POWS to camps in the U.S.

ROBERT KARRER was an Army Technician 5th Grade. He served in France with a Military Police unit in 1945.

FRANCIS KLUEBLER, was an Army Private First Class in Germany in 1944.

PAUL KNUE was a Corporal in the U.S. Army 94th Infantry. He served in the Trier Triangle, the offense that brought the end of the war with Germany.

JOSEPH KNUE, of Lawrenceburg, served in the U.S. Army as a Corporal in the European Theater as part of the 12th Army Group, under Gen. Omar Bradley, in France and Germany for 25 months. He earned 5 battle stars with the Field Artillery.

ROBERT V. KENNEDY, of Lawrenceburg, served as a Staff Sergeant in the infantry at Ft. Wolters, and in the Anti-Aircraft Artillery at Ft. Bliss in the American theater in 1944 to 1946.

PATRICK KENT, of Aurora, was in the Army at Camp Crowder. He later was a Corporal in a construction unit in Wales in 1944. He married Doris Coulthard of Liverpool, England.

OAKLEY KIDWELL was an airplane Mechanic Technician with the 386th bomber group in France.

JOSEPH KINNETT was a Private First Class in the Army. He was killed in action in France in July 1944.

EARL KITTLE was a paratrooper in the Army for a year in the ETO. He received a medical discharge in 1945 after being wounded in the face, neck and scalp.

FLOYD KITTLE was with an Ordnance Maintenance Company in France in 1944.

STANLEY KNECHT, of the Sunman area, was an Army Sergeant with the 301st Infantry Regiment, entering the Army in December 1942. He was an Assistant Squad Leader, seeing action in France and the Rhineland. He was wounded while fighting in Germany in 1945.

FRED KNITTENBRINK was a Corporal in the Army at Camp Perry in 1944.

EZRA KLEPPER, of Lawrenceburg, was a Corporal in the Army Signal Corps at Camp Crowder in 1944.

Joseph Knue

BERNARD KOCHER, of Harrison, was a Staff Sergeant in the 464th bomb group entering the Army Air Force in December 1942. His duty was a Radar Mechanic with action over Italy, France, and Central Europe. He received the Distinguished Unit Citation and 8 battle stars.

Robert V. Kennedy

LESTER KONRADI, of Guilford, entered the Army Air Force in 1944 and became a Private First Class in the 389th Bomber Group. He served as a Truck Driver in Central Europe, receiving a battle star.

RUDOLPH KLUEBER, of Wilmington, was a Seaman 2nd Class in the South Pacific in 1944.

HARLAND KRATZER, of the Sunman area, was a Staff Sergeant with the 95th Port Platoon in the European Theater of Operations in August 1944.

LEO KRAUS, of St Leon, was a Private First Class serving with an Engineer Unit of the Army Air Corps. He earned four battle stars.

DALE LAAKER, of Dillsboro, entered the Army in March 1943 and served as a Private until February 1944.

ORVILLE LAMPE, served with a Petroleum Distributor Company of the Army Engineering Corps at Camp Claibourn in 1944.

LAVERN LAFOLLETTE, of Lawrenceburg, was a Corporal in the 534th Anti-Aircraft Artillery Weapons Battalion. He served in Italy, Rhineland, France and Central Europe and merited 5 battle stars.

JOHN LESLIE, of Moores Hill, was in the U.S. Army at Camp Polk in 1944.

EARL LEVI, of Aurora, was a Corporal with the 370th Field Artillery Battalion. He served as a Telephone Operator in Normandy, France, Ardennes and Central Europe.

ALONZO (LONNIE) LEWIS, of Lawrenceburg, was awarded the Silver Star medal for gallantry in action in September 1944. When his platoon leader was wounded during an attack upon the enemy, Staff Sergeant Lewis assumed command and moved through heavy enemy fire to reorganize the platoon and carry on the attack. The battle occurred near Arbrey, France. At that time Lonny was serving with the 45th Army Division.

VIRGIL LOTTON entered the U.S. Army in 1943, but only served through basic training for six months and then received a medical discharge.

DONALD LOCKWOOD, of Aurora, was an Army Private. He served with the 6th Company of the Second Regiment, U.S. Army.

CHARLES LUKE, of the Dillsboro area, was a Private First Class in the 304th Infantry Regiment. He served as an Airplane and Engine Mechanic in Central Europe.

PAUL LUSK, of Aurora, was a Private First Class with the 456th Military Police Escort Guard Company. He saw action in the Rhineland and received a battle star.

ROBERT MACY completed the Navy's V-12 training at Emory University and then went to midshipman school at Asbury Park for advanced training in 1944.

ALBERT MANGOLD served in the European Theater in an Engineers Battalion, as a Technical Sergeant. He received a battle star on his European ribbon in 1944.

ROBERT MARKLAND was a Staff Sergeant with an Army Roadway Operating Battalion working in France in 1944.

ROBERT MARKS was a Staff Sergeant serving with the 92nd Signal Battalion in France, Belgium, Germany.

RUSSELL MEYER was a Seaman 2nd Class in the U.S. Navy. He received a medical discharge in 1945.

DONALD R. MILLER was a Private First Class in Patton's Third Army. He served in an Anti-Aircraft Artillery unit and was in Germany in 1945.

HOWARD ASHCRAFT, of Moores Hill, was a Chaplain's Assistant with the 9th Reinforcement Depot Training Center. He saw action in France and Germany, earning 2 battle stars.

GRIFFIN McELFRESH, of Lawrenceburg, served as a Technical Sergeant for three years in Europe with the 51st Division. He was in North Africa, Italy, Sicily and landed in France on D-Day.

JAMES McALLISTER, of Lawrenceburg, was a Surgical Technician in an Infantry Unit. He served in the Ardennes, Rhineland and Central Europe, receiving 4 battle stars.

WILLIAM McKEE served as a Sergeant in Germany crossing the Rhine in 1945.

IVAN McCLAIN was awarded a Silver Star posthumously for gallantry in action in an assault on a German outpost. He was fatally wounded in this action.

VIRGIL McCONNELL was an Army Private First Class, serving with the 101st Paratrooper Division. He suffered from frozen feet, as a result of spending three days in a foxhole in Belgium.

WILLIAM McKAIN, of Lawrenceburg, served as a Lieutenant in the Army Air Force, piloting a P-47 Thunderbolt in the European Theater of Operations. He was wounded when his plane was shot down over Germany and was hospitalized in France.

GARNET McMULLEN spent 27 months as a Corporal in the Army in Africa, Italy, France and Germany. Received operational medal for proficiency in the operation of a squad vehilcle in 1945.

RICHARD McMURRAY was a Technical Sergeant serving as a Tank Mechanic in 1945.

Vincent McCann

GEORGE McREYNOLDS, of Lawrenceburg, became a Lieutenant in the U.S. Navy. He was an instructor of naval indoctrination at the base at Hollywood, Florida.

WILLIAM McSWAIN, of Aurora, was a Private First Class with the 80th Infantry Division. He served as a Heavy Mortor Crewman in France, Andennes and Central Europe. He was wounded in the Battle of the Bulge.

HANSEL MIRICK, of Aurora, was Private First Class in an Armored Cavalry Squadron in Germany. He was wounded in combat in Czechoslovakia and transferred to the General Hospital, Louisville, Kentucky.

ALVIN MOODY was an Army Private with the 1st Division. He was reported missing in action, but later was confirmed that he was a prisoner of war in France.

THOMAS EDWARD MILLER, of Aurora, entered the Navy in March 1944 and became a Motor Machinist Mate 3rd class. He served at the Naval base in Norfolk and in the Atlantic Fleet.

HOBART MOREHEAD, of Moores Hill, was a Corporal in the Army Infantry Replacement Center at Camp Blanding, Florida. He served as a Rifle Instructor.

JOHNNY MANGOLD, of Lawrenceburg, was a Private First Class with the 1264th Army Air Corps base unit. He served as an Airplane and Engine Mechanic in the ETO.

WILLIAM R. MACKER, was an Army Captain serving on the island of New Guinea in 1944.

WILLIAM MAHAFFEY served in the U.S. Army Air Force as a Staff Sergeant. He was a photographer over Germany, a member of the crew of the flying fortress "Knockout Dropper," the first heavy bomber in the European Theater to complete 75 missions.

JAMES McADAMS was an Army Private First Class. He had duty in New Caledonia and elsewhere in the South Pacific.

JOHN McADAMS, of Lawrenceburg, was a Private First Class with the 467th Engineers. He was discharged at Camp Sherman, Ohio in March 1944.

VINCENT McCANN served in the U.S. Army in the European Theater from March 1944 to January 1945, when he was killed in the Battle of the Bulge.

EDSEL McCONNELL was a Seaman First Class. He served on a minesweeper in European waters and then on a destroyer in the Atlantic Fleet.

THOMAS McCOOL was an Army Private who served in France and Germany. He made seven parachute jumps and took part in the invasion of France.

ROBERT McKAIN, of Lawrenceburg, served two years in the South Pacific as a Staff Sergeant in the ground crew of the Army Air Force. He also served in Iran, Egypt and India.

HAROLD McCLANAHAN, of Moores Hill, was a Flight officer in the European Theater. He was missing in action on a bomber raid over occupied France in 1944 and later a prisoner of the Germans. He was awarded the Air Medal and two oak leaf clusters.

WILMER MOLTER entered the U.S. Army Air Corps and became a Corporal. He served with an Air Force ground crew.

GLENN MILLIGAN was a Private First Class in Marines in 1945.

LLOYD J. MILLER, of Aurora, graduated from pilot training at Randolph Field, Texas, and became a Second Lieutenant. He then served as a Flight Instructor at an Army Air Force flight school.

PAUL MATTINGLY, of Aurora, was a Lieutenant in the Army Air Force as a pilot of a bomber. He ferried his B-24 and crew from New York to West Aftica in 1944. Thereafter, he flew missions out of North Africa into Italy. He flew over targets in France, Germany, Austria and Yugoslavia. He was part of the 460th bomb group.

LOREN MARTIN, of Moores Hill, was a Private First Class in the 263rd Infantry. He was a Rifleman with duty in France, receiving a battle star.

ERCEL MARTIN was in the Army Air Force as a Corporal in the 537th bomber squadron in England. He was part of the ground crew.

ELLSWORTH MARTIN was in the U.S. Army in 1944. He served in the rank of Sergeant.

Harold McClanahan

Terrance McCann

Paul Oberting

DELTON MARKSBERRY, of Lawrenceburg, served as a radio operator-gunner with a B-52 bomber crew who was cited twice by the President for outstanding performance of duty in combat with the enemy, and an attack on a Nazi aircraft factory. A cluster was added for a mission over the Ploestic oil refinery in Rumania. Delton was a Technical Sergeant.

DORMAN MARTIN was an Army Corporal with a Tank Battalion. In 1944, they were located in England prior to moving to Europe.

CLETUS MARTIN was a Corporal in the Army Air Corps. He served as a Mechanic for a B-24 group.

VERMONT MARQUA was a First Lieutenant serving with an Anti-Aircraft unit in combat in Germany. He merited 7 battle stars and a Distinguished Unit Citation.

THOMAS McLEASTER, of Lawrenceburg, was a Hospital Apprentice 1st class in Bremerton, Washington in 1945. Later, he became Seaman 2nd Class assigned to a Navy hospital training station at Farragut, Idaho.

TERRANCE McCANN, of Guilford, was a Private First Class in the 741st Railroad Operation Battalion, U.S. Army. He served as a Brakeman in the Ardennes, Rhineland and Central Europe.

WILLARD NOWLIN was an Army Lieutenant. He had combat service in France with a tank battalion in 1944.

PAUL OBERTING, of Lawrenceburg Junction, served with the 743rd Tank Battalion, driving a 2-1/2 ton army vehicle transporting personnel and supplies in combat areas. He landed in Normandy on D-Day. His unit received 3 citations for excellent performance of duty. Later in a letter to his uncle, Bob Oberting, he wrote "I'm doing the same things you did in the other war (WWI). So I guess you know what I'm going through." He served in Normandy, France, Ardennes and Central Europe as a Private First Class.

CHARLES (TED) OHLER, of Lawrenceburg, entered the Navy in 1944 and became an Aviation Metalsmith 3rd Class. He served at the Naval Air Station at Barber's Point, Hawaii.

RICHARD OPPEN received his pilot wings at Corpus Christi, Texas in 1945. He was an Ensign in the U.S. Navy.

ROBERT PERPINGTON, was a Technical Sergeant with the 25th Cavalry Ordnance Department. He served in France and Luxembourg.

FRANCES PETERS, of Aurora, served in the 303rd Infantry as a Sergeant. He was a Rifleman in the Rhineland and Central Europe.

FLOYD PIEPER, of Dillsboro, entered the Merchant Marines. He would serve in the engineering department of merchant ships.

MARTIN PRATHER, of Lawrenceburg, served as an Ammunition Handler with the 100th Division in Central Europe. He had 1 battle star and was a Private First Class.

HENRY PETERS, of Aurora, saw action in a tank unit in the ETO. He also had duty as a Radio Operator Instructor for the 749th Tank Battalion. Later in Europe, he was injured and returned to the states for hospitalization.

EDWIN PETERS was a Sergeant in the U.S. Army in 1944. He was assigned to an armored Division.

WILLIAM RUTH, of Lawrenceburg, was a Storekeeper First Class in the U.S. Navy. He had duty in Trinidad in 1944.

BARRY RYAN was a Private in the Artillery in Germany in 1944.

PAUL ROCKWELL, of Lawrenceburg, entered the U.S. Navy and became a Yoeman 3rd Class. He served in the Pacific aboard the U.S.S. *Vestal* and at Bremerton Navy Base.

DALLAS ROSS was a Staff Sergeant with the 54th Infantry Training Battalion in 1944. He received a letter of commendation for superior performance of duty.

CHARLES RICE, of Aurora, was a Corporal in the Army Air Corps serving in a ground crew in 1944.

WESLEY RICE was a Private First Class with the 87th Division in France, Belgium, Germany and Luxembourg.

HARRY RIESE was a Private First Class in the Army Medical corps. He participated in the Battle of the Bulge in 1944.

Henry Peters

William Robinson

Norman Steele

Albert Schuman

LESTER RILEY, of Lawrenceburg, was a Private with the 803rd Replacement Battalion. He served as a Rifleman in Central Europe.

HOWARD RODGERS was missing in action in France in October 1944.

WILLIAM ROBINSON, of Aurora, was an Army Corporal with the 8th Armored Division of the 9th Army. He served in Germany and Czechoslovakia.

JOHN SATCHWELL was an Army Private who was wounded in his leg and eye in combat in France in 1944.

NORMAN STEELE, of Aurora, was a First Lieutenant in the Army. He fought in the European Theater where he was awarded the Bronze Star for heroic achievement in combat.

ALBERT SCHUMAN, of St. Leon, was an Army Sergeant. He was awarded the Bronze Star Medal for duty in the Third Armored Field Battalion. He was an observer on a hilltop in Luxembourg during an enemy attack. The telephone line to his unit was blown out and Schuman regained contact by radio, calling for artillery fire. With enemy fire racking his position he continued to call for his unit. He was wounded, but held to his position until his mission was accomplished.

LEROY SCHUMAN, of St. Leon, enlisted in January 1944. He was wounded at the Battle of the Bulge in Luxembourg and received a Bronze Star Medal for heroic action during combat.

PAUL SCHOLLE was a Private First Class in the U.S. Army. He was killed in action in France in 1944.

CARL SCHWIER, of the Sunman area, was an Army Technician 5th Grade with the 94th Cavalry Reconnaissance unit. He was wounded in Germany in 1945.

WALLACE SCHOTT, of Lawrencburg, entered the Army in March 1943 and became Corporal. He served with a Military Police Escort Squad Company in the Rhineland, receiving a battle star.

WILLIAM STRONG was commissioned a Second Lieutenant in the Army Air Corps and served as an Aerial Navigator.

WILLIAM STANDRIFF was a Private First Class in the Army. He was stationed at a base in England in 1944.

ROBERT (BUD) SWALES, of Bright, entered the Army in October of 1942. He served in the ETO, in France and Germany with the 9th Army Air Corps. He drove many different types of military vehicles, including motorcycles.

ERNEST SHORT, Army Private First Class, was wounded while fighting the Germans in France in June 1944.

RUSSELL H. SMITH was drafted into the Army in 1944 and served in the 226th Infantry Division in Belgium, Holland and Germany. He took part in the Battle of the Bulge and the Rhine Valley.

LEO SNELLING was an Army Sergeant in 1944. He served with the 506th Parachute Troops.

CLARENCE SNYDER, of Dillsboro, served as a Cook at the Army's 186th General Hospital. He was a Technical Sergeant in the ETO.

FRANCIS TEEL, of Lawrenceburg, became an Army Technician 5th Grade, serving with the 386th Quartermaster Training Company. He would drive a truck in the Rhineland and Central Europe Campaigns.

DAWSON TIBBITS, of Dillsboro, was a Sergeant in the Army. He served as a Mechanic Instructor at Ft. Knox in 1944.

HARRY TIBBITS was a Sergeant in the Army Air Corps. In 1944, he was stationed at Cochran Field, Macon, Georgia.

FRANK TIBBITS, of Lawrenceburg, entered the U.S.Army as a Private in March 1944, and served briefly before being discharged in April 1944.

RAYMOND TODD entered the Army and became a Technical Sergeant in the Quartermaster Corps. He served in Paris, Cherbourg and Bologne.

ALBERT WEHMEYER was an Army Corporal. He served with a medical unit in Germany. He had also seen action in Africa, Sicily and Normandy. He was awarded the Silver Star and Bronze Star medals for action on D-Day.

ANTHONY WALTER, of Lawrenceburg, was an Army Private serving with the Infantry. He saw action in France, meriting a battle star.

Robert Swales

Russell Smith

Raymond Todd

Alfred Webb

LEWIS WATERS, of Lawrenceburg, was a Staff Sergeant with the 223rd Infantry Regiment. He was a mortar NCO and saw action in the Ardennes, Rhineland and Germany, where he was wounded in 1944.

ALFRED (HAP) WEBB, of Wilmington, entered the U.S. Army in April 1944. He was trained in Cooks School at Fort Benning, Georgia. He served in the Army until December 1945.

WILLIAM WELLS was a Staff Sergeant serving as a Mechanic on a transport plane in 1944.

FRANCIS WESSEL, of Lawrenceburg, was a Sergeant with the 81st Engineering Combat Battalion. He saw action in France, Ardennes and Central Europe, receiving 4 battle stars.

WILFORD WHALEY was a Corporal in the U.S. Army. He had duty in both Italy and Germany, and was killed in combat in Germany in 1945.

EARL WHITEFORD was an Army Private First Class. For his performance of duty during combat in Germany, he was awarded the Bronze Star.

HARRY WILLIAMS was serving in the Army in England as a Staff Sergeant with the 9th Air Force as a Payroll Clerk in 1944.

ALBERT WILTBERGER was a Private in the Army in 1944.

JAMES WILTBERGER, of Greendale, was a Private in basic training in 1944.

CARL WINGATE was an Army Sergeant and was wounded in Belgium. He was with the Infantry and earned 3 battle stars in the ETO.

JAMES WINKLE was a Private First Class serving overseas with the Army in 1944.

EDWARD WINTER entered the Army in March 1943 and became a Technician 4th Grade. He served with the 66th Cavalry Reconnaisance Troop in northern France and received a battle star.

FRANCIS WINTER, of Guilford, was in the Quartermaster Corps, in the Army Service Forces Training Regiment Camp Lee, Virginia.

Three Wunderlich brothers: (r.) George, John, Fred (l.) and their brother-in-law Richard Mattingly

CLARENCE WITTE was an Army Air Corps Corporal. He served as a Radioman on a B-17 bomber in 1944.

HAROLD WITTE was a Private in the Army for 27 months. He earned 3 battle stars in 1943.

LEO WOLKER, of Aurora, was inducted into the Army in 1943. He served as a Sergeant as a Canoneer with the First Army in France, Belgium and Germany.

FRED WUNDERLICH, of Aurora, was a Captain with the 101st General Hospital in England.

CLARENCE WILSON was a Technical Sergeant serving in European Theater of Operation as a Radio Operator on a B-17 in 1945.

Earl Minger

Clarence Minger

Robert Minger

SWIFT WUNKER, of Lawrenceburg, graduated from OCS at Ft. Sill as a Second Lieutenant in 1944. He served in the South Pacific.

CURTIS W. VINEUP was a Staff Sergeant in an Army Demolition unit in Northern France. He also served with Headquarters Company, Supreme Headquarters. He received the Bronze Star medal.

EVERETT YORK, of Aurora, was a Technician 5th Grade in a Medical Detachment. He served as an Orthopedic Mechanic in the American Theater.

DELTON LANGE, of Aurora, was drafted into the Army in 1943. He became a Staff Sergeant and served in the European Theater of Operations.

BUELL (BILL) LAMBERT, of Bright, was a Captain in the Army Air Corps. He served in the European Theater as a Bombardier on a B-17 bomber, flying over enemy territory.

HENRY HUDSON, of Bright, served with the 82nd Airborne Division. He took part in the June 6th invasion of Normandy, and also jumped in Holland, at Arnheim. He made several top secret jumps during WWII.

EARL MINGER enlisted in August of 1943 in the Marine Corps and took basic training at San Diego. He became a Corporal in 1945, and was stationed at the Naval Air Station, Vero Beach, where he was discharged in May of 1946.

CLARENCE MINGER was inducted into the Marine Corps in May of 1943, taking his basic training at San Diego. He then took part in several battles in the Solomons, Guam and the Mariana Islands. He was wounded in action in July of 1944. After recovery, he was assigned to the Fleet Airforce Fire Company in Hawaii, until discharged in October of 1945.

ROBERT MINGER, of Lawrenceburg, enlisted in the U.S. Navy in January of 1943 and became a Dental Technician First Class. He served on the cruiser, U.S.S. *Atlanta*, in the Pacific, receiving the China Service Medal and Navy Occupation Medal. He completed 6 years of service in the Navy.

LEROY ECKLER, of Dillsboro, entered the U.S. Army and served some three months when he received a medical discharge.

WILBUR ECKLER, of Dillsboro, went into the Army with the first Draft. He served with the Artillery in Iceland and England.

NORMAN CONAWAY, of Dillsboro, served in the Alaska Theater during his Army tour of duty in WWII.

PRESTON CONAWAY, of Dillsboro, entered the Army Air Corps and became a Sergeant. As an Airplane Mechanic, he was stationed at various fields on the East Coast of the U.S. He served four years and nine months.

DELVER GEISLER served in the Army from July of 1941 until June of 1945. He became a Staff Sergeant and also a Mess Sergeant. He had duty at Camp Wheeler, Georgia.

OWEN LOWE was a Sergeant in the Army Air Force. He served with a Fighter Command station in England for over 18 months.

PAUL SCHUMAN was an Army Private who was killed in action in France in December 1944.

WILLIAM FORD, of Lawrenceburg, served as an Auto Mechanic in the Field Artillery in the European Theater in 1945. He was a Technician 4th Grade.

GEORGE TSCHAEN completed 24 missions in the ETO in 1945 as a Sergeant.

Paul Schuman

ROBERT VETTER, a Private in the Army, drowned at Napier Field Dothan, Alabama in 1944.

WILLIAM TURNER was a Private with the Escort Guard Company at a redeployment camp in France.

HARRY FABER entered the Marines in 1944 and served in the Pacific Theater. He was a Private First Class.

ANTHONY WEBER was a Private in the 214th Infantry at Camp Blanding, Florida in 1944.

THOMAS LIDDLE Private First Class, served with an Armored Division at Ft. Knox in maintenance repair in 1944.

Buell Lambert

MELVIN SELMEYER was with the Army Engineers in France, rebuilding wrecked bridges and railroads. He was a Private First Class.

ROBERT GLENN, of Lawrenceburg, a Private First Class in the Army Infantry, was wounded for the third time during the battle for the Hertegen Forest in the Central Europe Campaign.

Harley Uhlmansiek

James Farrar

SAMUEL WARD, of Lawrenceburg, was a Private First Class serving at Stout Field, Indianapolis in 1945.

BENJAMIN McALLISTER was a Private First Class in 1944 at a camp in Franklin, Lousiana.

PAUL POWELL was a 2nd Class Motor Machinist mate in the Navy serving in the Aleutians and in the invasion of France on D-Day. He served a total of 22 months.

THADDEUS GEISERT JR., of Greendale, was a cadet in the Army Air Force at Austin College, Texas. He completed aerial gunnery school and became a Private First Class at March Field, California in 1945.

JAMES FARRAR, of Lawrenceburg, was a Private assigned to the Intelligence Service Unit, which trained men for the Army of Occupation, based in Paris, France in 1945. He had been in a hospital in Belgium previously suffering from wounds caused by enemy fire.

VINCENT LONG was the first casualty in WWII for St. John's Parish, Dover. As a Private in the Army, he was killed in action on New Year's Eve, December 31, 1944, fighting Nazis in Luxembourg. Vincent was in the Infantry with the 5th Division of General Patton's Third Army.

SIDNEY LONG, of Lawrenceburg, served in the 8th Army Air Force Command in Ireland as a Master Sergeant. Later he served in Europe for 30 months.

OREAN LANE, of Dillsboro, was a Sergeant in the 8th Army Air Force serving at a B-17 Base in England in 1944.

NELSON LAWRENCE, of Lawrenceburg, was a Sergeant and had duty in Paris, France and Germany in 1945.

MARCUS LAWS, of Dillsboro, was a Corporal serving as a Surgical Technician in a station hospital in the South Pacific.

FOREST SNELLING was an Army Air Force Sergeant and a member of an Airborne Infantry Regiment. He was a passenger on a plane that left England on a mission to an undisclosed destination. The plane was shot down by enemy flak over southern Holland. All passengers bailed out, but no one saw Forest after they bailed out, and he was presumed dead.

ROBERT SCUDDER, of Dillsboro, was a seaman in the Merchant Marines in 1944.

ROGER FUGATE, a Technical Sergeant in the Army Air Force, was awarded the Flying Cross in 1944.

EDWARD POWERS served in the Army in 1944.

RUSSELL WELLS served with the 78th Cavalry and was commissioned a Second Lieutenant.

FRED TRAUE was a Private 1st Class who served in France, Germany and Italy.

ROBERT STANDRIFF a Private First Class in the Army was wounded on Christmas Eve while serving in Germany. He had served in the Army for 29 months.

ROSCOE BUCHANAN was a Corporal in the Army Air Force at Drew Field, Florida in 1944.

GERALD SUTTON, of Aurora, a Technical Sergeant in the 9th Army Air Force, was a ground crew member serving in France, Belgium, Holland and Germany.

CHARLES THOMPSON was a Private First Class in the 44th Army Infantry Division under General Patton. The division received a citation for outstanding performance. He was wounded while serving in Germany.

HARLEY UHLMANSIEK, of Aurora, was a Leader of the Motorcyclists of a Military Police Platoon and frequently escorted General Patton in the ETO. He was awarded the Bronze Star for heroic service in France, Luxembourg, Germany and Austria during the period of September 1944 to May 1945. Harley was a Sergeant.

JAMES JACKSON served in Iceland and in Europe where he was captured and became a German war prisoner.

ALBERT WALKER, was a Private First Class in the 3rd Army serving in Germany. He was wounded in 1944.

JOHN McCLANAHAN, of Moores Hill, a Staff Sergeant in the Army Air Force was reported missing in action over France since June 17, 1944. Sergeant McClanahan held the Air Medal with Clusters and was a Radio Operator-Gunner on a bomber.

A.R. (AL) STRYKER, Lawrenceburg, was commissioned as Captain after he entered the Army. He was assigned to the Specialist Reserves. He was trained to be a Public Utilities Specialist. He was sent overseas to assist the Allied Military Government. His unit was to go into occupied countries and aid in the rehabilitation of gas, water and related utilities.

Russell Wells

Al Stryker (l.) and John Stryker

Donald Marshall

David Tanner

DR. GEORGE FERRY, of Lawrenceburg, was in Germany, France, and Africa as a Captain in the Army Dental Corps.

HUBERT ESTAL BARNES, of Lawrenceburg, was killed in action in Germany. He had been in the Army more than three years and was assigned to a Tank Battalion as a Staff Sergeant.

DELMAR TUCKER was a Technical Sergeant 5th Grade in the Army was at Lincoln, Nebraska in 1944.

JAMES EDWARDS was a Private First Class in the Infantry 7th Army. He received 2 Battle Stars serving in the Aleutians, France and Germany.

FREDERICK EDWARDS graduated from Naval Reserve Officer Training and was commissioned an Ensign in 1944.

MARCUS MORRIS, of Aurora, was an Army Sergeant. He was wounded in the knee in France in November of 1944.

ERNEST SCHILLER, of Aurora, was a Fireman 3rd Class and served on a Destroyer Escort in 1944.

DAVID GLENN TANNER was a Sergeant who served in Bermuda as a Mechanic in 1945 and 1946.

DONALD MARSHALL, of Aurora, was with the 34th Combat Engineers. He saw action in North Africa, Sicily, Italy, Germany, France and Austria.

CHARLES SNYDER was a Staff Sergeant in the Army Air Corps. He was Crew Chief of his company and was stationed in England in 1944.

GLENN SNYER served with the 669th Army Air Corps Band. He was a Technical Sergeant and was promoted to Assistant Band Director.

DONALD LAND, of Aurora, a Private in the Army, landed in France on D-Day. While serving with an infantry unit, he was wounded in France in 1944.

CARL LAWS was a Fire Controlman in the Navy, stationed in Chicago in 1945.

LEROY BECKMAN a Staff Sergeant in the Army was missing in action while flying over Germany. He was a member of a B-17 crew.

GEORGE SNELLING was in the Navy, a Seaman Second Class, serving at the Norman, Oklahoma Naval Air Base in 1944.

LEON LeCLERC, of Lawrenceburg, a paratrooper with the 101st Airborne Division, died Dec. 23, 1944 of wounds suffered in action at Bastogne, Belgium (Battle of the Bulge). He was buried in an American cemetery in France. Memorial services were held at St. John's Lutheran Church, Aurora. His commanding officer wrote his parents, "...his personal courage and ability will always be a source of inspiration."

MAURICE HUNTER was an Army private and he was wounded in Germany in November 1944, with shrapnel in the left leg.

LESTER RENNER, of Aurora, was a Corporal with an Anti-Aircraft unit in Europe. He was hospitalized for a foot ailment in 1944.

HAROLD RENNER was Private in the Army Air Corps and served at Lowery Field, Denver, Colorado in 1945.

FLOYD SACKETT, of Bright, served as a Radio Mechanic with the 349th Bomber Squadron.

FLOYD SAILOR was a Sergeant with the Signal Corps overseas in 1944.

WILFORD WHALEY served as a Corporal with the Army in Italy and was killed in Germany in 1945.

FERRELL LIVINGSTON, of Lawrenceburg, was a Corporal and served as a member of an Airborne Division of Paratroopers at Camp McCall, North Carolina in 1944.

Virgil Trennepohl

VERRELL SHOOK, of Aurora, a Private First Class in the Army Air Corps was killed on November 8, 1945 in a collision with another plane, after participating in a Victory Bond show in Elmira, New York. He was stationed at the Army Air Base, Greenville, South Carolina. A military funeral was conducted the following week in Aurora with burial in Riverview cemetery.

VIRGIL TRENNEPOHL, of Moores Hill, served in Normandy, France, Germany and Central Europe. He was in a motor pool and transported military equipment and personnel. Virgil received the Bronze Star for his duty in 5 major battles as a communications Driver.

ARTHUR SHELL, a Private First Class, in the Army was a prisoner of war in Germany in 1945.

Clyde Fairfield

Dan Whiteford

Paul Mulroy

FRANCIS BARROWS was a Private in the Army at Fort Ord, California in 1944.

GILBERT BAKER, of Aurora, was a Seaman Second Class in a Naval Armed Guard unit in 1944.

CLYDE FAIRFIELD, of Aurora, arrived in England in December 1943. He served as an Aircraft Armorer with the 446th Bomber Group of the 8th Air Corps. He participated in air offensives over Normandy, France Rhineland, Central Europe and North Apenines in Italy. He was a Private First Class.

CHESTER FOX, of Harrison, served in the 150th Ordnance Battalion of the 3rd Army as a Medic. He was a Staff Sergeant earning 5 Battle Stars fighting in France and Central Europe.

ALBERT J. SCHUMAN entered the Army in the 9th Armored Division 3rd Armored Field Artillery in 1941. He gained the rank of Staff Sergeant serving in the battles of the Ardennes, Rhineland and Central Europe. He was wounded in the Battle of the Bulge. He received the Purple Heart, a Bronze Star and three battle stars. He served 4 years and 9 months.

PAUL B. MULROY, of Lawrenceburg, served in the Army as a Private First Class in the 94th Division of General Patton's Third Army in the European Theater of Operations, he saw action in France, Germany and Czechoslovakia. He had an infantry badge and two battle stars.

WILLIAM WORKMAN served 2-1/2 years in the South Pacific then served in the Army Air Force as Transportation Supervisor in 1944.

DAN WHITEFORD, of Aurora, was a Private in the 813th Tank Battalion Destroyer in the ETO.

LAWRENCE MORAND was one of the first inductees. He was sent into the Army and became a Corporal in the Quartermaster Corps serving in the Battle of the Bulge, Belgium and France.

PAUL NOWLIN trained as a Radio Operator and Mechanic at Scott Field, Illinois and became a member of a bomb crew.

RALPH BAKER served in an engineering battalion as a Carpenter Specialist. He died in France in November 1944.

HAROLD BAKER was a Staff Sergeant serving with the 500th Collection Depot in France in 1944.

ROBERT SLINKARD a Private First Class was injured on Okinawa when a tank he was riding in overturned. He suffered a broken leg and arms and had to be evacuated to a hospital on Guam.

TOM MILLER served as Private First Class in the Army at Reno, Nevada in 1944.

LLOYD SHUTER, born on a farm near Aurora, entered the Army in October 1942. He was assigned to the Infantry in the 90th Division, which came to be known as General Patton's "Tough Hombres." In August 1943, he was assigned to a Field Artillery unit to drive a supply truck hauling gasoline and ammunition to the "Tough Hombres." His division had been based in England where he met a lassie by the name of Gladys Foster and they fell in love. Shuter sailed from Cadiff, Wales aboard a supply ship on June 6, 1944, they crossed the channel and rode at anchor off Utah Beach. Lloyd watched the invasion from the deck of the ship while shells thundered overhead. On June 8, they unloaded on the beach. Lloyd was with the vanguard of Patton's army as it broke out of Normandy. He was in the Battle of Falaise Gap, when 100,000 Germans were captured. The 90th Division drove across France into one of Europe's worst winters and into the Battle of the Bulge. Finally in May 1945, the 90th met the Russians in Czechoslovakia as the war ended. Lloyd returned to England and convinced Gladys Foster to marry him and go to the U.S.

Lloyd Shuter

Leo Schuette

LEO SCHUETTE, of Dillsboro, entered the Army on October 9, 1943. He received basic training at Camp Chaffee, Arkansas and served with the 397th Field Artillery Battalion as a Supply Clerk in the European Theater for 7 months.

CHESTER SHARP, a Private First Class, was wounded twice when fighting in France.

GEORGE SHERMAN, of Lawrenceburg, was a Technical Sergeant who served in France, Belgium and Germany.

CHARLES MORRISON, of Manchester, was at Sheppard Field, Texas in 1944 as a Private First Class.

JOHN BARRY was a Private First Class serving at Camp Phillips, Kansas in 1944.

EUGENE PERMAR, of Aurora, was a Technical Sergeant who lost his life in a bomber crash in the ETO. His plane had bombed Bremen, Germany and they were only 50 miles from the English coast when the crash occurred in 1944.

THEODORE SCHULENBERG served as a Captain in the Army. He was an Artillery Battery Commander in Europe and earned 4 battle stars.

ELMER LAKER, of Dillsboro, graduated as a Second Lieutenant in the Army Air Force Central Flying Training Command at Randolph Field, Texas 1944. He was a B-24 Bomber Pilot.

CHARLES JAMESON was a Private First Class with the Army Medical Corps and also trained in camera photography in Culver City, California.

Charles Jameson

WILLIAM WELLS was a Mechanic for transport in the Army Air Corps. He served as Staff Sergeant.

CHARLES TAYLOR, of Lawrenceburg, served as an Army Sergeant in Belgium and France earning one battle star.

CHARLES K. TAYLOR, of Guilford, was in the Naval Air Force in 1944 having completed flight training in Pensacola and becoming an Ensign.

RUSSELL THUERMER served in the Army in the European Theater. He saw action in France and was wounded by a sniper in Germany in 1944.

Robert Lemm

WALTER HEMMING, of Greendale, served in France and Belgium as a Private First Class in the Army Air Force stationed in England in 1944.

ROBERT HARTMAN was wounded in France. He was a Private First Class with a Tank Battalion in Belgium in 1944.

AUSTIN SMITH, of Aurora, served with the 78th division of the First Army in Germany as a Technician 4th Grade. He received a Unit Citation of Merit.

ACELL HORTON was in the Army serving in France in 1944

WILLARD LOH was a Corporal in the Army Air Force who served as an Aerial Gunner in 1944.

ROBERT LEMM, of Lawrenceburg, was a Lieutenant in the Army. He served two years in France with an Army Transport unit.

LESLIE HORTON, of Aurora, was a Private First Class in the Army who had duty in Germany. He was assigned to a Field Artillery unit.

WILLIAM HUBER was an Army Corporal in Germany in 1945. He had also served in Africa and Corsica with the 214th Quartermaster Company.

FREDERICK SCHULENBERG was a Captain in the Field Artillery in 1945.

ROBERT PETERS, of Aurora, was an Army Sergeant who had duty in Havana in 1944.

EUGENE WHITE, a Private in the Army, was listed as missing in action while serving with Patton's Army in Germany.

JOHN HORTON was Private First Class who served in France in 1944.

DOUGLAS R. BURKHAM entered the Army in 1943. As a Private First Class, he was a member of the 106th Infantry Division and was taken prisoner by the Germans during the Battle of the Bulge. He was released about April of 1945.

LLOYD BAKER was a Sergeant in France where he did duty as an Airplane Mechanic. He was awarded 7 battle stars.

CLAYTON STEVENS, of Moores Hill, was a Private First Class who served in the 83rd Division who relieved the 101st Airborne Division in Normandy in June 1944. He was wounded on July 16th in the hedgerows near St. Lo and sent to a hospital in England and then to the States. Upon return to duty, he guarded German prisoners. He was awarded the Bronze Star and was discharged in January 1946.

CHARLES FLETCHER, of the Moores Hill area, entered the Army in March of 1942. He saw action in France, Rhineland and Central Europe as a Telephone Lineman. He earned 3 battle stars.

HUGHES HALL entered the U.S. Navy in August of 1944 and became a Seaman First Class. He served on the ship, S.S. *John Gibbon*, which made ports in Scotland, England and Russia. He served until December of 1945.

ROBERT HOLMAN, of Aurora, was a Sergeant in the Fifth Army and saw action in the Italian campaign.

ARTHUR THEBO was a Machinist Mate First Class who served in the 19th Naval Construction Battalion in the South Pacific. He had duty in the following places: New Guinea, Russell Islands and New Britain.

Charles Fletcher

Hughes Hall

Delmore Hizer

Dolan Seaver

Elmo Darlington

EUGENE GULLEY, of Lawrenceburg, entered the Army Air Corps in 1944 and became a Sergeant. He was based first in England and then in Germany in 1945. After WWII, he reenlisted and made a career in the Air Force.

RICHARD DENNERLINE, of Aurora, entered the U.S. Army. He was hospitalized from illness, and served entirely in the American Theater.

DR. CHARLES OLCOTT, of Aurora, was promoted to the rank of Commander in the Navy Medical Corps in March of 1944. He served as Regimental Surgeon with the 16th Marines in the Pacific Theater.

DARCY ADELMORE (DELMORE) HIZER, of Aurora, entered the U.S. Navy in May of 1944. He completed his Boot training at Great Lakes Naval Station in June and became a Fire Controlman 3rd Class. He was discharged in December of 1945.

DONALD POUND was inducted into the Army in January of 1943. After training, he was sent to the Fiji Islands then to New Guinea and the Philippines. His unit had the duty of bringing back prisoners who had fled into the hills after the Philippines were liberated.

CHESTER RARDIN, of Lawrenceburg, was a Seaman First Class in the Navy. He served in the cruiser, U.S.S. *Honolulu*, in the Pacific. His crew received a Navy Unit Commendation for outstanding duty in the Battle of Tassasaronga in 1942, Kolombangara in 1943 and Leyte in 1944.

DOLAN SEAVER, of Aurora, was a Sea Bee and a member of a Navy gun crew on the following merchantmen: U.S.S. *R.H. Davies* and *C.L. Wheeler*. He served as a Carpenter's Mate in Alaska, Guam and the Philippines, and on the Naval ship U.S.S. *Betalguese*. He received the Purple Heart for being wounded in action.

ELMO DARLINGTON enlisted in the U.S. Marine Corps several days after the bombing of Pearl Harbor. He served in the 4th Division in the Pacific. He would later be recalled for the Korean War.

CLAYTON ACRA had duty as a Truck Driver with the Army in the Pacific Theater. He hauled both material and troops in all types of weather and under combat conditions, and over all kinds of terrain. He earned the Philippine Liberation Ribbon with a battle star and 2 other stars for major battles in the Pacific.

STANLEY FRITCH was a Corporal with the 1st Cavalry Division in Australia. He received an honorable discharge in January of 1944, to take care of his father's farm since his father was unable due to an injury.

LEE FOLSOM enlisted in the Army Air Corps in 1942 and became a Staff Sergeant. He served with the 8th Air Force, based in England, and was discharged in November of 1945.

WILLIAM CORNING, of the Dillsboro area, entered the Army in November of 1942. He was in a Headquarter Supply unit at Fort Bragg and also had duty at Kessler Field. He became a Sergeant with demolitian duty.

WALTER DAVIDSON entered the U.S. Army in March of 1943 and served until July of 1946. He was a Sergeant in the Quartermaster Corps with an assignment at Camp Atterberry.

JOHN WILLMAN, of the Dillsboro area, joined the U.S. Navy in February of 1942. Most all of his service was spent in the European Theater. He was discharged in 1946.

ORVILLE FISCHVOGT was born in Ohio County, but moved to Dearborn County after high school and entered the U.S. Navy from Lawrenceburg. Most of his service was at the Naval Base, Groton, Connecticut where he met his wife and lived after WWII.

CHARLES D. GRIMSLEY, of Moores Hill, entered the Army Air Corps in July 1943. He served as a Mechanic at a base in England repairing and overhauling fighter and bomber engines. He served until March of 1946.

ANTHONY HASSMER, of Greendale, entered the U.S. Army in 1943. As a Private, he took his basic training at Camp Wolter in Texas.

VIRGIL ANDRES was in the 770 Field Artillery Battalion in General Patton's Third Army. He served as a Heavy Machine Gunner in Normandy, France and Central Europe. In December of 1944, his unit raced to Bastogne to support the 101st Airborne who were surrounded during the Battle of the Bulge. In 1945, they crossed the Rhine into Germany. Virgil's last duty was guarding German POWs in Stalag 7A, a German prison camp. Virgil received 5 battle stars and the French medals: Fourgerre and Croix DeGuerre for his service in the ETO.

Clayton Acra

Charles Grimsley

Austin Smith

Virgil Andres served with the 770th Field Artillery in the ETO.

RICHARD KLEPPER, of Greendale, was a Captain in an Army Ordnance Battalion. He served for more than three years in the North Africa and Italian campaigns.

LIONEL KNAUS was a First Lieutenant in the Army Air Corps. His crew received the Air Medal after completing 50 missions over Europe. He also received the Purple Heart for being wounded in action with the enemy.

NORBERT KNUE, of Dover, entered the U.S. Navy in 1943 and advanced to the rating of Torpedoman 3rd Class.

GARNET RICE, of Moores Hill, was a Second Lieutenant in the Army Air Corps. He trained as a Bombardier at a base at Sioux City, Iowa.

DONALD LEFFLER, of Aurora, entered the U.S. Army early in 1942 and served until October of 1945. He was a Truck Driver in the ETO, and attained the rank of Corporal with the 818th Engneering Battalion.

EUGENE ORTMAN served in the U.S.Navy from 1943 to 1946. He had duty as an Air Machinist Mate, with most of his service in Hawaii.

HOWARD (JACK) PORTER entered the U.S.Army in 1942. He trained at Biloxi, Mississippi and left there for duty overseas, serving in Luxembourg, Germany, and Switzerland until October of 1945.

WILLIAM (BILL) LYTTLE, of the Bright area, entered the U.S.Army in 1941. He had duty in the Army's Signal Corps.

Willam Lyttle

Howard Porter

NELSON DAVIS, of Dillsboro, an Army Private who served with the 368th Army Engineering Regiment who landed at Normandy on D-Day. He also served in the South Pacific.

VICTOR KRAUS entered the U.S. Army and served for four years, ending the war with the occupation forces in Japan.

ALBERT KRAUS entered the U.S. Navy and had duty aboard a destroyer in the South Pacific Theater of Operations.

JOHN (JACK) HANNAN, of Lawrenceburg, was a fighter pilot in the Pacific who was credited with shooting down two enemy planes. He was a Captain with the 5th Air Force. He flew over 100 combat missions and was awarded the Air Medal with four clusters.

RAYMOND HARMEYER was drafted into the Navy in 1944. He served in the Pacific at New Caledonia, the Hebrides and Guam plus other bases. At Iwo Jima, he was sent ashore after the bombardment, with a crew to set up a radio station for transmission to the invading ships.

FRANK HOPPING, of Aurora, was a First Lieutenant in the Army Air Corps. He did photo-interpreter duty in analyzing film brought in by reconnaissance planes from enemy territory. In 1943, he was in charge of a meterology group.

LEO KRAUS entered the U.S. Army and served in the European Theater of Operations. At the war's end, he was fighting in Germany.

LESTER BLASDEL entered the U.S. Army and became a Technical Sergeant. He served from September of 1942 to January of 1946.

DR. JAMES PFEIFER, of Greendale, entered the Army Air Corps Medical Service and attended Flight School at West Palm Beach. He had duty in the Pacific Theater as a Flight Surgeon, stationed at bases on Guam, Christmas Island, Samoa, Cook Island and the Philippines. He became a Major and returned to duty in the States.

Nelson Davis

Dr. James Pfeifer **John Hannan**

Raymond Harmeyer **Frank Hopping**

ROBERT (BOB) RAMEY, of Aurora, entered the Navy in 1943 and trained as a Corpsman. He was attached to a Marine unit based in China.

GLENN (HICKORY) RUMSEY served in the Army in the Pacific Theater. He fought in the Admiralty Islands and the Philippines and with the occupation troops in Japan.

RAYMOND THURMAN was drafted into the Army in 1943. He had basic training at Camp Carson, Colorado where he was assigned to the 10th Mountain Division. This was a unique outfit, the only group of its kind, who prepared themselves for combat in the high mountains in the Aleutians and Italy. Ray's unit fought in Italy. Senator Bob Dole was also in the 10th Mountain Division.

WILLIAM (BILL) HOPPING, of Aurora, was a Pharmacist Mate 3rd Class in the Navy. He had duty at Seattle Naval Hospital, and then transferred to the 25th Special Sea Bees in New Guinea. They moved up to the Philippines in 1945.

JACOB RIDER, of Aurora, entered the Army in 1944 and became a member of the 10th Infantry. He saw active combat in the ETO, including Germany. He was trained as a Military Policeman and served as a Rifleman as a Private First Class.

ANTHONY WEBER was an Army Private serving in the ETO. He was wounded in France in 1945.

SAM WHEELER, a Private in the Army, was overseas in 1944.

Robert Ramey (right)

William Hopping

Raymond Thurman

Jacob Rider

Glenn Rumsey

CHAPTER 9

Final Victory

The Defeat of Germany

Following its defeat in the Battle of the Bulge, the German's position was near hopeless. On January 3, 1945, Eisenhower's armies went on the offensive again. In early February, the military situation required the Big Three Allied leaders to meet for final strategizing. They chose a port on the Black Sea, Yalta.

While Roosevelt, Churchill and Stalin conferred in Yalta, their armies squeezed Germany ever tighter. Everywhere Hitler exhorted his troops to stand fast and everywhere they were overwhelmed, largely due to the lack of an air force, fuel and manpower, even though Hitler had conscripted a Peoples Army for all able-bodied men from the ages of 16 to 60.

By the end of February, the Allied armies were closing on the Rhine and the Germans were blowing up the bridges over this river which was a natural defense for Germany. On March 7 when the U.S. Ninth Armored Division closed on the massive bridge at Remagen, south of Cologne, to the amazement of the Americans, it stood intact. In one of the most daring actions of the war, GIs dashed across the bridge in the face of machine-gun fire even as the Germans tried to blow it up; they took the bridge and preventing its destruction. The Allies were now able to cross the Rhine and Eisenhower pushed reinforcements to the bridgehead. To the north, the Canadians and British were also able to cross the Rhine, some by boat and pontoon bridges, and Patton was able to cross the river in the south. The Germans were unable to cope with the Allies assaults; however they still fought hard and the Allies had to take them out house-to-house fighting. Meanwhile to the east, the Russians had taken Vienna and were racing toward Berlin.

Churchill pressed Eisenhower to beat the Russians to Berlin and take it before the Red Army could. But the General thought otherwise, believing his forces had little chance to beat the Soviets and the risk in troops was too costly, besides he wanted Patton's Army to move quickly into the Austrian Alps before the Nazis

The Germans were defeated first and about three months later were the Japanese to bring us final victory in World War II. (Opposite page) Japanese sign surrender documents aboard the U.S.S. *Missouri* in presence of General MacArthur and Allied military leaders.

conferring with Churchill, Ike informed Stalin that the Allies would halt at the Elbe River. Meanwhile back in the States, President Roosevelt died on April 12. Most all service people and civilians were shocked. Harry Truman, a modest but decisive man, stepped up from Vice President to take F.D.R.'s place as Commander-in-Chief of the U.S.A.

At the end of April, American and Russian troops met at the Elbe. On May 2, Berlin fell to the Russian Army. The rape, pillage and looting that followed was very great, even by Nazi standards. On May 7, 1945, all German forces surrendered unconditionally to the Western Allies and the Russians simultaneously in a school-house which Eisenhower was using for his headquarters. The next day, the ceremony was repeated in Berlin; thus making May 8 the historical V-E Day. In New York, London, Paris, the entire world (except Japan and Germany) celebrated with dancing in the streets, sirens and fireworks with an end to blackouts. It was eleven months since the Allies had landed at Normandy that they had accomplished what they set to do. Supreme Commander David D. Eisenhower had led the most successful military operation which defeated the Axis that had held Europe in its grip for four years.

Americans greet Russians on the Elbe in Germany.

V-E Day in Dearborn County

Surprisingly, the celebration of V-E Day in Dearborn County was fairly quiet. Although bells rang and whistles blew, there were no parades nor dancing in the streets and plants kept working. Nearly everyone in Dearborn County heard President Truman's broadcast of the V-E proclamation on May 8, 1945. He added that Sunday, May 13 would be a national day of prayer.

Mayor Robert Baker of Lawrenceburg declared a holiday in that community and urged all stores to close. By mid-morning, his request was carried out, while churches were opened for prayer and meditation. V-E Day services were then held at the Hamline Methodist Church and the Zion Evangelical and Reformed Church. Most other churches held services that evening.

With a vast feeling of relief and thankfulness, the big question now in most people's minds was when will our sons, husbands or sweethearts be sent home? Many had been absent for two years or longer. Or, how many will be sent to the war in the Pacific?

The Air War Against Japan

With the Philippines under control and the Mariannas secure in the Pacific, U.S. Engineers and Sea Bees worked quickly to construct airfields on Guam, Saipan and Tinian from which the new B-29 Super fortresses could operate against Japan. The first B-29 raid on Japan from these bases took place on November 24. The major concern of these raids was to destroy Japan's war industry. But the bomber casualty rates were too high because the distance was too far for U.S. fighter plane protection and the fuel requirements were too great for the amount of bombs that could be carried.

General Curtis LeMay decided on a new strategy: flying night attacks at lower altitudes. On March 9, 1945, the XXI Bomber Command put 300 B-29s into the air and in the early morning darkness, over a thousand tons of incendiary bombs were dropped on Tokyo. When the fires died out several days later, more than 80,000 Japanese had been killed and 250,000 buildings had been ruined. From March to August in 1945, the B-29s covered Japan with destructive fire-bombings which crushed Japanese industry and brought the war home in ways no other operation could have done.

Last Battles in the Pacific

Plans now called for seizing the islands of Iwo Jima and Okinawa. They were needed as advanced bases where U.S. fighter planes could escort B-29s attacking Japan; and later as staging areas for the invasion of Japan.

The invasion of Iwo Jima took place on February 19, 1945. Despite the saturation of naval and air bombardments prior to the landings, the Japanese survived by burrowing into caves and tunnels on the volcanic island. They were able to pin down the Marines on the beaches for it was nearly impossible to dig foxholes in the shifting sands, so the Americans took heavy casualties before they could move inland.

By the third day, the Marines controlled one-third of the island and climbed Mount Suribachi to raise the Stars and Stripes. The Japanese resistance was fanatical, and before total surrender, the battle became the most costly in Marine Corps history. In return for the Marine's sacrifice, the U.S. gained two serviceable airfields within 600 miles of Japan.

Raising the Stars and Stripes on Mt. Suribachi, Iwo Jima

Part of the casualties, especially on U.S. ships, were due to an acceleration of kamikazes (suicide plane attacks). The carriers, *Yorktown* and *Intrepid*, were damaged, and the U.S.S. *Wasp* took a kamikaze through the hangar deck, killing over 100 sailors. The carrier, *Franklin*, sustained hits on both sides. Although she did not sink, the ship had to be towed out of combat and back to the States for lengthy repairs.

D-Day for Okinawa was April 1, 1945. It was preceded by five days of naval and air bombardment. At first, there was a relative lack of Japanese resistance and U.S. infantrymen moved unopposed toward the first town on the island. It wasn't until four days later that the Americans met strong enemy defensive positions and increased opposition.

From April 6 until June, the naval forces, especially the destroyers on radar picket duty with the carrier task forces, were subjected to large kamikaze attacks, over 300 sorties were launched against U.S. naval ships. Total casualties were nearly 500 killed and 600 wounded. Japanese losses were also high: 350 kamikazes and 340 conventional bombers were lost.

The reserve infantry was landed on April 9th to increase American troops ashore up to 160,000. They were needed for tough ground fighting that now was beginning. Many Japanese caves had steel doors impervious to flame-throwers. Naval gunfire continued to support American ground troops. It was employed in greater quantities at Okinawa than in any other battle in history. It complimented the artillery from the day of the landing until the action moved to the extreme tip of the island where the combat area was restricted that there was danger of shelling American troops.

On May 11, Army General Buckner began an intense general offensive. On June 18, General Buckner was killed by enemy gunfire. Hundreds of Japanese civilians jumped to their deaths from steep cliffs rather than become prisoners; and the Japanese Army generals committed hara-kiri (suicide) in their command caves. On June 22, Okinawa was declared secure. By July 4, U.S. bombers were operating from Okinawa airfields against the Japanese home islands.

End of the Japanese Empire

Although the large-scale bombing raids, combined with the naval bombardments, had isolated Japan, there were no signs yet that the Japanese government was contemplating surrender. Instead they were preparing to resist the American invasion with what military units were left, plus guerrilla warfare by all citizens.

However necessary the projected invasion of Japan, the assaulting troops would confront hundreds of thousands of soldiers backed by a patriotic civilian population – all prepared to die defending their homeland. Allied casualties were projected about one million, but thanks to other events, all plans for the Japanese invasion would be cancelled.

A team of U.S. scientists had tested the most destructible bomb yet devised – the atomic bomb – in July of 1945. The information on this bomb and the tests were given to President Truman as he was on his way to the last conference of the Big Three at Potsdam. It would be his decision when or if the bomb would ever be used. Soon thereafter, Truman issued the Potsdam Proclamation which promised "utter destruction" to the Japanese homeland if they did not surrender. When they ignored the ultimatum, the use of the atomic bomb was inevitable.

On July 26, the cruiser, U.S.S. *Indianapolis*, delivered to Tinian "Little Boy," code name for the A-bomb. On August 6, the bomber Enola Gay took off for Hiroshima, Japan. At 8:15 a.m., the plane's bombardier released the bomb over Hiroshima and that city was practically wiped off the face of the map. The count of dead was 71,379 and an estimated 80,000 were wounded while 80% of all buildings were destroyed.

Again Truman called for the Japanese to surrender. When there was no reply, preparations were made for the drop of a second atomic bomb. This one, nicknamed "Fat Man," was dropped on the city of Nagasaki, again destroying the population and the buildings of a principal city of Japan.

On August 14, Emperor Hirohito instructed the Japanese cabinet to accept the U.S. terms of unconditional surrender, thus ending the war that began at Pearl Harbor forty-five months before. An official surrender ceremony was conducted on board the battleship, U.S.S. *Missouri*, in Tokyo Bay. On September 9, an American flag which had flown over the Capitol in Washington on the day Pearl Harbor was attacked, was raised over Tokyo. General MacArthur, in charge of the occupation of Japan, said, "Let it wave in all its glory as a symbol of hope for the oppressed and as a harbinger of victory for the right."

Atomic bomb explosion over Hiroshima, Japan

A Japanese lady stands among her city's bombing ruins.

Jackie Nocks

Donald Schmeltzer

HENRY ECKSTEIN, of Lawrenceburg, served in the 1st Infantry in the Pacific Theater in 1945, as a Private First Class.

JACKIE NOCKS, of Aurora, was a Seaman First Class in the Navy entering in November 1943. He served in the Pacific on LCT 1321, with Amphibious Forces operating in the Philippines.

HOWARD SHOOK served as a Private in France with General Patton's 3rd Army in 1945.

HENRY SERVICE, as an Army Private, took basic training at Camp Blanding, Florida in 1945. He was attached to a Medical Supply Unit at Kitamo Hospital, Osaka, Japan.

GEORGE JARVIS was a Private First Class with the Signal Corps. He landed in Normandy on D-Day, and then fought in Germany.

JAMES FARMER served in the Navy for a few months in 1944 before receiving a medical discharge for a disabled knee.

RUSSEL FETTE, of New Alsace, served in the Navy as a Motor Machinist Mate 2nd Class on the auxiliary ships U.S.S. *Cook* and U.S.S. *Starling*.

HAROLD FOGLE served in the Philippines and then in the occupation of Japan in the Army Intelligence Office of the 33rd Division as a Technical Sergeant.

CHESTER MORLING served as an Emergency Technician at Great Lakes, Illinois in 1945.

DONALD SCHMELTZER took Navy boot training in 1945 and became a Seaman 2nd Class.

ROBERT HARPER, of Lawrenceburg, served as a Seaman 2nd Class in the Pacific Theater.

CURTIS TRANSIER, an Army Technical Sergeant was stationed in Korea during WW II.

LOUIS SHIPPER was a Seaman 2nd Class with duty in the Pacific.

ARTHUR (BO) HARTWELL, of Lawrenceburg, was a Staff Sergeant in the Army Air Corps as a Gunner with the 8th Air Force. Arthur served with distinction, flying on 35 missions out of England over the ETO, including Berlin. He was credited with shooting down an enemy fighter plane.

JAMES GRUBBS was drafted in the Army in 1944. He served in 753 Tank Battalion as a replacement Gunner in M-24 Tank. He saw action in one major battle in Central Europe and spent 12 months in Army of Occupation near Munich, Germany.

CHARLES EAGLIN, of Dillsboro, served in the Army of occupation in Germany in 1945-1946. He was a Technical Sergeant.

WILLIAM CHILDERS was a Staff Sergeant in Army Air Force, serving as an Engineer Gunner on a B-24. He flew 30 combat missions over Europe and received 3 battle stars. He also received the Air Medal with 3 clusters for Meritorious service in the ETO.

LOUIS CHEEK, of Aurora, served as an Army Supply Clerk with the 576 Ordnance Ammunition Company with the Army of Occupation in Germany.

DORMAN BUSSE, of Mt. Sinai, a Staff Sergeant serving as an Engineer-Gunner on a bomber, was taken prisoner by the Germans in 1943. For exceptional performance of duty while flying missions over Germany, he had been awarded the Air Medal.

CLAYTON SMITH was in France and Belgium with the Army Signal Corps in 1944.

OMER SLAYBACK, of Lawrenceburg, was an Army Private First Class with the 3169th Quartermaster Laundry Detachment. He served as a Rifleman in Central Europe, earning 3 battle stars.

GLENN SHUTER, of near-Aurora, was a Private First Class with the 14th Constabulary Regiment. He served in the Army of Occupation of Germany.

ELMER SHARP was a Private First Class in the Army. He was wounded in France in 1944.

James Grubbs

ROBERT FRANK, of Aurora, Second Lieutenant, was killed in December 1945 when a plane he was piloting crashed into a hill two miles outside of Aurora. He had been home on leave and was returning to Patterson Field when the accident occurred. He was buried in Riverview Cemetery with full military honors.

VIRGIL COTTON, of the Bright area, entered the U.S. Army and became a Technician 5th Grade.

LLOYD CHATHAM enlisted in the Marines and trained at Parris Island in 1945.

WILLIS CHALK, of Manchester, joined the Merchant Marines at age 17 upon graduating from Aurora High School, and took basic training at Sheepshead Bay, Brooklyn in August 1945.

Glenn Konradi (7th from left, 2nd row) and Willis Chalk (1st, rear row) with basic training group of Merchant Marines August 24, 1945.

(l.-r.) Bob Spanagel, Lew Ogden and Gould Warneford

GOULD WARNEFORD, of Lawrenceburg, was a Master Sergeant in the 33rd Air Depot Group, a mobile logistic air arm to go into combat zones. When Patton's Third Army broke out of France, the 33rd was called upon to keep the Army supplied with fuel. They modified B-24 bombers by stripping them and installing fuel tanks from nose to the tail. The pilots would fly into the front areas and land. Tanks would pull up to these planes and refuel. Gould took part in campaigns in France, Rhineland and Central Europe.

CLYDE STEELE, of Aurora, was wounded twice in 1944 in the European Theater. He was a Private First Class with the 34th Infantry Division.

EDWARD SORTWELL, of Guilford, served 41 months with the 3rd Army and earned 5 battle stars in the ETO.

CARROL SNYDER entered the U.S. Army. He participated in combat in France and elsewhere in the European Theater of Operations.

FRANCIS RUMSEY, of near-Aurora, was a Parts Clerk with the 86th Ordnance Company. He served with the occupation forces in Germany.

Ralph Rees

George Knue

ROBERT ROSEMEYER, from near-Sunman, was a Private First Class with the 288th Engineers Battalion. He served as a Rifleman in Central Europe and with the occupation forces in Germany.

DELMER PINDELL was an Army Private First Class with the 781st Tank Battalion. He served from August 1944 to October 1946 in Italy, Rhineland and as a member of the Army of Occupation in Germany.

JOHN LEWIS, of Moores Hill, enlisted in the Army Air Corps and entered pilot's training in November 1942. He graduated as a pilot in June 1943 and was sent to Foggia, Italy. He flew bombing missions over German targets; and on D-Day in Southern France, he flew 3 missions on Toulon Harbor. After more bombing missions in Europe, he was rotated back to the States and assigned as a flight instructor at Douglas, Arizona. Later, he would fly in Korea and Vietnam.

GEORGE KNUE, of Lawrenceburg, served in the U.S. Army from March of 1943 to February 1946, spending almost two years in Europe, including the invasion of Normandy at Omaha Beach and the Battle of the Bulge. He was in the Signal Corps for the 12th Army Group as a Technical Sergeant. When he returned to the USA he was with the 49th Infantry Division. He received battle stars for Ardennes, Rhineland and Central Europe.

PAUL KOLB, of Harrison, was a Private First Class in the 564th Army Quartermaster Truck Detachment. He served in the Army of Occupation in Europe as a Truck Driver.

LESTER KIETER was a Staff Sergeant who served as a Mechanic in the ground crew in the Air Force in 1945.

EUGENE HURD was a Corporal in the Army serving in Belgium in 1945 when severely wounded in chest, arms and legs. He was returned to Indianapolis for recovery of these wounds.

GEORGE GREEN, of Lawrenceburg, was a Staff Sergeant with the Army Quartermaster Truck Corps. He received 2 battle stars for Normandy and Germany serving with the 9th Army. Wounded in Germany, he was hospitalized in England, then in the U.S.

ENOS L. BARROTT, of Lawrenceburg, Technician 4th Grade, served in the 355th SGO band at Wakeman Hospital in 1945 as a Bandsman in the American Theater.

VICTOR MONTGOMERY, of Aurora, was a Private First Class with the 70th Infantry Division. He served as an Automatic Rifleman in the Rhineland and Central Europe, receiving 2 battle stars.

MILLER MOSLEY, JR., of Moores Hill, entered the United States Army in November of 1945 and became a Private First Class. He served as a Rifleman with the Occupation Forces in Germany.

JAMES (JIM) WEDDLE, of Lawrenceburg, received officer's training and a commission in the U.S. Navy. He was Navigator on LST 928 at Iwo Jima. Then, he became the Executive Officer on an LST at the landings on Okinawa. As a full Lieutenant, he was made Captain of LST 928 in San Pedro, California. This ship was fitted-out as a refrigeration ship in preparation for the invasion of Japan, but the war ended before it sailed.

CHARLES BOBRINK, of Lawrenceburg, was a Naval Lieutenant serving aboard the U.S.S. *Dickens* during the Philippines, Iwo Jima and Okinawa campaigns. He served as an Assistant Beachmaster and was awarded a Bronze Star, "For heroic achievement as Officer in Charge of the initial beach landing from the U.S.S. *Dickens* against Japanese forces at Iwo Jima."

ROBERT (BOB) PARKER, of Aurora, had graduated from the U.S. Naval Academy as an Ensign. He served in the Gunnery Department aboard the Cruiser, U.S.S. *Cleveland*. He had duty during the Philippine campaign, Dutch East Indies invasion, Okinawa invasion, and occupation of Japan.

EDWARD REED, of Guilford, was a Private First Class serving in the 139th Field Artillery Battalion in the Philippines.

CHARLES RENSCHLER was a Second Lieutenant serving in the Pacific Theater of Operations in 1945.

RALPH REES served at the 20th Air Force on Saipan, used for the bombing of Japan.

JOSEPH RUMMEL was an Army Corporal with the 35th Division in New Guinea and the Philippines in 1945. He served as a Jeep Driver in a headquarters company.

Robert (Bob) Parker (l.) and shipmate in Japan

James Weddle (2nd right)

Robert Savage and ship he served on: U.S.S. *Springfield*

ROBERT SAVAGE, of Lawrenceburg, entered the Navy in April of 1944 and became a Radioman 2nd Class. He served aboard the heavy cruiser, U.S.S. *Springfield*.

EVERETT SAMS served in the navy as a Hospital Apprentice 2nd Class and was discharged in October 1945.

JAMES HENDERSON, of Dillsboro, was a Captain in the Marines in 1945.

ALVIN HELLER, of Moores Hill, as a Seaman 2nd Class, had duty at the naval Armory in Chicago in 1945-46.

GUY GREATHOUSE, Private, of Aurora served with the 9201 Transportation Command as a Radar Crewman in the American Theater from 1944 to 1946.

WILLARD GRAVES, Sergeant, of Aurora served at the Replacement Training Center at Ft. Knox as a Medium Tank crewman in 1945.

LOUIS GOBLE became an Aviation Radioman 3rd Class in the navy and served on the aircraft Carrier *Princeton* and at the Naval Air Station in Glenview, Illinois.

TONY SCOTTI was a Seaman 2nd Class in the Navy with duty in Tokyo in 1945.

STANLEY SCOTT entered the U.S. Navy and became a Ship's Cook 2nd Class. He served until November 1945.

WALTER SCHUCK was a Private in the Army and was wounded in action in his right arm and face.

CLIFFORD SCHWING, of Lawrenceburg, participated as a Sergeant, in the Battle of Iwo Jima.

DALE LAAKER, Technician 5th Grade, was killed in action in Germany in 1945. He had been serving with an Engineering Battalion.

HOWARD WALSER, of Greendale, was a Second Lieutenant in the U.S. Army.

HARLEY SUTTON, of Aurora, attended an instruction school for veterinarians at East Lancing in 1944, and served with the 120th Calvary as Second Lieutenant.

JAMES SLAYBACK, of Moores Hill, served with the 110 Airborne Division Paratroops as a Staff Sergeant. He was among the first Americans to enter Tokyo after the Japanese surrender. He had been awarded the Air Medal while operating from a base in the CBI Theater.

GEORGE WITT served in a Naval Hospital and also on the Marshall Islands. He was present when the atomic bombs were tested at nearby Bikini Atoll.

RAYMOND EAGLIN, of Dillsboro, served with an Anti Aircraft Gun Battery in the Pacific Theater in 1945-46 as a Private First Class.

JOSEPH WALLACE, as a Radioman First Class, participated in the first carrier raid over Tokyo.

DALE T. NOWLIN was one of three brothers serving their country. He entered the Army Air Force in July 1944 and was honorably discharged in 1945 from Keesler Field, Mississippi as a Private.

HOWARD MURDOCK was a Lieutenant in the Army and served in North Africa in 1945.

Louis Goble

Dale Nowlin

CARROLL SUTTON, of Aurora, left high school at midterm in 1942 to enroll in the Navy V-6 Program. He became a Pharmacist Mate First Class and served on the hospital ship, U.S.S. *Consolation*, in Wakayama Bay, Japan at war's end. The ship picked up Australian, British and American former POWS of the Japanese. Some had been in the Bataan Death March. Few weighed more than 85 pounds.

WILLIAM SAILOR became a Corporal in the Marine Corps. He served at Camp Pendleton; and was wounded during the Iwo Jima campaign in the Pacific.

SYLVESTER (DUTZ) NEARY, of Lawrenceburg, entered Midshipman Training at Northwestern University on December 31, 1942. He graduated as an Ensign and was assigned to duty aboard the battleship *Pennsylvania*. Beginning at the Aleutians and seeing action in the mid-Pacific islands, the Philippines and Okinawa, Neary spent 33 months at sea. His battle station was in the Plotting Room for target direction of the ship's larger guns. While he was in Buckner Bay, Okinawa in August 1945, a Jap plane got through the picket line and placed a torpedo in the side of the *Pennsylvania*. Fortunately, Neary was not injured and the crew was able to save the ship. Two ships towed her to Guam for temporary repairs. In company with other ships, but with only one screw, the battleship went on to Puget Sound Navy Yard.

Sylvester (Dutz) Neary

DR. EDWIN LIBBERT served as a Lieutenant Colonel in the Army Medical Corps. He as Chief of the X-Ray Department at the 239th Army Hospital in Assam, India in 1945.

DONALD GREEN was a Seaman First Class in the U.S. Navy. He served with an Armed Guard Crew in the Pacific Theater of Operations in 1945.

WALTER PYLES was a Private First Class who was killed in Action on Okinawa in January 1945.

ERNEST (ERNIE) PALMER, of Guilford, entered the Army in 1941 and became a Corporal in an Engineering Group. He would drive a Gas Truck in combat zones and help build air fields in the Philippines and go on to Japan in the occupation force.

JOSEPH McCRIGHT was an Army Private First Class who served in the Pacific Theater for 3 years in 1945.

VERNON AND VIRGIL STUTZ, of Guilford, were both Corporals in the Army. Although they did not enter the Army together, their mother's request that they serve together was honored. Virgil entered the Army in July 1942 and Vernon went in August. Both would serve in the 38th Division of the Third Army in Europe where they would earn four battle stars each. They would be discharged together at Fort Dix in December 1945.

FRANCIS JOE WALSER took Naval Officer Training at Notre Dame. He graduated as an Ensign. He served in the Pacific Theater aboard the Destroyer *Brestie*. After Japan's surrender, he had occupation duty in Japan.

STANLEY VICKROY served in the First Armored Division throughout the European War. His division was the Honor Guard at General George Patton's funeral. One night, he climbed the Leaning Tower of Pisa in Italy and rang the bells in the tower.

GERALD (JERRY) LEMM, of Lawrenceburg, was a Staff Sergeant in the Army Infantry. He was a Platoon Sergeant and special instructor of 60 millimeter mortar and the Browning automatic rifle.

JOHN (JACK) LEMM, Fire Controlman Second Class, Navy enlisted in June 1945 and was discharged in April 1948.

ROY (SLICK) LAMBERT, of Aurora, Seaman First Class, Navy was a crewman aboard the Landing Craft 33. He saw action at Iwo Jima. He witnessed the flag raising on Mt. Suribachi from his position aboard ship. The ship was sunk during the siege of Okinawa. A Japanese dive bomber or Val, pierced the ship below decks setting off explosions resulting in the ship sinking. The survivors were rescued by an LCS when the Vals were finally cleared from the area. Slick was awarded the Purple Heart for injuries sustained (seriously burned) in the Val attack.

CHARLES SKIDMORE, of Aurora, was taken prisoner by the Germans. He was among the POW's liberated by the advancing Allied Armies in 1945. He was returned to the States for a happy reunion with his family, and then was assigned to Camp Atterbury as a Sergeant.

WILLIAM (BILL) JACKSON was a Seaman 2nd Class with duty on a minesweeper that operated in the Atlantic.

Brothers Virgil (l.) and Vernon Stutz

F. Joe Walser

John Lemm

Orville Draper

Adrian Chatham

Robert Conrad

RUSSELL CARR was a Technical Sergeant in the Army. He was awarded the Bronze Star for heroic achievement in Germany in 1945. He earned 5 battle stars.

DONALD CART, of Greendale, was a Technical Sergeant with a ground crew of the Army Air Force in Germany in 1945.

ADRIAN CHATHAM was inducted into the Army in December 1943. He became a Private First Class with the Infantry. He served in Italy and Southern France. He was wounded and taken prisoner by the Germans in September 1944, spending time in several POW camps. He was liberated by U.S. troops on May 2, 1945.

ROBERT CONRAD, of Lawrenceburg, was a Staff Sergeant. He was in a crew of a Flying Fortress of the 8th Army Air Force as a Turret Gunner. He was awarded the Air Medal and Oak Leaf Cluster for raids over Germany in 1944.

RICHARD CRANDALL was a Private First Class in the 78th Division of the Army. He was awarded the Medical Badge for serving as a Medic in the front lines in 1945.

FREDERICK DAUSCH was a Staff Sergeant with the 974th Engineering Maintenance Company. He saw action in Normandy, Ardennes, Rhineland as well as in the Pacific Theater. He earned 4 battle stars.

BERNARD DALL, of Guilford, was a Technician 5th Grade. He served as a Clerk Typist with the U.S. Constabulary in the Army of Occupation of Germany.

CARL DENNIS, of Lawrenceburg, served as a Corporal in the Second Armored Division in Berlin in 1945. He fought with the 1st and 2nd Armies.

DONALD DILS, of Lawrenceburg, was a Captain in the Army. He served as Assistant Director of Ordnance Motor Transportation Schools, Baltimore. He also served at ordnance bases in France and Germany in 1945.

ARTHUR DOGGETT a Technical Sergeant received the Bronze Star for Meritorious service in France, Luxembourg, Belgium and Germany. He also received 5 battle stars.

ORVILLE DRAPER, of Aurora, was a Staff Sergeant with the Base Air Depot 1 in England, serving as a Sheet Metal Worker.

WILBER GLOWKA, of Lawrenceburg, was a Sergeant at the Eighth Army Air Force Bomber Station in England. He received a certificate for performing his duties as a Sheet Metal worker in a superior and outstanding manner. He was responsible for the repair of damaged planes which returned from bombing attacks over Germany. He entered the Army in March 1943.

IVAN R. GRUBBS, of Bright, was a Technical Sergeant in the 97th Infantry Division Co. D. 387th Infantry Regiment in France, Belgium, Holland, Germany and Czechoslovakia where he was when the war ended in 1945. He was awarded the Bronze Star for leading an attack on an airfield in Czechoslovakia.

Ivan Grubbs

WALTER HOOPER, of Aurora, was a Sergeant in the Army Air Force with the 1380th Base Unit. He served as a Truck Driver in the European Theater of Operation.

CARL WARD, of Route 2 Aurora, was a Major in the Army Medical Corps, 54th Field Hospital in France and Germany. He received the Bronze Star for Meritorious Service in direct support of Combat Operations in 1944 to 1945 as Commanding Officer of a second hospital unit. Major Ward displayed superior qualities in organization and foresight in the care of severely wounded personnel of the Infantry Division.

EDWIN WALDON entered the Army in September 1943. He served in Germany with the 3160th Signal Service Battalion as an Ammunition Handler and then as a Cook. He served until July 1946.

Jess Todd

JESS TODD, of Lawrenceburg, entered the U.S. Army and became a Staff Sergeant. He served in the Infantry in France in the European Theater of Operations. After WWII, he would also serve with the Army in Korea.

ROBERT THUERMER, of Aurora, was a Technician 5th Grade in the 8th Army. He served as a Stock Clerk with the Occupation Forces in Germany and received a Meritorious Unit Citation.

HAROLD SEAMAN enlisted in March 1945 in the U.S. Navy but served briefly due to a physical disability.

Edwin Waldon

Ervin Bishchoff

CHARLES HAMILTON, of Aurora, was a Private First Class with the 17th Infantry. He served as a Rifleman in the Army of Occupation in Japan.

RICHARD OBERTING, of Lawrenceburg, was a Seaman 2nd Class in the Navy. He served in the Atlantic as a Radarman on a Destroyer Escort; and then in the Pacific.

CORNELIUS KNIGGA, of Dillsboro, was a Technical Sergeant serving as a Construction Equipment Mechanic in the Pacific Theater of Operations during 1943-1946.

ELMER HOLDCRAFT served in the U.S. Navy as a Seaman 2nd Class. In 1945, he was aboard the U.S.S. *Delta* in Tokyo Bay.

EDWARD (BOOB) HOFFMAN, of Lawrenceburg, was a Seaman First Class in the Navy on an LST serving in the invasion of Iwo Jima in the South Pacific in 1945.

ERVIN BISCHOFF was a Seaman 3rd Class in the Southwest pacific. He served on Tulagi, Guadalcanal and Okinawa. He also served aboard the carrier, U.S.S. *Gloucester*.

WILLIAM WRIGHT was a Seaman First Class in the U.S. Navy in the Pacific Theater of Operations. He served with Utility Squadron One.

JOHN WOLIUNG was a First Lieutenant in the Army Air Force, operating as a fighter pilot with the Air Force in the Pacific in the Philippines and Okinawa. He received the Air Medal with 2 clusters.

LESTER WASHBURN, of Aurora, was a Technician 5th Grade in the Army. He served as a Clerk with a Military Government Team in the Occupation Army in Japan.

WAYNE THOMAS, of Dillsboro, enlisted in the U.S. Navy in December 1942, and became a Seaman First Class. He would serve aboard the U.S.S. *Wolverine*, U.S.S. *Leyte* and U.S.S. *Maui*. He took part in the Philippine Liberation.

RALPH SCHANTZ entered the U.S. Navy in November 1944 and became a Radioman 3rd Class. He served in the American Theater at New London and Ledo Beach, Long Island.

RAYMOND McCARDLE, of Aurora, served as a Radarman First Class in the Navy. He was discharged in October 1945.

THOMAS B. McLEASTER, of Lawrenceburg, enlisted in the U.S. Navy in January 1945 and became a Pharmacist's Mate 3rd Class. He served at its Naval Hospital in Bremerton, Washington.

DONALD MILLER was a Gunners Mate 2nd Class, U.S. Navy, who became an instructor at the Naval Station at Great Lakes in 1945.

GERHARD ORLAMUENDE entered the U.S. Navy in April 1944 and became a Carpenter's Mate 3rd Class. He served in the American Theater at Camp Parks, California.

PHILIP PLUNKET entered the U.S. Navy and became a Seaman First Class. He served from 1944 to 1946 in the Pacific Theater on the U.S.S. *Lipan*.

WILLIAM (BILL) PLATT, of Aurora, was an Army Private serving as a Clerk Typist in 1944-45 in the American Theater.

JESSE POWELL entered the U.S. Navy and became a Seaman 2nd Class. He served on board the U.S.S. *Puget Sound* and at the Naval Hospital, Great Lakes Naval Base.

EDWARD McCARDLE, of Aurora, was a Sergeant in the 29th Bomber Group, serving as an Airplane Instrument Mechanic with duty in the Air Offensive against Japan. His unit received the Distinguished Unit Badge for outstanding performance of duty.

WILLIAM NEAD was an Army Private who had duty with the 287th Army Ground Force Band. He was stationed in Yokohama, Japan at war's end in 1945.

RICHARD TRAUE was a Seaman First Class who served 20 months in Panama by 1945.

HENRY SMASHEY was a Sergeant serving as a Truck Driver with an Army Division in San Diego in 1944.

LESLIE KLUEBER earned two battle stars as a Fireman 1st Class in the Philippines in 1945.

Thomas McLeaster

Jerry Lemm (l.) and William Platt

Roy Lacey

Alfred Lang

GEORGE HAFENBRITLE, of Lawrenceburg, was an Army Sergeant. He served in France and Belgium in 1945.

DONALD BANSBACH, of Harrison, was a Private First Class in the Army with duty in the Panama Canal Zone.

GEORGE SORTWELL, of Sunman, was in the Navy.

WILLIAM A. GARNER, of Lawrenceburg, was a Seaman Second Class. He was assigned to the Navy Music School at Washington, D.C. In 1945 he had duty on the cruiser *Richmond* during the occupation of Japan.

AMOS HALL served in the infantry in the Philippines as a Private First Class in 1945.

CLINTON BAKER was in the Army Air Force as a Private First Class.

FREDERICK WOLFRAM was an Army Ordnance unit in the Army of Occupation in Germany.

HARRY LAWRENCE was a Radioman Second Class in the Navy. He was discharged in November 1945.

RAYMOND LAMBERT was a Seaman First Class in the Navy and served until discharged in October 1945.

ALFRED LANG was a Motor Machinist Mate, Second Class in the Navy. He served on a Landing Craft Infantry in the Pacific Theater. He was in the battles of Okinawa and Iwo Jima.

ROY LACEY was a Gunner's Mate First Class and served on the cruiser *Oakland* for 20 months in the South Pacific, taking part in battles at the Gilberts, Tinian, Saipan and Guam.

JOE LACEY, a Seaman Second Class in the Navy was in radar school at Bremerton, Washington in 1945.

GEORGE WALKER, of Bright, served with the Army Air Corps in the Pacific Theater. He had occupation duty in Japan.

SPENSER SEAVER entered the navy in April 1945 and became a Seaman 2nd Class. He served with a Construction Battalion at Camp Endicott, Rhode Island and at Port Hueneme, California.

GEORGE TERRILL, of Lawrenceburg, was a Private 1st Class with a paratrooper unit in Europe in 1945.

LESTER EHLERS, Seaman 2nd Class, served on the U.S.S. *Hilary Jones*, a destroyer in the Pacific.

RICHARD STADTLANDER entered the service in 1944. After the surrender of Japan, he did occupation duty in that country.

NORMAN WARNER, served with Glider Troops, entering Japan with the 44th Airborne, the first troops to occupy Japan. He was a Private First Class.

ROBERT SHAMBLIN served in the Sea Bees as a Motor Machinist Mate 2nd Class in 1945.

JAMES BARRY served as a Staff Sergeant in the South Pacific with a Field Artillery Unit.

ORVILLE TURNER served with the Sea Bees in the Philippines as a Seaman 2nd Class in 1945

JOHN TODD, of Lawrenceburg, served in the 3917 Quartermaster Corps Gasoline Supply Company as a Technical Sergeant. His unit entered Berlin with the 1st Airborne Army in 1945.

HUGH SNOW was a Seaman First Class with the Navy. He saw considerable action on the U.S.S. *Gendreau* in the Pacific. His gun shot down three Jap planes in the Okinawa invasion.

WILLIAM SNYDER was a Private in the Army. At stateside he was trained at Langley Field. He was sent overseas for occupation duty in the European Theater.

DAVID SCHWIER, of Sunman, was an Army Private who served on Iwo Jima in 1945.

CLETUS WATTS, of Aurora, he was a Corporal with an Armored Division. He was appointed Secretary to General Rogers in Paris, and his company was one of the first to cross over the Rhine at Remagen, Germany.

ROBERT WEAVER was an Army Private at Ft. Belvoir, Virginia in 1945.

Richard Stadtlander

George Walker

LAWRENCE MORRIS, of Lawrenceburg, was a Corporal in the Army. He was stationed at Johnson Field in Goldsboro, North Carolina.

ROBERT PERCIVAL, A Private First Class, was assigned duty at a POW camp for German prisoners in the United States.

LEE R. ELLIOTT, a Fireman 2nd Class in the Navy, served in the repair ships, U.S.S. *Briareur* and *Ampheon* in 1945-48.

ROBERT SHINKLE, of Lawrenceburg, entered the Army in April 1945. He served in the Pacific Theater of Operations.

JOE LACY, Navy Seaman First Class took training as a Radio Operator. He served on the U.S.S. *Badoeng* from March 1945 to July 1946.

JOHN LIDDLE, Machinist Mate 2nd Class in the Navy, served in the Pacific Theater in 1945.

EDWIN LIBBERT, JR. was a Pharmacist Mate 3rd Class in the Navy. He served at Okinawa with a fleet hospital unit. He experienced the great typhoon that swept the island in September 1945.

LAWRENCE SANDBRINK, of Dillsboro, was Private First Class in the 6th Army Infantry Division. He distinguished himself in combat against the Japanese. In February of 1945, he received a Bronze Star medal.

ROBERT FETTE entered the Navy in December 1944 and became a Fireman First Class, serving on the destroyer, U.S.S. *King*.

VERNON ELLIS, of Aurora, served as a Finance Clerk at a Field Artillery headquarters during the occupation of Germany. He was a Technician 4th Grade.

RUSSELL EAGLIN served as a Medical Technician, a Corporal in the Army. He served at Tilton General Hospital and also in the Pacific Theater in 1945.

JAMES WEST, of Lawrenceburg, was a Technician 5th Grade with the 599th Anti-Aircraft Weapons Battalion. He saw action in the Rhineland and Central Europe, receiving 2 battle stars.

Philip Schuler

ROBERT TURNER entered the Army Air Corps, became a Sergeant and served as a Radioman based in England in 1945.

RAYMOND TRESTER was a Private in the Army Medical Corps in England in 1945.

RAYMOND TIBBETTS, of Lawrenceburg, was a Technician 4th Grade. He served in an Army Hospital in England.

JOHN SWIFT, of Aurora, served with the 382 Engineering Regiment. He served as a Construction Foreman in Central Europe and the Army of Occupation in Germany.

CARROL STEVENS, of Aurora, entered the Army and became a Cook's Helper in 1943. He served with the 1252nd Combat Engineers Battalion in France, Rhineland and Ardennes.

CLIFFORD STEGEMILLER was a Corporal in the U.S. Army and was wounded in Germany in 1945.

ROBERT SHOCKLEY was a Technician 5th Grade in the Army, 90th Infantry Division in the ETO. He was awarded a Bronze Star.

CLARENCE SELMEYER was an Army Private First Class who served in a ground crew of the 9th Air Force and then in the First Army a Gunner. He had duty in Iceland, Scotland, England, Normandy, France, Holland, Germany and Austria. He earned 5 battle stars.

WILLARD SCUDDER was a Seaman 2nd Class on a destroyer in the Atlantic in 1944.

PHILIP SCHULER, of Aurora, used his ability as a machinist in the Army Engineers. His innovations kept machines running which otherwise would have remained inoperable. He had duty in England and in Europe.

CLARENCE SCHMIDT, of Lawrenceburg, was a 1st Lieutenant in a Tank Destroyer unit in England in 1944.

RAYMOND SCHOLLE, of Lawrenceburg, was a Private in the Army at Camp Stewart in 1944.

CHARLES SCHNEIDER, of Aurora, was a Captain in the Army Air Force.

Raymond Tibbetts

George Taylor

Sylvester Stenger

GEORGE TAYLOR, of Guilford, was a First Lieutenant with the Army's 859th Engineer Battalion. He served in England and Germany on active duty until 1945. He left the Reserves in 1950 with the rank of Major.

SYLVESTER STENGER, of St. Leon, and his unit, the 90th Infantry Division, rescued 1,700 German civilians from a living grave in the Saar Valley. The Germans had defied Heinrich Himmler's orders to abandon their homes in the path of U.S. troops and flee. Instead they took refuge in a mile-deep cavern. The Americans located the cave just as the Nazis were ready to dynamite the entrance. The German civilians were overjoyed at being rescued.

MARK SMITH was in the Navy on a Torpedo Boat in the area of Cherbourg, France in 1944.

SYLVESTER SCHEIBEL, of Guilford, was a Private in the 43rd Calvary Reconnaissance Squadron. He was wounded, fighting in Germany in March 1945 and received a Purple Heart.

CHARLES ROLLINS was an Army Corporal. He served in Germany in 1945.

ROY YOUNG, of Lawrenceburg, was a Private First Class. He served the 7th Army in France, Germany and Austria.

WALTER WESTRICH, of Bright, was stationed at Rome with a Military Police unit. He was a Clerk working on the duty roster and payroll. As an M.P., he was one of 12 guards to take 3 German generals back to Germany for the war crimes trials. He was a Technical Sergeant.

RUSSELL RULLMAN served with an Army Anti-Tank Division in France in 1944.

LESTER NORDMEYER was an Army Sergeant with the 376 Infantry of the 94th Division. He was a Truck Driver in France, Ardennes and Central Europe. He had 4 battle stars.

WILFRED NEGLEY, of Aurora, was a Private First Class with an Anti-Tank Company in the 345 Infantry. Negley served as a Rifleman in the Ardennes, Rhineland and Central Europe.

LEONARD SIEMANTEL, of Aurora, entered the Army on the first anniversary of the bombing of Pearl Harbor, December 7, 1942. He served as a Supply Clerk in the Pacific and in China, as a Sergeant.

JAMES CHASTAIN was a Coxswain in the Navy. He was lost in action in the Pacific in 1945.

RICHARD CHASE was a Private First Class in the Marines. He took part in five engagements in the Pacific as an Aerial Gunner. He earned three battle stars.

FRITZ CALLAWAY, of Bright, served with the 16th Infantry Division in the Pacific. His unit took part in three major campaigns, including the Philippines. He was in combat for 219 continuous days. As far as it was known, his division fired the last shot of World War II.

DONALD DAWSON was a Seaman First Class in Hawaii in 1945.

RALPH CLIFTON was a Seaman First Class with the U.S. Navy. He served at stations in Sampson, New York; Domsullen, Rhode Island and in the Pacific.

GEORGE HALL, of Lawrenceburg, was a Heavy Equipment Operator in the Occupation Army of Japan in 1945.

BENJAMIN CUNNINGHAM, of Aurora, served with 305th Infantry as a Sales Clerk in the Army of Occupation of Japan in 1945-46.

LEROY WARNER, of Lawrenceburg, was an Army Private with the 3139th Signal Service Battalion. He served in the Army of Occupation in Japan.

HENRY CORNELIUS, of Lawrenceburg, served as a Sergeant with the 3129th Signal Service in the Occupation Forces in the Pacific.

NORMAN LEE UTTER was a Corporal in the Marine Corps serving for three years in the Pacific Theater at Iwo Jima, Volcano Islands, and occupied Japan.

GORDON TRESTER was a Yeoman Second Class who served with Halsey's Third Fleet for 16 months in the South Pacific.

Sylvester Scheiber

Fritz Callaway

Emmert Kirsch

John Largent

RALPH JEFFRIES, of Lawrenceburg, a Staff Sergeant flying as an Armorer Gunner aboard a Liberator bomber, was forced down in Switzerland, returning from a mission over Augsburg railroad yards. He was awarded the Air Medal and two Oak Leaf Clusters for Meritorious service. He destroyed 27 enemy fighters and damaged many more.

EMMERT KIRSCH was a Sergeant in the Army. He served in France and Germany and then in Manila in 1945 in an Engineering Unit.

PERIN LANGDON III, of Aurora, was a Private First Class who served in France and Germany with Patton's Third Army.

JOHN LARGENT, of Kyle, entered the U.S. Army and became a Technician 5th Grade as a Military Policeman in the 759 MP Battalion. In November 1945, he had duty in Berlin, Germany with the occupation troops.

FRANK LENK, of Sunman area, was a Private First Class with the 818 Engineers Battalion Aviation. He entered the service in February 1942 and would serve in Normandy, France, Ardennes and Central Europe, earning 5 battle stars.

GEORGE LOVELACE was a Navy Cook 2nd Class. He served aboard a landing ship in Europe on D-Day.

WILLIAM MARSHALL, of Dillsboro, was a Private First Class in the 187th Glider Infantry, 11thAirborne Division. He served from February 1943 to September 1945.

BEN McADAMS, of Aurora, was an Army Staff Sergeant serving as a Supply Sergeant during the occupation of Germany. He served from July 1945 to January 1947.

MILTON McCOOL, of Lawrenceburg, was an Army Sergeant with the 773 Tank Destroyer Battalion. He served in Normandy, France, Ardennes and Central Europe, receiving 5 battle stars.

FRED MENNING entered the U.S. Army and became a Staff Sergeant. He received the Silver Star medal for outstanding performance of duty in the ETO. He also received a Purple Heart for wounds taken in Germany.

LESTER GILLISPIE, Private, of Harrison, served with the Armored Replacement Training Center in the American Theater in 1945.

ALEX FRANZ was a Staff Sergeant in the Army Air Force at Randolph Field in Texas. He served for 3 plus years by 1945.

HAL DRIVER, of Aurora, attended Officer's Candidate Infantry School at Ft. Benning and was a commissioned Second Lieutenant. He became an instructor in small weapons at Ft. Benning in 1945.

WILLIAM DAU, of Aurora, was a Second Lieutenant in the Army Air Force. He won his wings at Alve Air Field, Victoria, Texas in 1945.

FRENCH COMBS was a Navy Pharmacist Mate 3rd Class who served at the U.S.N. Hospital at Treasure Island, California and the U.S.N. Air Station at Alexander, California in 1945.

IRVIN SLAYBACK, of Aurora, was an Army Private with the 1520 Area Service Unit at Fort Hayes. He served as a Military Policeman in 1945.

CHARLES SLAYBACK, of Aurora, was in the Army Medical Corps in 1944.

GEORGE SIMMERMAN was a Sergeant in the 8th Army Air Force.

EDGAR SIEBENTHAL was a Ship's Cook 3rd Class in the Navy. He served aboard the U.S.S. *Bates*, U.S.S. *Prarie* and at the Fleet Hospital 115. He was discharged in October 1945.

HAROLD SHOOK was a Private serving with Patton's 3rd Army in 1945.

FRANCIS SHELTON was a Private in the Army serving at a base in Bermuda in 1945.

William Marshall

Robert Lamkin

Hal Driver (r.) and Don Ritter

Edgar Stevens

John Miller

Richard Kaffenberger

JOHN C. MILLER, of Yorkville, entered the U.S. Army in February 1945 and was honorably discharged in June 1945, due to a disability. As a Private, he had been a member of Company C, Twenty-second Battalion IRTC, before he was discharged at Regional Hospital, Fort McClellan, Alabama.

WINIFRED MARKSBERRY, of Lawrenceburg, served as a Private in the Quartermaster Corps at Camp Lee, Virginia in 1945.

CHARLES LANE was a Seaman First Class in the Navy. Some of the ships he served aboard were: SS *Thompson*, SS *Charles Paddock*, and at the base in Port Said, Egypt.

ROBERT LAMKIN, of Moores Hill, was a Staff Sergeant. He served as a Mess Sergeant in the American Theater, being discharged in May 1946.

CLIFFORD KUHLMEIER, of Aurora, was a Corporal in the U.S. Army. He served as a Clerk-Typist in the American Theater.

LEO KOCHER, of Harrison, was a Technician 5th Grade, serving as a Clerk-Typist in the 165th Army General Hospital in 1945-1946.

ROBERT KELLER, of Lawrenceburg, was a Second Lieutenant in the Army Quartermaster Corps at the Charlotte Quartermaster Depot in 1945.

GILBERT KIETH, of Aurora, was a Private in the Marines at Camp Lejeune in 1945.

ROBERT KLEMM was a Merchant Marine, Seaman 2nd Class assigned to a radio training station at Gallup Island in Boston in 1945.

JACK KENNEDY served with the Sea Bees at Port Heumame, California in 1945.

RICHARD (DICK) KAFFENBERGER, of Lawrenceburg, entered the U.S. Navy and became a Yeoman 3rd Class, serving at Naval Air Station at Patuxent River, Maryland.

HENRY JOHNSON, of Wilmington, a Private First Class, was wounded twice while serving with the Army in Germany. He was wounded in the arm and both legs.

ANTHONY WESTERKAMP, of Guilford, entered the Army in September 1942 and became a Sergeant. He served with the Medical Depot of the 1884th Service Unit as a Military Policeman until September 1945.

JOHN WEBB served in the U.S. Army from August 1944 to June 1946.

HARRY WALTON, of Lawrenceburg, served in the Army as a Private for a brief period. He entered the Army in March 1945 and was discharged at Camp Atterbury in June 1945.

MARVIN VOGELSANG was an Electrician's Mate 3rd Class in the U.S. Navy. He served aboard the U.S.S. *Sierra* (AD 18) in the Pacific.

PAUL TURNER was a Seaman First Class in the U.S. Navy. He served until October 1945, receiving his discharge at the Naval Base in Norman, Oklahoma.

HOWARD TRENNEPOHL served in the Merchant Marines.

EDGAR STEVENS, of Lawrenceburg, was a Seaman First Class in the Navy and was transferred from duty in the British Isles to the Naval Base in Charleston in 1945.

RAHE SPECKMAN, of Aurora, was a Technician 4th Grade in the Paratroopers in 1944.

HOWARD SMASHEY entered the Navy in May 1944 and became a Storekeeper 2nd Class. He was stationed at Treasure Island, California until his discharge in 1946.

ROBERT E. SMITH, of Dillsboro, entered the Army with his twin brother Alan in 1943. Both served as Medical Technicians in the American Theater, being discharged in 1946.

ALAN F. SMITH, of Dillsboro, entered the Army in December 1943. He served as a Surgical Technician with an Army Medical Detachment at the Salt lake City Air Base; Peterson Field, Colorado Springs; and at Fort Sheridan.

FLOYD ROUSH entered the U.S. Navy and became a Seaman 2nd Class. He served aboard the heavy cruiser, U.S.S. *Columbus*. He was discharged in April 1949.

Howard Smashey

Twin brothers Robert and Alan Smith

Louis Rullman

Clyde Myers

John H. Schott

DORMAND KAISER was a Staff Sergeant with the Army Air Corps in India. He served with the 28th Headquarters Squadron in 1945.

CARL S. REED, of Guilford, completed his basic or boot training at the Great Lakes Naval Training Station in July 1945.

GEORGE YAUGER, of Lawrenceburg, was with the Infantry Replacement Training Center at Fort McClellan, Oklahoma in 1945.

FOREST SACKETT served about 6 months in 1944 as a Private with the U.S. Army Headquarters Company T at Fort Francis in Warren, Wyoming.

HENRY RYAN was a Private in the Army at Camp Rucker, Alabama, in basic training in 1945.

ARTHUR RYAN was a Private in the Army at Shepperd Field, Texas in 1945.

JAMES RUNYAN served as a Sergeant in the Army Hospital Corps at the 51st Evacuation Hospital in France, serving units of the 6th Army Group.

THERON RULLMAN was a Staff Sergeant in the Army Air Force. He served at Lowrey Field and in Alaska in 1945-1946.

LOUIS RULLMAN was an Army Staff Sergeant who received training at the University of Pennsylvania for duty with a Civilian Investigation Detachment. The C.I.D. handled disputes between the Army and civilians and Japanese or different Army Groups in dispute.

ARNOLD RULLMAN, of Lawrenceburg, was a Private in the Army Signal Corps. He served as a Switchboard Operator at Camp Crowder, Missouri. In 1945, he transferred to Army School of Photography.

WARD ROGERS, of Lawrenceburg, was a Corporal in the Army Air Force Base Unit in 1944. He served as an Auto Equipment Operator in the American Theater.

PHILIP ROBBINS was a Chief Radio Technician at the Naval Air Station, Patuxent River, Maryland. He had served 29 months in the Pacific Theater.

RAYMOND REED was a Seaman First Class in the U.S. Navy. From Manchester, Ray was training at Camp Peary, Virginia in 1945.

DAVID (CROCKETT) RADAR, of the Aurora area, entered the Army Air Force and became a Private First Class. In 1945 he served at Chanute Field, Illinois.

MILLARD MYER was a Private at Ft. Riley, Kansas in 1945.

JOHN McWETHY, of Lawrenceburg, was a Pharmacist mate 3rd Class serving in a Naval Dental Clinic in Cleveland.

FRED KITTENBRINK, of Aurora, served as a Military Policeman in the American Theater. He was a Sergeant in 1945.

HARLAN KING, of Dillsboro, was a Private First Class serving as a Machine Gunner with the 71st Infantry in the American Theater.

WILBUR JOHNSON entered the U.S. Navy and became a Water Tender 2nd Class. He was honorably discharged in November 1945.

WALTER JONES was a Seaman 2nd Class in the U.S. Navy. He was honorably discharged at the Naval Center in Farragut, Idaho in February 1946.

JAMES JARVIS was an Army Sergeant assigned to the 129th General Hospital in England in 1944.

RODNEY HODGES, of Dillsboro, served with the Headquarters Company of the Army Ground Force as a Clerk-Typist in 1945-1946.

RICHARD YOUNG entered the U.S. Navy in March 1945 and became a Painter 3rd Class with the Sea Bees.

FRANK YAUGER entered the U.S. Navy and became a Seaman 2nd Class. He served until December 1945, released at the Naval Hospital in Seattle.

JAMES WITT, of Logan, entered the U.S. Navy and became a Seaman First Class. He was stationed at the Navy Yard at Pearl Harbor in Hawaii.

David Radar

William Gilb

Philip Given

Ray Miller

Robert Myers

ROBERT F. MYERS, of Aurora, was in the Marines. He served in the Pacific at Oahu, Iwo Jima and the occupation of Japan with the Fifth Marine Division.

OMER BARTON, of Manchester, was a Third Class Petty Officer in the U.S. Navy. Two of the ships he served aboard were sunk and a third one was badly damaged. While he went through all these dangers unharmed, he was killed in an automobile wreck within a few miles of home.

PHILIP GIVEN, of Lawrenceburg, was in the U.S. Marine Corps and saw action in major battles with the Japanese in the Philippines, on Iwo Jima and Okinawa.

WILLIAM GILB, of Lawrenceburg, entered the U.S. Navy and became a Chief Petty Officer who served on a tanker in the Pacific. He was at Iwo Jima for the flag-raising event.

HAROLD FRENCH enlisted in the Marine Corps in 1942 and participated in many battles and actions in the Pacific Theater including the following: Guadalcanal, Guam, Okinawa, and China. He served until December 1945.

BRUCE BOYD, of Lawrenceburg, was a Fireman First Class, U.S. Navy, who served aboard the cruisers: *Mobile* and *Santa Fe*. He earned 13 battle stars in battle in the Philippines and other places in the Pacific Theater of Operations.

NEWTON BELL, of Moores Hill, was a Machinist First Class in the Navy Sea Bees. He saw action at the invasion of Okinawa.

WILLIAM SCHUMAN, of St. Leon, entered the Army in March 1945 and became a Technician 4th Grade. He served as an Automotive Mechanic in the Pacific Theater.

JOHN SCHOTT entered the Army in March 1943. As a Private he served in various stateside camps and then went into the Pacific for the invasion of Okinawa with the 152nd Heavy Equipment Company as a Staff Sergeant.

EARL SEEVERS, of Guilford, was a Sergeant with the 8th Bomber Squad, 3rd Bomber Group. He served in the Philippines and the Air Offensive against Japan as a Carpenter.

LESLIE SELLERS, of Harrison, was a Tank Crewman with the 28th Tank Battalion. He served in the Pacific Theater from October 1943 to February 1946.

WARREN ROSENBAUM entered the U.S. Navy and became an Aviation Radio Technician First Class. He was discharged in November 1945.

LYLE PITTS entered the U.S. Navy and became a Chief Motor Machinist Mate. He was honorably discharged at Sampson, New York in December 1945.

CLARENCE LAND, of Aurora, entered the U.S. Navy in 1945. After he completed his boot training at Great Lakes Naval Station, the war was soon over and he had no opportunity to see combat.

GLENN KONRADI, of Manchester, joined the Merchant Marines at age 17, upon graduating from Aurora High School, and took basic training at Sheepshead Bay, Brooklyn in August 1945.

OLLIS KING, of New Trenton, was a Teletype Operator Instructor with the 3505th Army Air Force Base Unit in the American Theater.

GEORGE HURD served as a Machinist Mate 2nd Class in the Navy and was discharged in November 1945.

WILLIAM HOUSTON, of Lawrenceburg, enlisted in the Navy in 1945. He completed Basic Training and was a Seaman 2nd Class.

JOHN HANNAH was a Machinist mate First Class in the U.S. Navy, serving in the Ordnance Department in 1945.

EDWARD McCARTY was a Sergeant in the Army in 1945.

CARROLL McCARTNEY served in the Quartermaster Corps in 1945.

RAYMOND MILLER, of Yorkville, entered the U.S. Army in March 1945, and was honorably discharged in December 1946, as a Technician 5, Automotive Mechanic. In the Philippines he inspected and performed maintenance service and repairs on gasoline and diesel powered vehicles, drove a wrecker and operated a crane.

ELDON BAKER, of Aurora, was a Cook with the Army's 25th Headquarters Special Troops in the Second Army. He served as a Technician 5th Grade in Central Europe.

Omer Barton

Harold French

Newton Bell

Dorman Lange

Noel Hess

ALVIE McCLAIN, of Dillsboro, was an Army Private First Class. He was in the 81st Calvary and served in both the Pacific and Europe, doing occupation service in Germany.

RALPH MILLER was a Staff Sergeant with the 3rd Army in Germany in 1945.

CLYDE MEYERS was a Private First Class in the Army and was wounded in Germany in 1945.

DORMAN LANGE, of Aurora, was a Private in the 913th Field Artillery Battalion. He served as a Radio Operator during the occupation of Germany.

ORVILLE KENT, of Aurora, Seaman First Class served in the Navy in both the Atlantic and Pacific Fleets.

CLARENCE WESSEL, of Harrison, entered the Army in June 145. He served in the American Theater with the 42nd Air Force Base Unit until November 1946.

FRED WEHMEYER was killed in action in August 1944 while serving with the Army Infantry in combat in France.

NOEL HESS, from the Sunman area, entered the U.S. Army and became a Warrant Officer. He served with the Information Control Division Office of Military Government in the U.S. Zone of Europe.

JAMES HANCE was an Army Technician 5th Grade. In 1945, he was serving in an American Hospital in Germany, doing statistical work.

GLENN ENGLISH, of Wilmington, was a Private First Class. He was wounded when a truck in which he was riding ran over a mine and exploded. He served in Africa, Sicily, France and Germany.

ARTHUR BRUNNER served in the U.S. Army as a Messenger and then a Medic. He took part in the Normandy Invasion and went on from there to fight throughout France.

FLOYD HORNBACH, of Yorkville, was a Staff Sergeant in the U.S. Army Air Force. He served in England and France as a Meteorologist for 25 months.

MARVIN HOLLIDAY, of Lawrenceburg, had Army duty for 22 months in 1945 in Panama, the Canal Zone.

LESLIE HOPPER, of Dillsboro, was an Army Truck Driver. He served at the 40th General Hospital in 1945.

JOHN WUNDERLICH, of Aurora, was in the V-12 program of the U.S. Navy at Ohio Wesleyan University. He later served as a Navigator and Radioman.

ROBERT WIRTH, of Lawrenceburg, was a Cook, serving with the Headquarter Company of the No. 2 Infantry Replacement Training Center in the American Theater.

EDWIN STEVEN, of Moores Hill, was a Signalman 2nd Class in the Navy serving on a destroyer in 1945.

WILLIAM RICE was in training at Ft. Bragg, North Carolina in 1945.

RICHARD SMITH was at the Technical Training Center at Norman, Oklahoma in 1945.

RAYMOND SMITH, of Dillsboro, was in Army Ordnance.

ALBERT SMITH, of Wilmington, was a Staff Sergeant at Ft. Benjamin Harrison in 1945.

JAMES SATCHWELL was an Army Private with duty in 1945 at Camp Jackson, South Carolina.

LUTHER SAPPENFIELD was a First Sergeant with an Infantry Unit in Panama and then had duty training replacements for overseas service in 1945.

DAVID SAPPENFIELD was a Fire Controlman 3rd Class in the Coast Guard and then was assigned pre-flight training to become a Navy pilot in 1945.

GLENN RANDALL, of Lawrenceburg, was taken into the Army in March 1944 and served some 4 months before receiving an honorable discharge.

GEORGE POWERS, of Aurora, entered the Army in April 1944. He was a Private serving as a Canoneer in the American Theater until April 1945.

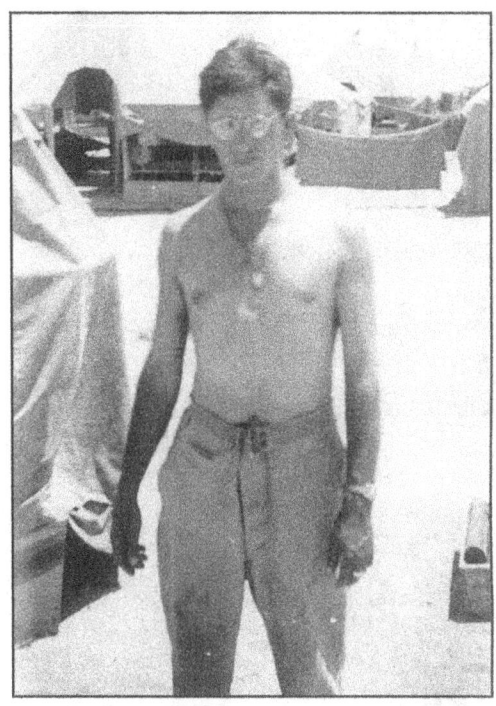

Arthur Brunner

Floyd Hornbach

Henry Nanz

Elmer Rumsey

Robert (Bob) Robinson

ELMER RUMSEY, of near-Aurora, was an Army Technician 3rd Grade serving with a Heavy Automotive Maintenance Company. He served in both the ETO and the Pacific in the occupation of Japan.

ROBERT RUPP was a Technician 4th Grade with the 1345 Engineering Construction Battalion. He served in Okinawa in 1945.

EDWARD ZIMMERMAN was an Army Corporal with the 187 Glider Infantry. He served in the Asiatic-Pacific Theater in the Philippines and the Army of Occupation in Japan.

WAYNE WILLIAMS was a Sergeant in the Marine Corps who was wounded at Iwo Jima. He was in the Fourth Marine Division and also fought in Saipan and Tinian.

HENRY NANZ was a Seaman First Class in the U.S. Navy. In 1945, he served as a Signalman aboard an LST in the Pacific.

EVERETT RIMSTIDT, of Lawrenceburg, was a Technician 5th Grade, with the 31st Infantry. He was a Clerk and served with the Army of Occupation in Japan.

ROBERT (BOB) ROBINSON, of Aurora, was a Pharmacist's Mate 2nd Class in the U.S. Navy, serving with the 9th Battalion of the Third Marine Division on Guam in 1944.

JOSEPH STACY, of Moores Hill, was a Staff Sergeant with the 1395th Engineering Construction Battalion. He was a Power Shovel Operator with duty in Ryukyus Islands in the Pacific.

JOHN SEAVER was a Private First Class with the 28th Marines in the 5th Division in the South Pacific in 1945.

TALBERT TEKE was an Army Technician 5th Grade. He served on an Army Hospital Ship in both the Atlantic and Pacific, returning wounded soldiers to the U.S.

CHARLES REDMAN, of Aurora, was a U.S. Army Private. While serving in combat in the Philippines in 1945 he was killed in action against the Japanese.

HARRY E. HOFFMAN, JR, of Dillsboro, was an Army Technical Sergeant with the 137 Signal Intelligence Company of the Signal Corps. He served in the European Theater with the Seventh Army being discharged in January 1946.

RUSSELL THORNTON was an Aviation Electrician Mate in the U.S. Navy. He served aboard the carrier, U.S.S. *Franklin*, which was hit by suicide planes in the Philippines and at Iwo Jima. The crew saved the ship from sinking and another ship towed her to the States.

EARL SULLIVAN, of Lawrenceburg, entered the U.S. Navy and became a Seaman 2nd Class. He served 20 months in the South Pacific.

ROBERT STEINER, of Weisburg, enlisted in the Navy in September of 1942, and became a Sea Bee. He served on New Caledonia, Guadalcanal, New Hebrides and Bougainville. He was injured on the latter island by a shell explosion which ruptured both his ear drums in 1944. As a Machinist Mate 2nd Class, he was discharged January 1945.

MYRLE DUNN, of Lawrenceburg, was a Seaman 1st Class in the invasion of Leyte, Iwo Jima, and Okinawa.

MORRISON DOWNEY was a Corporal in the battle of Okinawa.

LESTER DAVIS was a Private First Class in New Guinea in 1945.

ALBERT DAVIES, of Dillsboro, was a Seaman 2nd Class in the Navy. He was on the U.S.S. *Birmingham* in the Pacific in 1945 fighting in the battle of Okinawa.

DILVER WALCOTT, of Aurora, was a Sergeant in the Headquarters Squadron of the 13th Division. As a Clerk-Typist he had duty in the Army of Occupation in Japan.

HERBERT GILBERT, of Lawrenceburg, was a Technician 5th Grade with the 341st Infantry. He served as a Rifleman in the Pacific Theater.

RAYMOND HEMKE, of Weisburg, served as a Radio Mechanic in the Army Air Force in the China-Burma-India Theater, taking part in the air offensive over Japan.

DALE W. GRIMSLEY, Machinist Mate 3rd Class served in the Navy in the Pacific aboard the aircraft carrier, *Enterprise* in 1945.

Talbert Teke (l.) and Earl Ferdon

Robert Rupp

Robert Steiner

Reynold Lanvermeyer

William Wittrock

CLIFFORD EDWARDS, Private First Class, served in the 112th Calvary at Tokyo in 1945. Previously had served in the Philippines and New Guinea.

REYNOLD LANVERMEYER, of Dillsboro, was a Corporal serving with a Mechanic Tractor unit at Ft. Crook, Nebraska in 1944.

URBAN JOSEPH KUEBEL, of Yorkville, was a Coxswain in the Navy. He entered the service in December 1943 and served at NTS Farragut, Idaho and aboard the U.S.S. *Gropac*.

CURTIS ESTER, from the Aurora area, served in the Navy from February 1944 to March 1946. He was a Flight Engineer flying bombers out of Norfolk. At the end of the war he had duty at Clinton, Oklahoma, the graveyard of airplanes being dismantled. He was an Aviation Machinist Mate 3rd Class.

WILLIAM WITTROCK, of Lawrenceburg, trained at Great Lakes Naval Station in 1945 and later became a Seaman 2nd Class.

WILBUR GLACKIN, of Moores Hill, was a Private in the Army. He served in France in 1945.

ARTHUR McCALLISTER of the Army Air Force was a Private First Class at Avon Park Air Field, Florida.

FRANK PLUNKETT was at Camp Atterbury in 1945 as a Private in the Army.

JOE VOTAW served in the Navy as an Ensign in the Pacific Theater in 1945.

GLENN NORMAN served as a pilot on a B-29 bomber in the Army Air Force over Germany in 1945.

RUSSELL MORRIS was a Sergeant with the 381st Division in the South Pacific.

BOBBY LISCHKGE, of Aurora, took Basic Training at Sheppard Field in 1945.

ALBERT HOPPING was in a special training program for the Army at Ohio State University in Columbus, Ohio.

WILLIAM BEARD, of Lawrenceburg, Technical Sergeant, served with the Air Transport Command European Division as a Draftsman.

ROBERT BADENHOP was a Sergeant in the Army Air Force, training with a ground crew at Patterson Field in 1943.

GUARD McADAMS served in the U.S. Army as a Private and was a Truck Driver for a medical detachment. He served from March 1945 to December 1945.

CHARLES PETERS, of Moores Hill, entered the U.S. Navy and became an Aviation Electrician Mate 3rd Class in 1945.

MILLARD MEYER of Aurora was a Private First Class in the 24th Infantry Division, February 1945 to June 1946, serving as a Mail Clerk.

WILLIAM BADENHOP was a Private in the Marine Corps who graduated from gunnery training in 1944.

DONALD BORGMAN was a Private in the U.S. Army, participating in a specialized training program in 1945.

LOUIS BOVARD was a Private in the Army at Camp Lee in 1945.

PETE DEMMONS was a Private in the Army. He received a medical discharge after six months service in 1945.

JOSEPH DOBER, of Lawrenceburg, was a military Policeman at Camp Ellis, Illinois. While acting as an escort guard for German prisoners of war, he accidentally slipped from the truck in which he was riding with the POW's and struck his head on the ground, suffering a severe intra-cranial injury. He was rushed to the hospital, then flown to General Hospital, Clinton, Iowa for surgery. He never regained consciousness and died.

JOHN GROSRENAUD was an Army Private First Class in 1944. He was a resident of Aurora.

DAVID HOLDCRAFT enlisted in the U.S. Navy in July 1944 as an Apprentice Seaman, took his boot training at Great Lakes and was discharged in August 1945.

Urban Kuebel

Albert Hopping

CLIFFORD SCHULER, of Aurora, was a Corporal in the 14th Replacement Depot. He served as a Heavy Mortar Crewman and was wounded in Germany in 1944.

JAMES SATCHWILL, of Aurora, entered the U.S. Army and served as a Private with the 787th Tank Battalion. He was a Mortar Crewman in the ETO.

WILLIS SANDBRINK, of Aurora, graduated from Officer's Candidate School as a Second Lieutenant in the Field Artillery. In January 1945 he was sent into combat in the ETO. Three months later, he was wounded in action. He received the Bronze Star and Silver Star medals for heroic service.

PAUL (TED) GILBERT, of Greendale, was a Technician 5th Grade in the Army serving in the 1st Armored Division as a Truck Driver in Central Europe. He earned one battle star.

THOMAS FOX, of Greendale, was a Technician 3rd Grade. He received the Bronze Star for Meritorious service from June 1944 – May 1945. He had 5 battle stars, serving as a Combat Engineer in France, Belgium, Germany and Czechoslovakia.

HARVEY CLARK, of Harrison, was a Technical Sergeant with the 1467th Engineering Maintenance Company. He served in both the ETO and the Asiatic-Pacific Theaters of Operation from May 1943 to February 1946.

SAMUEL BOYD, of Lawrenceburg, served as a Mortar Crewman. He was stationed in the Caribbean, North Atlantic and the Mediterranean regions.

JOSEPH NEFF, of Aurora, was a Corporal with the 10th Constabulary Regiment. He served in the Army of Occupation in Germany.

DELTON MARKSBERRY, of Lawrenceburg, was a Staff Sergeant with the 15th AAF in Italy. He received the Air Medal with three clusters for "Achievement in flight while in activities against the enemy." He was a Radio Operator-Gunner on a bomber that flew many missions over Germany, Yugoslavia, the Ploesti oil fields in Romania and other targets. He braved anti-aircraft fire, enemy fighter planes and engine failures of his own plane.

Willis Sandbrink

Harvey Clark

Four cousins (l. to r.): Dan Daley (Army), Bruce Boyd (Navy), Sally Polk, Samuel Boyd (Marines)

WILLARD WHITE, of Lawrenceburg, entered the U.S. Navy and served on many islands in the South Pacific Theater in 1944.

EDWARD HOFFMEIER was a Seaman First Class in the U.S. Navy. He served in the Pacific Theater aboard the U.S.S. P.C.C. 882 and Attack Transport 33.

THOMAS GROSS, of Lawrenceburg, was a Staff Sergeant with Air Force Quartermaster Corps in New Guinea in 1945.

KENNETH DEWERS, of Aurora, was a Sergeant in the Army serving in the Philippines. He also was in the occupying forces in Japan.

LOUIS GRIFFITH served as a Private First Class in the Marines in the Pacific in 1945.

JERRY DENNERLINE, of Aurora, was a Corporal in the Marines as an Anti-Tank Gun Crewman. He served in the Pacific at Iwo Jima and Japan.

H. S. CURTIS was an Ordnanceman First Class in the U.S. Navy. He was serving in Hawaii in 1945.

EDMON CUMMINS was a Ship's Serviceman 3rd Class in the U.S. Navy. He had duty at the Naval Air Station in Hawaii in 1945.

ESTAL CONAWAY, of Dillsboro, was a Corporal serving as a Tail Gunner of a bomber crew in the Army Air Force. He was killed in action in the South Pacific in 1945.

Paul Gilbert

Edmon Cummins

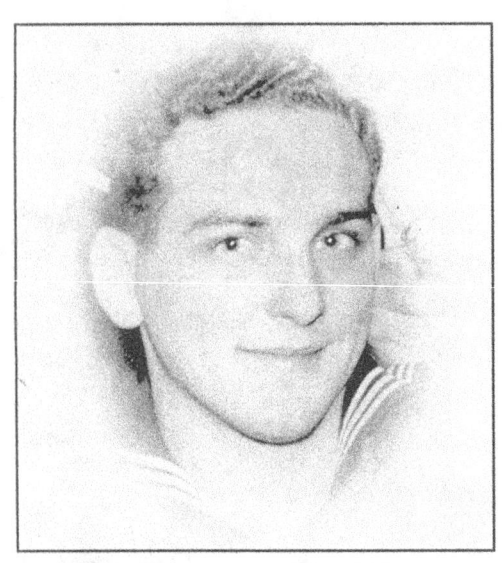

William (Bill) Jackson

Jean Knue

Edwin Enneking

WALTER JACKSON, of Aurora, was a Seaman First Class in the U.S. Navy. He entered the service in March 1944 and served on LSM and U.S.S. *Marlboro* in the American Theater.

HERBERT FOBLE was a Seaman First Class in the U.S. Navy. He was in the Palm Beach Hospital in 1945.

JAMES FEUSTEL served briefly as a Private in the U.S. Army at Fort Riley, Kansas in 1945.

NORBERT EVANS, of Aurora, served in the Field Artillery stateside in 1944-1945 at Ft. Sill, Camp Rucker and in Arizona as a Corporal.

CHARLES HORNBACH, of Lawrenceburg, went to Officer's Training School for the Merchant Marines in New London and was commissioned an Ensign in 1945.

CHARLES HUFF was a Water Tender First Class in the U.S. Navy who was discharged in November 1945.

BILL JACKSON, of Greendale, was a Storekeeper and then a Ship's Cook in the Navy. He served on a destroyer and a minesweeper.

LOREN JACOBS served at Fort Jackson, South Carolina, with the U.S. Army in 1944.

JAMES KENT, of Aurora, was an Army Private in a Training Unit in 1945.

JEAN KNUE, of Lawrenceburg, served in the U.S. Army from February of 1945, as a Private as a Fire Direction and Survey Instructor in the Field Artillery at Fort Bragg, North Carolina. He was stationed at Fort Riley, and was sent to Germany after the war ended.

EDGAR MATSON, of Lawrenceburg, became a Corporal in the Marine Corps in a Casual Company at Quantico, Virginia as a Bandsman in the American Theater in 1945.

ALBERT MATTOX was an Army Technician 4th Grade with the 232 General Hospital Unit in 1945. He became a Surgical Technician in an operating room in an Army Medical Corps General Hospital in Temple, Texas.

EDWIN ENNEKING was drafted at Lawrenceburg and reported for duty on December 30, 1942. First, he served in the offices of several bases, and later worked on a floating repair operation to repair parts for B-29 bombers in the Pacific. He was based at Tinian, Guam, Saipan and Okinawa.

WILLIAM (BILL) BRUNNER was a Boatswain's Mate in the U.S. Navy at San Diego. He was transferred to the Navy base at Key West where he served as a Clerk. As the war ended, he was shipped to the Philippines to help dismantle bases.

WILLIAM HOSKINS, from Aurora, was a Seaman First Class, U.S. Navy. He served on the *Saugus*, a vehicle landing ship which brought troops ashore in Japan for occupation duty.

ROBERT HUMBLE, of Lawrenceburg, entered the Marine Corps and became a member of the 4th Marine Division. He participated in the invasion of Iwo Jima on February 19, 1945, and was killed by the enemy a few days later on February 23.

KENNETH JACKSON, Medical Doctor, of Aurora, was a Lieutenant in the Navy Medical Corps, stationed in Nagasaki, Japan.

EARL JEFFRIES, of Lawrenceburg, a Boatswain Mate 2nd Class received five battle stars for service in the South Pacific.

RICHARD (DICK) KITTLE, of Lawrenceburg, served in the Navy during 1944-1946 in the Pacific Theater. He was stationed at Iwo Jima in 1945 for six months and was discharged at age 19.

WILLIAM KRIDER, of Lawrenceburg, a former teacher at Lawrenceburg High School, was an Ensign in the Navy, acting as an Executive Officer aboard a LST in Japan.

GARNET LONIAKER, of Lawrenceburg, entered the Navy in October 1942 and became a Storekeeper 1st Class. He served in the Pacific with duty at Pearl Harbor, Johnson Islands and Midway.

GLEN LUKE, of Dillsboro, was a Private First Class with the 27th Infantry serving as a Rifleman in the Pacific Theater and the Occupation of Japan.

Robert (Bob) Humble and wife

William Brunner

JAMES McKINNEY was a Seaman 2nd Class aboard a ship in Pacific Theater in 1945.

SAMUEL MELSON, of Aurora, in 1943 was a Hospital Apprentice First Class in the Navy. He trained with the Marines at Camp Pendleton and then shipped to the Pacific Theater. While at sea, he learned Japan had surrendered. He was sent to Nagasaki days after the atomic bombing and remained on duty until December 1945.

ROY R. LACEY JR., of Lawrenceburg, entered the U.S. Navy and became a Seaman First Class. He served aboard the ship U.S.S. *Okeland* and received 13 battle stars.

MELVIN KREMER entered the U.S. Navy and became a Seaman First Class. He served aboard the battleship, U.S.S. *Idaho*. This ship took part in the Aleutians campaign; and at Iwo Jima where Melvin would see the raising of the American flag on the island.

GILBERT KINDER was a Radioman 3rd Class serving in Philippines, Iwo Jima and Okinawa.

AMOS KEYES was a Technician 4th Grade in the U.S. Army, served with the 4025th Signal Detachment in the Pacific Theater of Operations. He also had occupation duty in Japan.

JAMES (JIM) KAFFENBERGER, of Lawrenceburg, entered the Army Air Force in 1942 and served as a Weatherman in the Pacific Theater. He was a Staff Sergeant with three battle stars. He was in the honor guard aboard the battleship *Missouri* when the Japanese signed the surrender ending WWII.

WILLIAM HINSON was a Staff Sergeant with the 874th Harbor Craft Company. He served in the Philippines and in Japan in 1945.

HAROLD HAVEY, was a Seaman First Class in the U.S. Navy, serving aboard the U.S.S. *Guam*. From Okinawa they went to Japan at the end of the war.

FLOYD GRUBBS, of Lawrenceburg, was a Sergeant in the Army. He was a Cook. Later he managed an Army hotel in Tokyo during the occupation after the war.

VERNON CHRISTIAN was a Corporal in the Army serving at various island bases in the Pacific Theater in 1945.

Samuel Melson

James Kaffenberger

BRUCE ARTHUR BOYD was a Fireman First Class in the Navy. He served on two cruisers: the *Mobile* and the *Santa Fe* in the Pacific, taking part in the Philippine liberation.

WILLIAM BLACK was a Seaman 3rd Class having received boot training at Great Lakes. He received motion picture training at Pearl Harbor and then served at Manila in 1945-1946.

EDGAR STEVENS entered the Navy in May of 1943. He became an Aviation Mechanic Repairman. In 1944, he had duty at Sub Base in New London. Later he served in the destroyer escort, U.S.S. *Brough*. He served in the ETO and the Pacific.

Edgar Stevens

Roy Lambert

Richard Kittle

Amos Keyes   **Garnet Loniaker**   **Charles Skidmore**

Harry Nocks

Lawrence Pelgen

Frank Heine

ORIN NOWLIN, of Mt. Pleasant, entered the Army in February of 1943 and became a Sergeant. As a medic, he served on a hospital ship serving North Africa and the Mediterranean.

HARLEY BLASDEL became a member of the Navy Air Force. He served as an Aviation Repair Mechanic, 3rd Class in Hawaii.

LEONARD BEATTY served in the Army for 4 years. He had duty on New Guinea in communications.

CHARLES G. NOWLIN entered the Army in 1942 and was assigned to the mechanized calvary as a Rifleman. However, he was released in 1943 for farm work.

LESTER BLASDEL entered the Army in October 1942 and was assigned to the Signal Corps. He had duty in New Guinea and the Philippines.

HARRY NOCKS was in the Navy Air Force in the Pacific Theater of Operation. He was a Flight Engineer and served as a Second Class Petty Officer.

LAWRENCE (LARRY) PELGEN, of Aurora, enlisted in the Army in 1942 and was assigned to the Field Artillery. He had duty in the South Pacific on Guadalcanal and served as a Cook. He served until 1944.

HENRY EVANS was a Torpedoman, serving on the destroyer, U.S.S. *Jenkins*, from December of 1943 to November of 1945. He saw action in the invasion of the Marshall Islands, Western New Guinea, Borneo and the Philippines.

FRANK HEINE, of Aurora, entered the Army in 1942 and saw service in the whole German Campaign with the 330th Infantry Regiment. On the European invasion, his unit was to relieve the 101st Airborne who had just jumped behind the lines on D-Day; however, these plans weren't carried out for storms over the English Channel kept them offshore for a week. His unit made it ashore, despite German firing, and relieved the 101st. After a month of heavy fighting, they broke out of the hedgerows. Heine was a Radio Operator, and he with his partner kept communications going 24 hours a day under battle conditions. After breaking the German lines in France, Frank's unit had four more major battles to do before Germany's capitulation. Frank would win the Bronze Star for valor in combat, plus five battle stars.

ROBERT (BUCK) CRONTZ, of Lawrenceburg, entered the Army Corps of Engineers in June of 1942. He served in Panama and Camp Stoneman in California, being discharged in February of 1943.

JOHN SWALES, of Bright, first sreved in the U.S. Maritime Service, and then enlisted in the Army. He was in the Infantry and served as a Military Policeman. He saw action in New Guinea and the Philippines, where he contacted a severe case of Malaria. He was discharged in December of 1946.

CHARLES WELLS entered the Army and served with the 613th Field Artillery Battalion in the Pacific Theater of Action.

John Swales

Charles Wells

Eugene Beebe

Robert Crontz

Henry Evans

Donald Anderson

Noah Albright

NOAH ALBRIGHT, of Lawrenceburg, was a Sergeant in the Army Paratroopers. He served with the 511th Air Group in the Pacific on Leyte and other islands of the Philippines.

DONALD ANDERSON, of Aurora, was a Machinist Mate, 2nd Class. He served aboard the submarine U.S.S. *Skate*, in the Pacific. In addition to patrols against the enemy, he took part in the invasion of Wake.

DELMAR ANDREWS joined the Marines in January of 1944, and by that summer was in combat in the Mariana Islands. He served in an anti-tank unit and fought in the last battle of Okinawa. He served in the occupation of Japan.

EUGENE BEEBE, of Lawrenceburg, was an Army Sergeant. He served as a Technician with the Engineers Base Battalion on New Guinea and in the Philippines.

BURTON BARNES, of Aurora, became a Signalman 2nd Class. He served in a transport ship, U.S.S. *Sioux* and the U.S.S. *Cape Palmo* and at the Pacific Armed Guard Center.

EDWARD BASCOM, of Aurora, served in the Navy as a Ship's Cook 3rd Class taking amphibious training in 1943.

HERBERT BASCOM, of Aurora, entered the Merchant Marine. He served in the South Pacific Theater.

CLARENCE (PETE) HORNBERGER served in the U.S. Army with duty in Manila, Okinawa, and Korea during WWII. He was also an instructor in Jujitsu defense.

WILFORD ANDREWS, of Mt. Pleasant, enlisted in the Marine Corps. He took part in the Pacific battles at Saipan, Tinian, as well as the occupation of Japan.

GEORGE FOX, of Aurora, after being rejected twice physically, tried again and entered the Army. He became a Sergeant, stationed in California with duty guarding German POWs and later he was transferred to Ft. Harrison.

WILLIAM PARKER, of Lawrenceburg, turned down a deferment, and entered the Navy in 1943 and took boot training at Great Lakes Naval Station. He became a Seaman 2nd Class with duty at the Naval Air Station at Norman, Oklahoma.

JAMES PARISH, of Lawrenceburg, was in the Army Air Corps. He took pilot's training at the base in Amarillo, Texas.

Clarence Hornberger

George Fox

Edward Knoebel

Wilford Andrews

Delmar Andrews

James Parish

Harold Merritt

William Parker

Ralph Courter (topleft)

Robert J. Kennedy

Robert Connelly

EDWARD KNOEBEL, of Lawrenceburg, was drafted into the Army Air Corps in December of 1942. He became a Sergeant and served in the Philippine Campaign and in the occupation of Japan. He was discharged in March of 1946.

ROBERT J. KENNEDY, of Greendale, entered the Army in 1942. He was then sent to the Southwest Pacific Theater and became the Sergeant Major of a Regimental Combat team with rank of Master Sergeant. He earned three battle stars for action in New Guinea and the Philippines. He was assigned to General MacArthur's headquarters in Manila. He took conference notes of the invasion planes for Japan. Actually, he was in the second American plane to touch down in Yokohama after the atomic bomb was dropped. He helped establish MacArthur's headquarters in Tokyo.

GEORGE CARR was an Army Private. He had duty at Fort Blanding, Florida and Fort Ord, California; but was released to work his father's farm near Bright.

ROBERT CONNELLY was a Private in the Marine Corps. He served in a mortar platoon of the 4th Marine Division. In 1944, he took part in the battle of Iwo Jima.

ROBERT COOK, of Greendale, entered the Navy and became an Aviation Machinist Mate First Class. He served in the Pacific Theater of Operations.

RALPH COURTER, of Lawrenceburg, served with the 4th Armored Division in their drive through France, Germany and Czechoslovakia. He met his wife while based in Scotland.

HARRY CHEEK, of Aurora, served in the Medical Corps of the Army. He was a Technician, 2nd Class, serving in the South Pacific from 1943 until 1946.

JOHN WHITEFORD, of Aurora, was an Army Private, First Class. Her served as a Military Policeman with the 593rd Army Air Corps Base Unit in the American Theater.

GEORGE HOLDEN, of Lawrenceburg, was an Army Private with the 53rd Armored Infantry Battalion, serving as a Heavy Weapons Crewman. He saw action in Germany, but received a disability discharge due to a severe case of trenchfoot.

WILLIAM O'SHAUGHNESSY, of Greendale, was an Instrument Survey Man with the Glider Troops, rating as a Technician 4th Grade. His unit was involved in the Normandy invasion where he was wounded. He received a Bronze Star for action in France, Rhineland, Ardennes, and Central Europe.

PAUL PRIBBLE, of Lawrenceburg, entered the Army in August of 1944 and became a Tank Commander, He saw action in the Ardennes, Rhineland, Central Europe and the occupation of Germany.

John Whiteford   Harry Cheek

Robert Cook   George Holden   Paul Pribble

Charles Ketchum

LOUIS LANDRUM, of Guilford, was an Army Private First Class. He served as an Aircraft Mechanic. He was given a discharge in 1943 to operate the family farm after the death of his father.

CHARLES WELLS, from the Guilford area, entered the Army and was assigned duty with the 613th Field Artillery. He saw action in the Pacific Theater, serving in the Army for 22 months.

CHARLES KETCHAM had the unusual experience of serving in three branches of the Armed Forces. In 1941-1942, he was an engineering aide in the Navy Department, Ordnance Bureau in Washington. He then entered the Army in December of 1942 and served for a year before transferring to the Air Corps. He was based in England and then France with an engineering squadron ground crew member.

RAYMOND KERN, of Aurora, graduated in June of 1945 from pilot's training at Corpus Christi, Texas and became an Ensign. He was assigned to the Jacksonville Navy Base where he flew Curtis Helldivers.

RALPH REISEN, of Dillsboro area, served in the Navy from 1941 to 1945. He was Chief Petty Officer on the destroyer U.S.S. *Summers*, spending much time in the Caribbean and Southampton, England. His duty was to operate the ship's office.

Raymond Kern

Louis Landrum

William Caldwell

Jack Craven   **Monroe Bowker**   **Ray Callon**

MONROE BOWKER, of Aurora, entered the Navy and trained to become a Motor Machinist Mate 3rd Class. He served until December 1945.

CLAYTON BENTLE was inducted into the Army in 1945. After boot training, he was assigned to the Medical Corps and trained to be an X-ray Technician.

WILLIAM CALDWELL entered the Army as a Lieutenant in the Infantry and later transferred to the Air Corps, taking his pilot's training at an A.A.C. field in Georgia. While serving in the ETO, he became a Captain and received the Air Medal and five battle stars.

FLOYD CAMPBELL entered the Army and became a Corporal. In 1944, he was serving with an anti-aircraft unit at Camp Cook, California.

JACK CRAVEN entered the Navy and became a Seaman, 2nd Class. He served aboard the Destroyer Escort 764 as a radioman.

RAYMOND CALLON, of Aurora, was a Corporal in the Army who served from 1942 to 1945. He saw action with the 255th Field Artillery, fighting General Rommell's army in France and Germany. He received the Bronze Star for "fearless devotion to duty under heavy shelling... to maintain a communications line."

EARLE DEAN was a Technical Sergeant with the 9th Army. He served as a Range Setter in an anti-tank battalion. He saw action in Germany at the Ruhr River Offensive.

CLAUDE DECKER, of New Alsace, was a Private in the Marine Corps. In 1944, he was in training as an amphibious tractor operator.

SHERMAN HOLLAND quit high school to join the Navy in 1945. He served 14 years, becoming a Chief Petty Officer, and then transferred to the Reserves.

THOMAS E. MILLER was a Motor Machinist Mate in the U.S. Navy. His duty stations were Naval Operating Base at Norfolk, Training Command with the Atlantic Fleet and Naval Training Station at Newport, Rhode Island.

LOUIS BEHR served as a Private in the U.S. Army Air Corps. He was a member of a ground crew in 1943.

Floyd Cambell

Earle Dean

Louis Behr

Claude Decker (l.)

The Uncle I Never Knew

(Loss of Life in WWII affected those left behind in Dearborn County in various ways. The following excerpt from a letter received by the editor is illustrative of one way.)

"Private First Class Wesley Forrest Roberson, U.S. Marine Corps was killed on Pelelieu Island in the Pacific on September 15, 1944. He was only 19 years old. He was married to my Aunt Toddy Swales of Bright. Toddy is the daughter of John Swales, Sr., a life-time resident of Bright, and in his later years, Guilford.

Because he was a Marine in WWII, I was attracted to him, even though I didn't know him. When I was a kid, instead of playing baseball or fireman or all the others careers boys dream of, I always wanted to be in the Army. I guess it was due to the stories I begged my uncles and other veterans to tell. Sometimes they did so with tears in their eyes.

I called this Marine, "the uncle I never knew," because as I was growing up, my uncles and aunts never talked much about him, not from shame because Aunt Toddy had remarried after the war. I think they always felt sad and awkward about him. Like other couples who were married during the war, Aunt Toddy and her Marine were not married very long and had no children.

Recently, my mother and her sisters and brothers had a family gathering. There Aunt Toddy gave my mother two pictures of her Marine husband, and she gave me his Purple Heart medal.

My great-great-grandmother gave me, when I was in grade school, a box of family mementos. In it were several items that my uncle had sent back from the war. Also, there was the framed letter from the War Department to Aunt Toddy about her husband's death. After all these years, I finally got to see what he looked like. Although I never knew him personally, I always admired him and wondered what he was like, fighting for his country on an island halfway around the world. Now, however, that I can put a face to that letter from the War Department, I do feel that I actually know him.

Sincerely,
Eric"

Wesley F. Roberson

They Were Also Called

Following is a list of some Dearborn County people who were called to serve in the military during WW II, but for whom we were unable to find other information during our time limits.

Abbot, Robert
Adsit, William
Anderson, Harry
Arbaugh, Dennis
Armbuster, Francis
Armstrong, Herschel
Arnold, Vincent
Ashby, Clifford
Ashcraft, Everett
Ashcraft, Ira

Back, Harlan
Baer, Paul
Banks, Joseph
Barker, Ford
Bauer, Earl
Bayne, John
Belker, John
Bird, J.C.
Bischoff, Cletus
Block, George
Bloom, Louis
Borgman, Harold
Bosco, James
Bowles, Anson
Bowling, Conley
Braden, Harold
Brown, Lloyd
Burgess, Leroy
Bussong, Harold

Caldwell, Alex
Caplinger, Harold
Carr, Ralph
Carter, Zephyr
Case, Ray
Caseltine, Louis
Chapin, Leroy
Coleman, David
Combs, French
Cornett, Chester
Crabb, John
Crable, Virgil
Criswell, Paul
Cross, Edward

Dason, Robert
Davis, Richard
Davies, William
Dawson, Frederick
Dennis, Edward
Dittmer, Larry
Dobs, Lawrence
Donn, Frank
Downey, Paul
Doyle, Lawrence
Dunn, Norbert
Dunn, Ennis

Eckler, Estel
Edwards, Johnson
Ellis, Walter
Elrod, Hugh
Elston, Delmar
Emerson, Raymond
Emmert, William
Ewing, Clifford

Farmer, Norbert
Feller, Cornelius
Feller, Leroy
Fenske, Albert
Fields, Roscoe
Findley, William
Flick, Harold
Foggle, Russell
Foley, James
Footon, Cecil
Ford, Raymond
Foster, William
Fowler, Ora
French, David
Frey, Lawrence
Fuestal, James

Gamble, Gale
Garrison, Howard
Gash, Charles
Gibbons, Robert
Gibbs, Samuel
Gilbert, Albert

Gillman, Robert
Glenn, Charles
Goodpaster, William
Goodwin, Charles
Gordson, Edward
Gotman, Robert
Graber, Louis
Grall, James
Green, Leroy
Greene, Lindon
Gridley, Robert
Grubbs, Howard
Guernsey, Carl
Gullion, Charles
Gutman, Charles

Haas, Clarence
Haggard, John
Hale, Cornelius
Hall, Willard
Hamill, James
Hamilton, George
Hanson, Arthur
Harper, Ellsworth
Harris, Jake
Hart, Joseph
Harves, Robert
Horwitz, Joseph
Hutcher, George
Hayes, Mark
Hanes, Hazron
Hearne, Charles
Heaton, Charles
Helm, John
Henke, Carl
Henson, Roy
Herring, Horace
Herndon, Charles
Herron, William
Herzog, Gene
Hess, Hendrick
Hickey, Everett
Hicks, Fred
Hiett, George
Hill, Charles

Hill, Eugene
Hill, Stanley
Hinson, Louis Hinman, Louis
Hodges, Edwin
Hoff, Ellsworth
Hogan, Albert
Horton, Chester
Houston, Ewell
Howard, Clarence
Hudson, Delmar
Huffman, Orville
Huff, Clifford
Hulett, Glenn
Hunter, Elmer
Huston, Robert
Hutton, Fred
Hyatt, Richard
Hyde, Edwin

Ison, Herman
Ison, Hiram

Jackson, Clinton
Jackson, Milo
Jacobs, Holland
Jarvis, William
Johnson, Harold
Johnson, Ralph
Jones, Gilbert
Jones, Lavern
Justice, William

Kaiser, Alvin
Kammeyer, Lloyd
Kern, Clifford
Kerr, Fred
Keyes, Thomas
Kidd, Thomas
Kidwell, Ralph
King, Rufus
Kinnett, Harold
Klepper, Robert
Klopp, Carl
Knigga, Ernest

Koehler, Phillip
Kolb, Kenneth
Koons, Charles
Korte, Anthony
Krah, Eugene
Kuhlman, Harold
Kuhlman, Harley
Kurte, Anthony
Kyle, Henry

Lageman, Clyde
Lamkin, John
Landman, Jack
Largent, Francis
Latimer, Donald
Lattire, Donsell
LeForge, Jesse
Lemmel, Dale
Lewis, Elmer
Liddle, Harold
Linkmeyer, Denton
Lloyd, Samuel
Lockwood, Eugene
Loftus, Donald
Loh, William
Louden, Carl
Lynn, Herbert

Marlin, Robert
Martin, Chester
Martin, Marion
Massing, Edward
McAdams, Leo
Maxwell, George
McAllister, Jack
McConnoll, Carl
McGlover, George
McKinley, Hans
McMurray, Virgil
McQueen, Noble
Medecke, James
Mendell, Donald
Mericle, Floyd
Merritt, Harold

Mess, Max
Meyer, John
Meyers, Clarence
Miller, Gerald
Miller, Morris
Mirick, Russell
Moon, Howard
Moore, Arthur
Morgan, Samuel
Morter, Omer
Mosley, William
Munch, Theodore

Nagel, Robert
Nelson, Fred
Newbold, Gilbert
Nicholas, Phillip
Noble, Clyde
Nolte, Clifford
Norris, Alvin
Nowlin, Charles
Nowlin, Norman
Nowlin, Lloyd
Nowlin, Raymond

O'Connell, Leroy
O'Conner, Thomas
Olman, Curtis
Olson, Kenneth
O'Neal, Hubert
Oppen, Richard
Owens, Chester

Parsons, Curtis
Parrott, Elmer
Pate, Chauncey
Payton, Cecil
Peelman, Herbert
Pelsor, John
Pease, Harry
Peters, Cecil
Peters, Morris
Petit, Clarence
Phillips, Donald

Pitts, Merle
Potts, Harvey
Pound, Edward
Powell, Roland
Powers, Lee
Pratt, Milton
Priest, George
Price, James
Proud, John
Pyle, Walter

Randall, Leo
Reamer, Virgil
Records, John
Redding, George
Redding, Leo
Redding, Keith
Repasky, Albert
Rice, Albert
Ricketts, Louis
Riggs, Ohmer
Roberts, Carl
Robertson, Wesley
Rodefer, Carl
Rogers, Paul
Rolf, Edward
Rosen, James
Roth, Edward
Rump, Arnold
Runnel, Joseph
Russell, Homer
Ryle, Percy

Sackett, James
Scherer, Clarence
Schmidt, Andrew
Schmidt, Francis
Schneider, Stanley
Schuck, Frank
Schole, Leroy
Schwier, Eugene
Scarber, John
Scudder, Ralph
Scott, Leroy
Sears, Thomas
Sedler, Clarence

Seekatz, Cain
Steele, Norbert
Sterling, Thomas
Stuart, Roy
Stevens, Franklin
Stewart, Leo
Still, Laurens
Stoll, Edward
Suit, Paul
Summer, Carl
Summers, Earl
Swales, Louis
Sellers, Charles
Shanks, James
Shantz, John
Sheldon, William
Shell, Chester
Shilling, Ralph
Shelton, Leroy
Shuman, Herman
Simon, Hugh
Simpson, Melvin
Slayback, Claude
Slayback, Elbert
Smith, Herman
Smith, Milton
Smith, Stanley
Snider, Jack
Snyder, Gene
Sounders, Ernst
Stang, Harold
Stedler, Gene

Taylor, Delmar
Taylor, Hubert
Thomas, Warren
Tibbetts, Kenneth
Tindle, William
Todd, Samuel
Trabel, Lawrence
Trabez, Jerome
Traver, Wilbur
Trester, Dale
Tucker, William
Tutt, Joseph
Turner, Buford

Tweed, Earl
Tyler, William

Uhlmansiek, Cletus
Uhlmansiek, Gerald

Van Winkle, William
Vaughn, Cecil
Viel, Richard
Viel, Harlan
Visnon, Ray
Vinup, Lester

Waldon, Francis
Waldon, Melvin
Walker, Carl
Wallace, Herbert
Walsh, John
Walston, Cletus
Walton, Floyd
Ward, Emmett
Warner, Loren
Watts, Clifford
Weaver, George
Weber, Cletus
Weist, George
Wells, Norvin
Whaley, Alford
Whaley, Ivan
White, John
Whitham, Herschel
Whitham, Verle
Wilhelm, Richard
Williams, Kenneth
Wilson, Carl
Winters, Paul
Wolf, Robert
Worden, Allen
Wright, Delmer

York, Ernest
York, Harold

Zernach, Gerald
Zernach, Clarence
Zimmer, Gerald

Clayton Bentle

Michael Johnson

Robert Todd

Herbert Bascom

Marvin Bowker

The back of Sergeant Major John R. Holland, USMC, showing the three wars he participated in: WWII, Korea, and Vietnam. He's the same man who was the youngest to enter WWII from Dearborn County (see Chapter 2).

The Day the War Ended

After six long and bloody years, World War II had ended. All over the Free World, including America, there were joyous celebrations with whistles blowing, church bells ringing, bars overflowing and people dancing in the streets. Differing from V-E Day, V-J Day in Dearborn County's Seat at Lawrenceburg was the noisiest and most exuberant celebration in the town's history.

Radio broadcasts of Japan's surrender came into homes in early evening on August 14, 1945. Quickly a parade formed, headed by the High School band, with Superintendent Harrison marching along with the musicians, with a motley procession of trucks and cars following, all filled with laughing and shouting men and women and children, extending for about a mile behind the band.

Religious services were held later in the evening in several churches. Most were attended by large crowds. The next day, the celebration continued with all stores and factories closed.

In Aurora, the same intensive celebration took place with lots of noise and parades. The next day, the Aurora High School band, followed by hundreds of decorated cars and trucks paraded through the town and to Lawrenceburg and back. On the corner of Second and Mechanic Streets, three service men home on leave: Louis Goble, Louis Fahey and Ralph Kleuber, hung an effigy of Japanese War Minister General Tojo outside of Fehling's Soda Shop. That night, a huge bon-fire was burned on the same intersection. A drum corps played as the flames leaped higher than the buildings. The crowd cheered and rejoiced that the war was over at long last.

Servicemen would be coming home to Dearborn County and changing their uniforms for "civvies" anxious to get on with their lives. Tomorrow they would face a new technological, atomic world with a baby-boom of some 30 million (until 1950) brand new citizens.

V-J Day – Fill 'Er Up, no more rationing: (l. to r.) Lil Cook, Martha M. Harris, Evelyn S. Schulz (rear), Sheila O'Brien Ritzmann, Marjorie D. Robinson and Sally R. Polk.

V-J Day Celebration in Aurora

Book Donors

The Dearborn County Historical Society thanks the following donors for their contributions to help make this publication possible:

AMERICAN LEGION POST No. 239, Lawrenceburg

AMERICAN STATE BANK

AURORA CASKET COMPANY

FIRSTAR BANK

FRIENDSHIP STATE BANK

HAAG FORD SALES, INC.

H.J. LYNESS CONSTRUCTION, INC.

KENTUCKY FRIED CHICKEN (Lawrenceburg)

MAXWELL CONSTRUCTION

MERCHANTS AND TRUST CO. BANK (W. Harrison)

SEAGRAM, JOSEPH E. & SONS, INC.

SOUTHEASTERN BEVERAGES, INC.

STEDMAN MACHINE CO.

UNITED COMMUNITY BANK

Acknowledgments

In addition to the Dearborn County Historical Society Book Committee for Volume II of our pictorial history series of Dearborn County, we received various kinds of help from other people to produce this book. We wish to acknowledge this assistance which we very much appreciated.

As we noted in Volume I, a pictorial history requires many authentic photos of that particular time period. Consequently we requested Dearborn County people, some of whom now live in other places, and others to share with us their photos of family members, friends and acquaintances who participated in the armed forces or in notable a way on the Home Front during World War II. Once again, the response was gratifying. Special recognition is given to these people, without whom the book would have been impossible, in the section entitled "Photo Credits".

To help us, a non-profit organization, with production costs, we not only thank the pre-publication purchasers of the book, but also the Sponsors who are shown in a special section. Moreover, we give thanks to Mary O'Brien Gibson for funds from the Cornelius and Anna Cook O'Brien Foundation; and for grant funds from the Dearborn County Community Foundation.

For many hours of research in the local newspapers, we are indebted to Mona Bryan of Lawrenceburg. For an inordinate amount of research through people-contact, we thank Mary June Kennedy of Greendale, Alan Smith of Versailles and Jackie Donley of Aurora. Also we appreciate the help and courtesy shown us as we spent many hours reviewing military records in the County Recorder's office. And to the various Veteran Posts of Dearborn County, we appreciate their help in promoting book sales. Also thanks to Dick Lewis for his work in producing gift certificates.

For the work of typing all the written material in this book, we are indebted to the Retired Senior Volunteer Program, especially to Annette Windsor, and to the following people: Marsha Elliott, Shirley McGhee, Linda Teke and Cathy Ward.

Others who helped in gathering photos, gathering and writing information, and in many general ways, we thank the following: Ruth Gray, Lois Harper, Alberta Parker, Lois Parker, Suzanne Ullrich, Tom Ward and Jean Witte. The Book Committee, over the period of a year plus several months, did great work in the promotion and production of this book to provide a pictorial record of Dearborn County during the greatest of all wars, World War II.

Book Committee: (l. to r.) Seated: Irene Bultman, Louella Brooker, Carolyn McManaman, Frances Egner, and Robert Parker: Standing: Mark Thompson of MT Publishing Company, Carroll Sutton, Nelson Elliott, and Eric Smith

Bibliography

Books

Ambrose, Stephen, Editor, *American Heritage New History of World War II*. Penguin Group 1998.

Astor, Gerald. *Crisis in the Pacific.* Penguin Group 1996.

Bailey, Ronald. *The Home Front: U.S.A..* Time-Life Books, Inc. 1978.

Goldstein, Dillon and Wagner. *D-Day Normandy.* Brasseys (U.S.) 1994.

Keegan, John, *The Second World War.* Viking 1989.

Lecke, Robert. *Okinawa, The Last Battle of World War II.* Viking Penguin 1991.

Morison, Samuel Eliot. *The Two-Ocean War.* B.B.S. Publishing Corp. 1963.

Murray, Patrick G. E. *Victory in Western Europe. M.* Freedman Publishing Corp. 1999.

Murray, William and Millett, Alan. *A War To Be Won.* Harvard University Press 2000.

Booklets and Articles

Indiana at War. Indiana War History Commission 1951.

U.S. News and World Report. Issue of August 27, 1990.

U.S. News and World Report. Issue of May 23, 1994.

Time, Issue of August 28, 1989.

Newspapers (Issues of 1940-1945)

Aurora Bulletin
Lawrenceburg Press
Lawrenceburg Register

Photo Credits

Credits for photos are shown by pages and separated from top to bottom and/or right to left by semicolons. Dearborn County Historical Society photos are shown as DCHS.

Dust Jacket

Front Cover - DCHS, photographed by Robert Mattingly. Back Cover - Eric Smith. Front Flap - DCHS; Frank Savage; DCHS. Back Flap - Robert Steiner; Larry Steigerwald; DCHS.

Front and Rear Matter

Front End Piece - U.S. Navy. 2 - N.Y. Daily News. 3 - U.S. Navy.
Rear End Piece - DCHS

Chapter 1

4 - Rita Knue. 6 - Louella Brooker. 7 - Dianna McDonald; David Crouch; (bottom) Walter Hallfarth; Suzanne Ullrich. 8 - Leesa Wittenstrom; Dorothy Sedam; Anne Hays; (bottom) Dorothy Dixon; Dodie Baker. 10 - Inez Ebel. 11 - Ruth Lipscomb; Wesley Taylor. 12 - Alan Smith. 13 - Edward Miller; Dorothy Elliott. 15 - Carolyn McManaman. 16 - Ralph Rees; Ms. W. Ester. 17 - Margaret Pitts; Betty Gehring; Russel Steele. 18 - Mary June Kennedy; Marlene Kocher; Charles Klump. 19 - Carolyn McManaman; Lyndon Moon. 20 - Irwin Miller; Eric Smith. 21 - Ruth Lipscomb; Walter Neary; Dodie Baker. 22 - Ralph Bentle; Marie Seitz. 23 - Ms. K. Darling; Loretta Bihr; Suzanne Ullrich; Marcella Gulley. 24 - Murl Fox; Arnold Brauer; (bottom) Jean Miller; Eric Smith. 25 - Debbie Zimmer; (bottom) Robert Oelker; Carolyn McManaman.

Chapter 2

26 - National Archives. 28 - DCHS. 29 - Ms. M. Seitz; Ruth Gray; (bottom) Marcella Gulley; Howard McKee; Clarence Fondong. 30 - Marcella Gulley. 31 - Leslie Boone; Donna Fischer. 32 - Carl Harmeyer. 33 - Jack Lemm; Eric Smith. 34 - Edith Callon; Mrs. Arlie Baer. 35 - Michael Klump; Marvin Schultz. 36 - Robert Schwing; Suzanne Ullrich. 37 - William Ritzmann, Jr.; Vivian Lyness. 38 - Wilma Wittrick; Ms. M. Seitz. 39 - Carolyn McManaman; Louella Brooker. 40 - Opal LaFollette; Sylvester Neary. 41 - Robert Stainer; Wallace Boyles. 42 - John Edrington. 43 - Margaret Pitts; Ronald Nocks. 44 - Frank Cottingham; DCHS. 45 - Louella Brooker. 46 - National Archives.

Photo Credits

Chapter 3
48 - DCHS. 49 - Evelyn Schulz. 50 - Avis Geisert; Willis Bentle. 51 - Evelyn Lischkge; Mary Cash. 52 - William Ewan; Paul Sartin. 53 - Eleanor Ewbank; Eleanor Ewbank; Pat Lacey. 54 - James McManaman; George Fox. 55 - Clayton Stevens; Jean Bielby. 56 - Ralph Shilling; Carolyn McManaman. 57 - Robert Gardening. 58 - Robert Ryle. 59 - Ms. P. Tittle; Marvin Sizemore. 60 - Dale Schoeff. 61 - Eleanor Longcamp. 62 - Mary Murtaugh. 63 - John Probst. 64 - Mary Thomas. 65 - Sheila Ritzmann. 66 - Evelyn Hornbach; Eric Smith. 67 - Martha Boese; Carl Sykes. 68 - Louis Goble; G. Wilson Bentle. 69 - Paul Leive; Carl Harmeyer. 70 - Doris White. 71 - Suzanne Ullrich; Mary Folke. 72 and 73 - All from Debbie Zimmer. 75 - U.S. Navy.

Chapter 4
76 - U.S. Army. 78 - Mrs. Ben Gould; Lucille Dittmer. 79 - Howard McKee; Eric Smith; (bottom) Army Air Force; Ms. Ebel. 80 - Mary Mattingly (both). 81 - Mrs. Ben Gould; Army Air Force. 82 - Marie Seitz; Evelyn Schulz; Betty McLaughlin; (bottom) Robert Fox. 83 - Anna Kirehgassner; Mrs. Ben Gould. 84 - Patty Houston; Tonya Carroll. 85 - Neysa Lambert; Carolyn McManaman. 86 - Eric Smith; Suzanne Ullrich. 87 - Charles Givan; Carl Sykes. 88 - Milred Sweppenheise; Mrs. Shelby Cumming; Edith Blasdel. 89 - Martha Boese; Billie Henry. 90 - Bob Britton. 91 - William Knue. 92 - Ann Gillespie. 93 - Opal LaFollette. 94 - Louis Taylor. 95 - Mrs. James Steigerwald; Mrs. John Leiendecker. 96 - Mrs. Robert Cheek; Barbara Platt. 97 - Mrs. Dennis Dixon; Suzanne Ullrich. 98 - Anna Kirchgassner; Evelyn Schulz. 99 - Eric Smith; John Renck. 100 - Richard Kaffenberger. 101 - Paul Woliung, Wilbert Taylor. 102 - Leroy Seevers; DCHS. 103 - Gayle Combs. 104 - Stanley Vickroy. 107 - Leroy Schman. 108 - DCHS. 109 - Mrs. Ben Gould. 111 - Mrs. Ben Gould.

Chapter 5
112 - Carolyn McManaman. 113 - Larry Giffin. 114 - E.G. McLauglin. 115 - William Barrott. 116 - DCHS. 117 - Charles Taylor. 118 - Charlotte Horn. 119 - DCHS. 120 - Louella Brooker (both). 121 - DCHS. 122 - Marie Seitz. 123 - Henry Nanz. 124 - National Archives; DCHS. 125 - DCHS; Robert Ewbank. 126 - W.J. Burk. 127 - Keith Schultz.

Chapter 6
128 - DCHS. 131 - Rosemary Witt; John Probst; (bottom) Virginia Hess; Evelyn Schulz; Edith Callon. 134 - Roberta English; Dodie Baker; Edward Hartwell (bottom) Evelyn Schulz; William Doerr; Marjorie Gannaway. 135 - Eloise Lambert; Judy Hughes. 139 - DCHS.

Photo Credits

Chapter 7
140 - National Archives. 144 - Martha Sedler; Tonya Carroll; Larry Steigerwald. 145 - Mary Adams. 146 - Ms. Stutz; Mary J. Terrill. 147 - Frank Savage - Suzanne Ulrich. 148 - Robert Miller; Ruth Stadtlander. 149 - Mary Grieve; Bobbie Knue. 150 - Carl Harmeyer. 151 - Leland Teaney. 152 - Carolyn McManaman (both). 153 - Evelyn Schulz; Margaret Scholle. 152 - Eloise Lambert; Carl Harmeyer. 153 - Robert Steiner. 156 - Bernice Wells; Willard Aust. 157 - Calvin Klingelhoffer; Ruth Lipscomb; Edward Miller. 158 - Mark Widolf, Walter Nelson. 159 - Carl Skykes; Cindy Holland; Eric Smith. 160 - Dodie Baker; William Barrott II. 161 - G. Wilson Bentle; Willis Bentle. 162 - Cindy Holland; Mrs. Tom Cook. 163 - DCHS; Mrs. Tom Watts. 164 - Frank Cottingham. 165 - Clara McCool; Mrs. K. Darling. 166 - Orpha Sykes. 167 - Martha Ziegler; Ms. L. HoIsclaw. 168 - Richard Horn; Evelyn Hornbach. 169 - Donna Hoff, Louella Brooker. 170 - Jean Fulton; John Klump. 171 - Carolyn McManaman; D.J. Fisher. 172 - Harvey Poshard. 173 - Donna Fisher. 174 - Nancy Bennett. 175 - Eric Smith; G. Wilson Bentle. 177 - Joy Rice. 178 - Helen Tettenhorst. 179 - Frank Savage; Leesa Wittenstrom.

Chapter 8
180 - National Archives. 183 - Robert Parker. 186 - Bernice Wells; Martha Sedler; Alan Smith. 187 - Elmer Bischoff; Jerri Gillespie; Adrian Chatham. 188 - Pauline Collier (both). 189 - John Connolly; Pauline Collier. 190 - Robert Dewers. 192 - Steve Fehling; Bonnie St. Germain. 193 - Mary Eisenshank; Dan Rider. 194 - Eric Smith, Marge Hartman. 195 - Doris Stutz. 196 - Willis Chalk. 197 - Edward Hartwell; Vernedine Gould; L. Jeffries. 198 - Richard Kaffenberger; Rita Knue. 199 - Rita Knue; Mary June Kennedy. 202 - Mary Thamann. 203 - Margaret McClanahan. 204 - Mary Thamann; Martha Schoeff. 205 - Henry Peters. 206 - Clyde Meyers; Kathryn Steele; A. T. Schuman. 207 - Eric Smith; Russell Smith; Mary Thomas. 208 - Thomas Largent. 209 - Mary Mattingly. 210 - Donna Beebe (all). 211 - Albert Schuman; Eric Smith. 212 - Harley Uhlmansiek; Donna Farrar. 213 - Dorothy Dixon; Marge Kittle. 214 - Don Marshall; Tonya Carroll. 215 - Virgil Trennepohl. 216 - Clyde Fairfield; Dan Whiteford; Jim Mulroy. 217 - Lloyd Shuter; Verna Schuette. 218 - Charles Jameson; John Lemm; Carolyn McManaman. 219 - Charles Fletcher; Suzanne Ullrich. 220 - Marie Hizer; Caroline Seaver; Mary June Kennedy. 221 - Thelma Acra; Caroline Seaver; Austin Smith. 222 - Lawrence Andres. 223 - James Lyttle; Mrs. Shelby Cummins. 224 - Mrs. Nelson Davis. 225 - Nancy Carrier; Bob Hannan; Eric Smith; Daniel Hopping. 226 - Mary Ramey. 227 - Daniel Hopping; Mary Ramey; Dan Rider; Gloria Rumsey.

Photo Credits

Chapter 9

228 - National Archives. 230 - U.S. Army. 232 - National Archives. 235 - National. Archives; Mrs. Harry Watts. 236 - Ron Nocks; Donald Schmeltzer. 237 - Eric Smith. 238 - Willis Chalk. 239 - Gould Warneford. 240 - Ralph Rees; Rita Knue. 241 - Robert Parker; Mary Weddle. 242 - Robert Savage. 243 - Louis Goble; Dale Nowlin. 244 - Slyvester Neary. 245 - Art Brandt; Joe Walser; John Lemm. 246 - Donna Fisher; Bernette Conrad; Adrian Chatham. 247 - Eric Smith; Sharon Todd. 248 - Wanda Waldon; Ervin Bischoff. 249 - Lucy McLerster; Rita Young. 250 - Pat Lacey; Alfred Lang. 251 - Ruth Stadtlanders; Eric Smith. 252 - Suzanne Ullrich. 254 - Martha Boese. 253 - Clara Lewis; Register. 255 - William Knue; Eric Smith. 256 - Mrs. E. Kirsch; Thomas Largent. 257 - Geneva Marshall; Robert Lamkin; Jeanne Klingelhoffer. 257 - Lucille Dittmer; John Miller; Richard Kaffenberger. 258 - Virginia Brown; Alan Smith. 260 - Elizabeth Rullman; Clyde Myers; John Schott. 261 - Andrea Marine; Juliana Gilb. 262 - Mrs. Philip Given; Robert Myers. 263 - Louella Brooker; Alan Smith; Joy Rice. 264 - Dorman Lange; Noel Hess. 265 - Martha Sedler; Evelyn Hernbach. 266 - Henry Nanz; Gloria Rumsey; Dan Whiteford. 267 - David Teke; Mary E. Rupp; Mrs. Robert Steiner. 268 - Mrs. Emmert Kirsch; Wilma Wittrock. 269 - Anna Kuebel; Daniel Hopping. 270 - Mrs. Willis Sandbrink; W.J. Burk. 271 - Sally Polk; Paula Gilbert; Mrs. Shelby Cummins. 272 - Bill Jackson; Rita Knue; E. Enneking. 273 - Louella Brooker; Rita Knue. 274 - Mrs. S. Melson; Richard Kaffenberger. 275 - Lucille Dittmer; Roy Lambert; Richard Kittle; Eric Smith; Garnet Loniaker; Charlotte Horn. 276 - Ron Nocks; Mary Lampert; Frank Heine. 277 - Eric Smith; Bernice Wells; Margaret Beebe; Ellen Crontz; Henry Evans. 278 - Charlotte Hoffman; Evelyn Schulz. 279 - L. Harmeyer; Murl Fox; Irene Bultman; N. Fondong; N. Fondong; Robert Parker; Virginia Brown; Mary Thomas. 280 - Eric Smith; R.F. Connolly; Mary F. Murray. 281 - Dan Whiteford; Harry Cheek; Evelyn Schulz; Wilma Holden; Jean Cook. 282 - Charles Ketcham; Mrs. Raymond Kern. 283 - Eric Smith; Betty McLaughlin; Janet Craven; Nancy Creech; Edith Rullman. 284 - Eric Smith. 285 - Suzanne Ullrich; Rita Knue; Claude Decker. 287 - Eric Smith. 291 - Ann Gillespie; Mary Thomas; Mary Thomas; Louella Brooker; JoAnn See; Nancy Creech. 292 - Sally Polk. 293 - Louis Goble (all).

Index

A

Abbot, Robert 288
Abdon, Edgar 110, Flo Hill 118, Frank 110, William (Bill) 155
Abshire, A.E. 115
Acra, Clayton 220, 221 Thelma 299
Adams, Mary 299
Adsit, William 288
Aikman, John 155
Albright, George (Honk) 156, Noah 278, Noah 278, William 156
Ambrose, Stephen 296
Anderson, Donald 278, Donald 278, Harry 288, Lloyd 97, Mary Fox 130, William 28
Andres, E. William 72, Edgar 72, 73, Edmund 25, Ella Florence 72, 73, Lawrence 299, Paul 72, Paul 25, 72, Richard 25, 72, 73, Victor 72, 73, Virgil 221, 222, Wilber 72, 73, William 72
Andrews, Carl 156, Delmar 278, 279, Wilford 278, 279
Arbaugh, Dennis 288
Armbruster, Leo 64
Armbuster, Francis 288
Armstrong, Edward 97, Herschel 288, Norman 110
Arnold, Vincent 288
Ashby, Clifford 288
Ashcraft, Everett 288, Howard 201, Ira 288
Astor, Gerald 296
Aust, Edward 186, Herbert 156, Willard 156, 299, William 39
Aylor, Robert 92

B

Bachelor, Harold 80
Back, Harlan 288
Badenhop, Melvin 92, Robert 269, William 269
Baer, Arlie 34, 35, 297, Paul 288
Bailey, Ronald 296
Baker, Armada Fisher 130, 134, Clinton 250, Delbert 179, Dodie 297, 298, 299, Earl 186, Eldon 263, Floyd 186, Ford 88, Frederick 150, Gilbert 216, Harold 216, Leroy 8, 16, Leslie 20, 21, Lester 160, Lloyd 219, Ralph 216, Robert 231, Russell 154, Walter 186, Willard 160
Bales, Edward 41
Banks, Charles 96, Joseph 288
Bansbach, Donald 250, Fred 189
Banta, Gale 115, 160
Barber, James 146
Barker, Ford 288, Gretna 131
Barnes, Burton 278, Frank 121, Hubert Estal 214, James 146, John 80, Robert 90
Barrott, Enos L. 240, Fred 96, William II 160, 299, William 160, 298, William, Sr. 115
Barrows, Carlos 90, Charles 88, Francis 216
Barry, James 251
Barry, John 186, 217
Barton, Omer 262, 263
Bascom, Alger 160, Edward 278, Herbert 278, Herbert 291
Batchelor, Harold 92
Bateman, George 127
Bauer, Earl 288, Leonard 90
Bayne, John 288
Beard, William 269
Beatty, Leonard 276
Beckemeyer, Marvin 186
Beckett, James (Jim) 36
Beckman, Leroy 214
Beckmeyer, Marvin 186
Becraft, Leslie 12
Beebe, Donna 299, Eugene 277, 278, Margaret 300
Behr, Louis 284, 285
Belker, John 288
Bell, Newton 262, 263
Bennett, Charles 6, 98, Delmar 84, 106, George 31, 40, Nancy 299, Paul 160
Benning, Elmer 39, Russell 160
Bentle, Clayton 284, 291, Elbert 50, 68, G. Wilson 160, 161, 298, 299, George 161, Gerald 92, Ralph 22, 297,

Willis 161, 298, 299, Wilson 175
Berning, Norman 186
Betscher, Richard 71
Bieker, John 15
Bielby, Chester 55, Chester 55, E. G. 14, Jean 298
Bihr, Albert 61, Edward 18, Edward 23, Jacob 61, Loretta 297
Billups, Christopher 68
Bird, J.C. 288
Birmingham, Mary Jane 130
Bischoff, Cletus 288, Elmer 186, 187, 299, Ervin 248, Ervin 300
Black, William 275
Blackburn, Earle 39, Robert 92
Blasdel, Edith 298, Elvin 80, 88, Harley 276, Lester 224, 276
Block, George 288, Martha 130
Bloom, Denton 63, Louis 288
Bobrink, Charles 241
Bocock, Carl 186, Earl 12, Earl E. 12, Gordon 61
Boehler, Norbert 161, Oliver 18, Oliver R. 18, Otto 51, Otto T., Jr. 56
Boese, Martha 298, 300, Robert 89
Booher, Lance 115
Boone, Leslie 31, 44, 297
Borders, Carl 28

Borgman, Donald 269, Harold 288
Bosco, James 288
Bossong, Harold 161
Bourquein, Russell 161
Bovard, Louis 269, Stowe 161
Bowker, Marvin 291, Monroe 283, 284,
Bowles, Anson 288
Bowling, Conley 288, David 186
Boyd, Bruce 262, Bruce 271, Bruce Arthur 275, Samuel 270, 271
Boyles, Robert 38, Wallace 36, 41, 297
Braden, Harold 288
Bradley, Omar 183
Brandel, Margaret Schneider 130, 134, 135
Brandt, Art 300, Bill 152, Mervin 40, William (Bill) 152
Brauer, Arnold 22, 24, 297
Braun, John 61, 90, Robert 161
Briggs, Marvin 40
Brightwell, Woodford 61
Britton, Bob 298, James 90
Brookbank, Robert 187, Victor 186, 187
Brooker, Louella 120, 295, 297, 298 299, 300
Brooks, Eugene 161, J.W. 187, James 41
Brossart, Charles 187
Brown, Charles 63, Harold 106, Lloyd 288, Raymond 161, Virginia 300, Watson 187
Browning, Earl 186, Philip 90
Bruce, Charles 150, Marion 10
Brunner, Arthur 264, 265, William (Bill) 273
Bryant, Louis 187
Buchanan, Roscoe 213, Steward 96, William 150, Edward 186
Bulthaup, Leroy 150
Bultman, Irene 295, 300
Burgess, Leroy 288
Burk, W.J. 298, 300
Burkham, Douglas R. 219
Burnett, Floyd 93
Burton, Dorothy 133, Von 90
Busse, Dorman 237
Bussong, Harold 288
Butler, Glenn 161
Butterly, Robert 161
Byrant, Mary Jane 130

C

Cain, William 162
Caldwell, Alex 288, James 88, Raymond 96, William 283, 284
Callaway, Fritz 255
Callon, Edith 131, 133, 297, 298, Ray 283, Raymond 284, Roy 34, Rullman 131
Calvert, Russell 162

Cambell, Floyd 284,
Canfield, Loren 22, 25
Caplinger, Harold 288
Carlson, Stanley 162
Carr, Charles 90, George 280, Harold 63, Ralph 288, Russell 246
Carrier, Nancy 299
Carroll, Tonya 298, 299
Cart, Donald 246
Carter, Evelyn 133, William 162, Zephyr 288
Case, Ray 288
Caseltine, Louis 288
Casey, Donald 189
Cash, Arnold 7, 11, Elzie 51, 62, Eugene 188, Herbert 12, Mary 298, Ronald 90
Cavendish, William 63
Chalk, Willis 238, 299, 300
Chambers, Francis A. 187, Ivan 17, Morton 64, Ralph 58
Chandler, Ralph 163
Chapin, Leroy 288
Charlton, Amos 161, 163
Chase, Clifford 187, George 90, Richard 255
Chastain, James 255
Chatham, Adrian 246, 299, 300, Dallas 187, Lloyd 238
Cheek, Charles 188, Clyde 188, Harry 280, 281, 300, Louis 237, Raymond 163, Robert 96, 298

Cheever, Russell 21
Childers, William 237
Christian, Bernie 90, Bill 189, Carl 90, Edward (Bud) 189, Thomas 63, Vernon 274
Clark, Chester 163, Earl 163, Ester 133, Harvey 270, Robert 175, Wilbur 88
Clause, J. Romain 9
Clifton, Ralph 255
Coghill, Harold 90
Coldwell, Alex 58
Cole, Carroll 162, Harold 162, 156
Coleman, David 288
Colen, Clifford 156, Rudolph 187
Collier, John 188, Pauline 299, Ralph 188, Richard 123, Tom 189
Collins, William 162
Combs, Clyde 16, French 257, French 288, Gayle 298, Taylor 22, 24
Conaway, Estal 271, James 94, Norman 211, Preston 211
Connelly, E. Ford 189, Harold 189, Robert 280
Connolly, E. Ford 189, John 299, R.F. 300
Conrad, Bernette 300, Harold 188, Robert 246
Conway, Emily Baker 133
Cook, Elmer 29, 30, Jean 300, Lil 292, Robert 280, 281, Thomas 162, Tom 299, William 162
Cormican, Roger 20
Cornelius, Henry 255, Russell 88, Walter 98
Cornett, Carter 94, Chester 288
Corning, William 221
Corns, Mildred Hilker 130, Roy 12
Cosby, Jerome 162
Cottingham, Alfred 162, Frank 63, 297, 299, Harry 40, Stanley 189
Cotton, George 94, Robert 189, Virgil 238
Coughlin, Frank 94
Courter, Ralph 280
Crabb, John 288
Crable, Virgil 288
Craig, Estal 98, Harold 187, Melvin 38
Craigmile, Malcom 163
Cramer, Clarence 25, John 9
Crandall, Richard 246, Robert 187
Craven, Jack 283, 284, Janet 300
Creech, Nancy 300
Crider, Gerald 163, 165, Oakey 163
Criswell, Paul 288
Crontz, Arthur 187, Ellen 300, Robert (Buck) 277
Cross, Edward 288
Crouch, David 297, Lee 10, Leonard 187, W. Lee 155, 7
Crowe, Eugene 6
Crowism, Jim 116
Cumming, Shelby 298
Cummins, Edmon 271, Roscoe 60, Shelby 299, 300
Cunningham, Benjamin 255
Curtis, H. S. 271, Robert 163
Cusick, Michael 189
Cutter, Charles 189, Lester 189, Richard 63, Robert (Bob) 36, Russell 189
Cuttingham, Alford 94
Czarniecki, Leonard 189

D

Daley, Dan 271
Dall, Bernard 246
Darbo, Robert 30
Darling, Arthur 190, Dale 190, Donald 171, Horace 69, K. 297, 299, Kenneth 163, 165
Darlington, Elmo 220
Dason, Robert 288
Dau, William 257
Daugherty, Kenneth 171
Dausch, Frederick 246, James 94
David, Joe 163
Davidson, Walter 221
Davies, Albert 267, Denver 190, William 288, Worthington 191, Alvin 59
Davis, Clare 65, Clarence 88, Elmer 124, Harold 34, Jim 34, Lester 267, Nelson 224, 229, Richard 288, Wilber 94
Dawson, Donald 255, Frederick 288, Richard 171, Robert 190, Roy 94
Day, James 171
Dean, Earle 284, 285
Deaton, James 41
Deck, Ernest 171
Decker, Claude 284, 285, 300, Walter 171,
Dell, Carl 83
Demmons, Pete 269
Denmure, Clayton 191
Dennerline, Earl 83, Forrest 171, Jack 171, Jerry 271, Richard 220
Dennis, Carl 246, Charles 190, David 190, Edward 288, John 191, Rudolph 190, William 63
Dent, John 190
Deron, Harry 191, Harvey 190
Detmer, Eugene 94
Detmer, Harley 61
Dewers, Kenneth 271, Robert 190, 299
Dibble, Johnson 163
Dicken, Courtney 151, Courtney, Jr. 171
Dickerson, Harry 191
Dieselberg, Frank 190
Diezman, Albert 189
Dils, Charles 171, Donald 246, Howard 171

Disbro, Warren 61
Dittmer, Gayle 78, 88, Larry 288, Lucille 298, 300
Dixon, Dennis 94, 97, 298, Dorothy 297, 299
Dober, Joseph 269
Dobs, Lawrence 288
Doegnes, John 94, Raymond 94, Leslie 94
Doerr, Virginia 133, 134, William 298
Doggett, A.H. 191, Arthur 246
Donley, Jackie 295
Donn, Frank 288
Donnelly, Tom 191, William 94
Dowdee, Robert 191
Downey, Frank 60, Morrison 267, Paul 94,
Doyle, Lawrence 288
Draper, Norbert 171, 173, Orville 246, 247
Draut, Oakey 56, 67
Driver, Edward 191, Hal 257
Drosgia, Edward 166
Duncan, Buford 191
Dunn, Ennis 288, Irvin 61, Melvin 166, Myrle 267, Norbert 288, Raymond 85, Thomas 191

E

Eaglin, Charles 237, Denzil 166, Raymond 243, Russell 252
Ebel, Inez 297, Philip 85
Ebnet, Adam 25
Eckler, Clarence 191, Estel 288, Fredrick 191, Leroy 210, Wilbur 210
Eckstein, Henry 236
Edrington, John 42, 297
Edrington, Leona 133
Edwards, Clifford 268, Frederick 214, Hugh 191, James 214, Johnson 288, Ralph 151, 158
Egner, Frances 295
Ehlers, Lester 251, Willard 192
Eisenhower, Dwight D. 77
Eisenshank, Mary 299, Robert 192, 193
Elbrecht, Quentin 88
Elliott, Dorothy 297, Lee R. 252, Loren (Hobe) 13, Marsha 295, Nelson 295
Ellis, Vernon 252, Walter 288
Elrod, Hugh 288
Elston, Delmar 288
Emerson, Raymond 288
Emery, Albert 192, Charles 126, Everett 88, Hubert 51, Roy 51
Emmert, William 288
Engler, Cletus 166
English, Glenn 264, Roberta 133, 134, 298,
Enneking, E. 300, Edwin 272, 273
Ennis, Alfred 62, Alfred (Squire) 51
Ent, Norman 166
Ernest, Donald 152
Ester, Curtis 268, Glenn 21, W. 297, Willard 16, Willard 16
Evans, Henry 276, 277, 300, Norbert 272
Everett, Carl 51, Eugene 41
Ewan, Richard 52, William 298
Ewbank, Eleanor 298, Gerald 52, 53, James 192, Robert 298, William 51, William (Bill) 125
Ewing, Clifford 288

F

Faber, Harry 211
Fackler, Paul 192
Fagaly, William 81
Fahey, Leo T. 166, Louis 192, 193, 292
Fairchild, James 88, 192 Clyde 216, 299
Farmer, James 236, Norbert 288
Farrar, Donna 299, James 212,
Fawcett, Willard 17
Fehling, Charles W. 19, Edward 115, Edward F. 192, Ep 192, Steve 299
Fehrman, Harold 166
Feller, C.E. 193, Cornelius 288, Leroy 288
Fenske, Albert 288
Ferdon, Earl 153, 267
Ferry, George 214
Fette, Robert 252, Russel 236
Feustel, James 272
Fields, Roscoe 288
Findley, William 288
Finney, Jack 21
Fiorito, Francis (Ted) 8, 18
Fischer, Donna 297, Erwin 156
Fischvogt, Orville 221
Fish, Oplet 88
Fisher, D.J. 299, Donna 299, 300
Fitch, Edith 30
Fitzpatrick, Charles 31, Walter 166
Fletcher, Charles 219, 299
Flick, Harold 288
Foble, Herbert 272
Foggle, Russell 288
Fogle, Harold 236, Leslie 20
Foley, James 288
Folke, Alvin 71, Mary 298
Folsom, Grace 132, Lee 221
Folzenlogen, Ralph 52
Fondong, Clarence 29, 31, 297, N. 300
Footon, Cecil 288
Ford, Gerald 49, Raymond 288, William 211
Foster, William 288
Fowler, Charles 52, James 166, Ora 288, William 52
Fox, Bernard 55, Chester 216, George 278, 279, 298, George H. 54, 67, Keith 89,

Murl 21, 24, 297, 300, Raymond 89, Robert 193, 298, Thomas 270
Frakes, Madison 193, Robert 238
Franz, Alex 257
French, David 288, Harold 262, 263
Frey, Lawrence 288
Frieberger, Lee 52
Fritch, Stanley 221
Fryer, Ben 156, 159
Fuchs, Frank 85
Fuernstein, Charles 193
Fuestal, James 288
Fugate, Robert 193
Fugate, Roger 213
Fugitt, Jerome 35, John 38, Reuel 167
Fulton, Jean 299, Walter 39, William 167, 170
Furtrick, Ralph 17

G

Gamble, Gale 288
Gannaway, Marjorie 298
Gardening, Robert 56, 57, 298,
Gardiner, Alex 30
Garner, William A. 250
Garnier, Robert 89
Garrison, Howard 288
Gash, Charles 288
Gaynor, Bernard 167
Gehrig, Betty 297, Carl 16, 17
Geisert, Avis 298, Thaddeus, Jr. 212, Ray 50

Geisler, Delver 211
Genter, Edward 9
Gentrup, Charles 66
Gerkepott, Elmer 62
Gerkin, Floyd 154, 165
Germain, Bonnie St. 299
Gibbons, Robert 288
Gibbs, Samuel 288
Giblin, Richard 193
Gibson, Mary O'Brien 295
Giffin, Clayton 167, Larry 298
Gilb, Juliana 300, William 261, 262
Gilbert, Albert 288, Herbert 267, Paul 271, Paul (Ted) 270, Paula 300
Gilland, Grover 169
Gillespie, Ann 298, 300, Frank 194, Glenn 167, Jack 167, 171, Jerri 299, Lester 257
Gillman, Harry 54, Paul 167, Robert 288
Gillum, Della 132
Gilmore, Delmar 194, Loren 156, Ralph L. 167
Givan, Charles 298, Philip (Zeke) 167
Given, Charles 87, 89, Philip 167, 262, 300
Glackin, Wilbur 268
Glenn, Charles 288, Chester 85, Robert 193, 211, William 153
Glowka, Wilber 247
Goble, Louis 242, 243, 292, 298, 300

Godfrey, Earl 193, Harry 6, 13
Goldstein, Dillon 296
Gompf, Edwin 193, Kenneth 167
Good, Kathleen 132
Goodman, Awanda Calvert 132
Goodpaster, Clayton 156, Elmer 193, Elva B. 132, Frank 193, Jack 12, William 288
Goodwin, Charles 288
Gordon, Howard 169
Gordson, Edward 288
Gotman, Robert 288
Gould, Ben 298, Vernedine 299, William (Ben) 83, 84
Graber, Louis 288
Graf, Wilbur 193
Grall, James 288
Granard, Harold 194
Granatir, Margaret Hartwell 132, 134
Graves, Dorothy 132, Perry 85, Willard 242
Gray, George 89, Lawson 58, Ruth 295, 297
Greathouse, Guy 242
Green, Donald 244, Earl 169, Fernindand 194, George 240, Leroy 288, Ollie 89, Robert L. 194
Greene, Lindon 288
Gregory, John 57
Greive, Glenn 156, Norvin 85, Paul 149
Grelle, Allen 149

Grenat, Joe 115
Gridley, Robert 288
Grieve, Mary 299, Norvin 55, Paul 169
Griffin, Charles 194
Griffith, Louis 271
Grimsley, Charles 221, Dale W. 267, Frank 194, James 169
Grizzel, William 36
Grosgia, Charles 58
Grosrenaud, John 269
Gross, Thomas 58, 271
Grubbs, Floyd 274, Howard 288, Ivan R. 247, James 237, Roger 194
Guard, Chester (Pie) 57, Leroy 89, Orville 194
Guermely, Carl 58
Guernsey, Carl 288
Gulley, Carlyle 8, 10, 29, Denver 29, 30, Eugene 220, Harry 29, 31, Leroy 149, Marcella 297, Melvin 194, Woodrow W. 8, 10
Gullion, Charles 288
Gutman, Charles 288
Gutzweiler, George 123

H

Haag, Lester 65
Haas, Clarence 288
Hafenbritle, George 250
Haggard, John 288
Hale, Cornelius 288
Hall, Amos 250, George 255, Hughes 219, Willard 288

Hallfarth, Walter 7, 10, 30, 297
Hamill, James 288
Hamilton, Charles 248, George 288, Hubert 194, Mary 132
Hance, James 264
Hanes, Hazron 288
Hannah, John 263
Hannan, Bob 299, John 224, 225
Hansell, Wayne 65
Hanson, Arthur 288
Harcourt, Lowell 69
Harmeyer, Carl 154, 297, 298, 299, L. 300, Raymond 224, 225
Harmon, George 53, 54
Harney, Kenneth 169
Harper, Ellsworth 288, Hubert 195, Lois 295, Robert 236
Harris, Jake 288, Martha M. 292
Harry, E.G. 114, 121, Emmet 82, 85
Hart, Carl 145, Joseph 288
Hartman, Alvin 194, Joseph 18, Marge 299, Robert 218
Hartwell, Arthur (Bo) 237, Edward 196, 298, 299, Ernest 196
Harves, Robert 288
Hassmer, Anthony 121, 221
Hastings, Edgar A. 54, Robert 23
Hauntz, Henry 65
Havey, Harold 274
Hawkins, Ernest 196
Hayes, Mark 288

Hays, Anne 297
Hearne, Charles 288
Heath, Clarence 149, Orville 85
Heaton, Charles 288
Heine, Frank 276, 300
Heitman, Carl 93
Heitmeyer, Horace 93
Heller, Alton 169, Alvin 242, Givan 126, Virgil 41
Helm, John 288
Hemke, Raymond 267
Hemming, Walter 218
Hempling, Henry 169
Henderson, James 242
Henke, Carl 288
Henry, Billie 298, Dale 196, Herschel 85, Ralph 169, Robert 89, Russell 169
Henson, Charles 74, Edward 74, Ernest 51, 74, John 74, Roy 74, Roy 288, Thomas 74, Thomas (Tom) 37, William 74
Hernbach, Evelyn 300
Herndon, Charles 288
Herring, Horace 288
Herron, William 288
Herzog, Carl 169, Gene 288
Hess, Hendrick 288, Noel 264, 300, Virginia 298, 131, 132
Hickey, Everett 288
Hicks, Fred 288, John 84
Hiett, George 288
Higgins, Eugene 149
Higham, Raymond 196

Hill, Charles 288, Edward 196, Eugene 289, Frank L. 168, Leonard 169, Stanley 289
Hinman, Louis 289
Hinson, Louis 289, Roy 41, William 274
Hizer, Darcy Adelmore (Delmore) 220, Marie 299
Hodges, Edwin 289
Hodges, James 168
Hodges, Rodney 261
Hoff, Alfred 168, 169, Donna 299, Ellsworth 289, Virgil 168
Hoffman, Charlotte 300, Edward (Boob) 248, Harry E., Jr 266
Hoffmeier, Edward 271, Victor 84, 91
Hogan, Albert 289, Paul 69
Hoisclaw, L. 299
Holdcraft, David 269
Holdcraft, Elmer 248
Holden, George 280, 281 Ben Jr. 195, Wilma 300
Holland, Cindy 299, Harley 39, John 44, 45, Sherman 284
Holliday, Marvin 265
Holman, Robert 219
Holzbacher, Lester 195
Honschell, George 168, Leonard 168, Robert 168
Hooper, Walter 247, Leslie 265

Hopping, Albert 268, 269, Daniel 299, 300, Frank 224, 225, William 226, 227
Horn, Charlotte 298, 300, George 118, Richard 168, 229
Hornbach, Charles 272, Evelyn 298, 299, Floyd 66, 264, 265, George 195, Joseph 168, Robert 96
Hornberger, Clarence 278, 279,
Horton, Acell 218, Chester 289, John 219, Leslie 218
Horwitz, Joseph 288
Hoskins, William 273
Houston, Elwood 84, Ewell 289, Patty 298, William 263
Houze, Ellis 195, Fred 195
Howard, Clarence 289, James 195, Paul 168, Walter 195
Hubbel, Mary Swift 136
Huber, Albert 56, Martin 56, 85, Robert (Mush) 150, William 219
Hudson, Delmar 289, Henry 210, Howard 168, John 84, 86
Huenefeld, Bernard 84
Huesman, Irvin 174
Huff, Charles 272, Clifford 289
Huffman, Donald 65, Dorance 175, Orville 289
Hughes, Edward 195,

James 23, John W. 7, 11, Judy 298, Judy Mckain 135, 136, Luther 149
Hugo, Herman 30
Hulett, Glenn 289
Humble, Robert 273, William (Bill) 168, 169
Hunefield, Robert 175
Hunter, Elmer 289, Frank 195, Jack 42, Maurice 215, Morris 195, William 85
Hurd, Eugene 240, George 263, Joseph 36
Huston, Robert 289
Hutcher, George 288
Hutchinson, Frank 123
Hutton, Fred 289
Hyatt, Richard 289
Hyde, Edwin 289, Louis 195
Hyman, Clyde 149

I

Ingram, Lloyd 65
Inman, Edward 196
Irvin, Lloyd 65
Ison, Herman 289

J

Jackson, Bill 272, 300, C.A. 114, Clinton 289, Elmer 196, James 213, John 6, 12, Kenneth 273, Milo 289, Robert 84, Russell 175, Thomas 145, Walter 272, William (Bill) 245, 272
Jacobs, Carl 56, Holland 289, Jim 146, Loren 272
Jacques, Earl 56, 84
Jameson, Charles 218, 299, Clarence 42, Harold 196, 197
Jarvis, George 236, James 261, William 289
Jefferies, Leroy 196
Jeffries, Earl 273, John 84, Leroy 197, 299, Ralph 256
Jobe, Herman 196
Johnson, Donald 196, Glenn 196, H.T. 115, Harold 289, Henry 258, John 84, Kathryn 136, Lyndon 49, Margie Carter 136, Michael 291, Ralph 289, Wilbur 261
Johnston, Charles 36, Dormand 97
Jones, Elmer 84, Gilbert 289, Lavern 289, Walter 261
Justice, William 289
Justin, William 3

K

Koons, Ada 136
Kreinhop, Margie 136
Kabakoff, Jacob 15
Kaffenberger, Edward 100, James 274, Raymond 198, Richard 258, 298, 299, 300
Kaiser, Alvin 289, Carl 84, Dormand 260, Howard 198, William 174
Kammeyer, Irvan 198, Lloyd 289
Kane, Leo 56
Karr, Burl 198, Max 56, Tilden (Til) 11
Karrer, Leroy 198, Robert 198
Karst, Hazel 136
Keegan, John 296
Keith, Cecil 149, Miller 18
Keller, Robert 258
Kellner, Leo 57
Kemper, Warren 149
Kennedy, Herbert 170, Jack 258, Mary June 295, 297, 299, Robert G. 97, Robert J. 280, Robert V. 198, 199
Kent, James 272, Orville 264, Patrick 198
Kern, Clifford 289, Raymond 282, 300
Kerr, Clifford 149, Fred 289, Jerald 170, Walter 14
Ketcham, Charles 282, 300
Keyes, Amos 274, 275, Thomas 289
Kidd, Thomas 149, 289
Kidder, George 170
Kidwell, Forest 79, 87, Oakley 198, Ralph 289
Kieffer, Lester 57
Kieninger, Lawrence 170
Kieter, Lester 240
Kieth, Gilbert 258
Kinder, Gilbert 274
King, Harlan 261, Ollis 263, Rufus 289
Kinnett, Harold 289, Irwin 149, Joseph 199
Kirchgassner, Anna 298, Robert 83
Kirsch, E. 300, Emmert 256, 300
Kittenbrink, Fred 261, Gene 176, Kenneth 157
Kittle, Earl 199, Floyd 199, Leo 170, Marge 299, Richard 273, 275, 300, Vernon 170
Klein, Bernard 170, Eugene 170
Klemm, Robert 258
Klepper, Ezra 199, Richard 222, Robert 289, William 87
Kleuber, Ralph 292
Kline, Allean 136
Klingelhoffer, Calvin 157, 299, Jeanne 300
Klinkerman, Martin 56
Klopp, Carl 289, Gene 157, Joseph 157
Klueber, Leslie 249, Rudolph 199
Kluebler, Francis 198
Klump, Charles 18, 297, John 170, 299, Michael 35, 36, 297
Knaus, Lionel 222

Knecht, Stanley 199
Kneuven, Clifford 81, 106
Knigga, Cornelius 248, Dale 36, Ernest 289
Knippenberg, Gene 97, Robert 170
Knittenbrink, Fred 199
Knoebel, Edward 279, 280,
Knue, Bobbie 299, Edward 170, George 240, Jean 272, Joseph 198, 199, Norbert 222, Paul 198, Rita 297, 299, 300, William 298, 300
Knueven, Howard 97, Joseph C. 146
Kocher, Bernard 199, Leo 258, Marlene 297
Koehler, Phillip 289
Kolb, Kenneth 289, Paul 240
Konradi, Glenn 238, 263, Lester 199
Koons, Charles 289, John 176
Korf, Fred 66
Korte, Anthony 289
Krah, Eugene 289
Kratzer, Harland 199
Kraus, Albert 224, John (Jack) 176, Leo 199, 224, Victor 224
Kremer, Louis 87, Melvin 274
Krider, William 273
Kroggell, Edward 87
Kuebel, Anna 300, Urban 268, 269
Kuhlman, Harley 289, Harold 289
Kuhlmeier, Clifford 258, Raymond 71
Kurte, Anthony 289
Kyle, Henry 289, Ray 123

L

Laaker, Dale 199, 243
Lacey, Joe 250, Pat 298, 300, Richard 145, Roy 250, Roy R. Jr. 274, Virgil 145
Lacy, Joe 252,
Lafollette, Gareld 93, Lavern 200, Opal 297, 298
Lageman, Clyde 289
Lake, Joseph 176, William 176
Laker, Elmer 218
Lambert, Buell 210, 211, Charles 154, Eloise 298, 299, Eloise Busse 135, Neysa 298, Raymond 250, Roy 245, 275, 300
Lamkin, John 289, Robert 257, 258, 300
Lampe, Orville 200
Lampert, Mary 300
Land, Clarence 263, Donald 214, William 147
Landman, Jack 289
Landrom, Donald 85
Landrum, Louis 282, 283
Lane, Charles 258, Orean 212
Lang, Alfred 250, 300, Lawrence 87
Langdon, Perin III 256
Lange, Delton 210, Dorman 264, 300, Freda 136, Ralph 97
Langon, Harry 58
Lanvermeyer, Reynold 268
Largent, Francis 289, John 256, Thomas 299, 300
Latimer, Donald 289
Lattire, Donsell 289
Lawrence, Donald 145, Harry 250, Nelson 212
Laws, Carl 214, Marcus 212
Lawson, Robert 70
Leasure, Robert 145
Lecke, Robert 296
Leclerc, Leon 215
Leffler, Donald 222, Earl 155
Leforge, Jesse 289
Leiendecker, John 95, 298
Leisure, Robert 152
Leive, Paul 69, 298
Lemm, Gerald (Jerry) 245, Jack 297, Jerry 249, John 245, 299, 300, John (Jack) 245, Paul 33, Robert 218
Lemmel, Dale 289
Lenk, Frank 256
Leonard, Raymond 157
Leslie, John 200
Levi, Earl 200
Lewis, Alonzo (Lonnie) 200, Clara 300, Dick 295, Elmer 289, John 240, Robert 176
Libbert, Edwin 244, Edwin, Jr. 252
Licking, Bobby 176
Liddle, Harold 289, John 252, Thomas 211
Liebecke, Robert 70
Liggett, Noble 147
Lindsey, Charles 97
Lingg, George 157
Linkmeyer, Denton 289
Lipscomb, Arthur 157, John 20, 21, Ruth 297, 299
Lischkge, Bobby 268, Curtis 115, Evelyn 298
Livingston, Ferrell 215
Lloyd, Samuel 289
Lockwood, Donald 200, Eugene 289
Loftus, Donald 289, Loren 88
Loh, Willard 218, William 289
Lommel, Carl 150
Long, James 58, Sidney 212, Vincent 212
Longcamp, Eleanor 298, Frank 155, Virgil 61
Loniaker, Garnet 273, 275, 300
Loomis, David 6
Losekamp, Bernard 123
Lotton, Virgil 200
Louden, Carl 289
Love, William 146
Lovelace, George 256
Lowe, Owen 211
Lower, Stanley 87
Luhrsen, John 71

Luke, Benjamin 56, Charles 200, Glen 273
Lusk, Paul 200
Lutherbeck, Joseph 70
Lutz, Robert 176
Lyness, Harry 37, Vivian 297
Lynn, Bennie 176, Herbert 289
Lyons, William W. 145
Lyttle, James 299, William (Bill) 223

M

Macker, William R. 202
Macy, Robert 200
Mahaffey, William 202
Mahler, Lloyd 93
Majorie, Kurtzman Mcdougal 137
Mangold, Albert 200, Clifford 91, Delmar 20, Johnny 202
Manning, Fred 91
Marine, Andrea 300
Markland, Harold 21, 92, Robert 201
Marks, Paul 91, Robert 201
Marksberry, Delton 204, 270, Orville 176, Winifred 258
Marlin, Robert 289
Marqua, Vermont 204
Marsh, Charles 153
Marshall, Don 299, Donald 214, Geneva 300, George 97, Stanley 70, William 256, 257
Martin, Chester 289, Cletus 204, Dorman 204, Ellsworth 203, Ercel 203, Harold 176, John 121, 177, Loren 203, Marion 289, Norman 97, Robert 6
Mason, Ralph 87, Roy 146
Massett, John 97
Massing, Edward 289
Mathias, Howard 67
Matson, Edgar 272
Matthews, C.H. 69, John 97, Omer 59
Mattingly, Mary 298, 299, Paul 203, Richard 80, 89, Robert 297
Mattox, Albert 272, Robert 55
Maxwell, George 91, 289
Mcadams, Ben 256, Foster 91, Guard 269, James 202, John 202, Kenneth 87, Lee 91, Leo 289, Raymond 91
McAllister, Benjamin 212, Jack 289, James 201, Arthur 268
McCann, Terrance 204, Vincent 202, 203
McCardle, Edward 249, Raymond 249
McCartney, Carroll 263
McCarty, Edward 263, James 165
McClain, Alvie 264, Ivan 201
McClanahan, Harold 203, John 213, Margaret 299
McClure, Shirley 123, William 91
McConnell, Edsel 203, Virgil 201, Carl 289
McCool, Clara 299, Julius 55, Leo F. 55, Milton 256, Thomas 203
McCright, Joseph 244, Mary Catherine 137
McCrory, Douglas 177
McDonald, Dianna 297
McElfresh, Griffin 201, Raymond 160
McGhee, Shirley 295
McGlover, George 289
McKain, Edwin 91, Robert 203, William 201
McKee, Howard 29, 79, 80, 297, 298, John 165, Paul 97, William 201
Mckinley, Hans 289, Harry 160, James 274
Mclaughlin, Betty 298, 300, E.G. 298
Mcleaster, Thomas 204, Thomas 249
McLerster, Lucy 300
McManaman, Carolyn 118, 295, 297, 298, 299, James 54, 298
McMullen, Alvin 92, Garnet 201, Grace 137, Ralph 97, Tommy Lou Strack 137, Wilbur 160
McMurray, Richard 201, Virgil 289
McNaughton, Vernon 95
McQueen, Noble 289
McReynolds, George 202
McSwain, William 202
McWethy, John 261
Medecke, James 289
Melson, S. 300, Samuel 274
Mendel, Walter 177
Mendell, Charles 91, Donald 289, Howard 157, Norman 91
Menning, Fred 256
Mericle, Floyd 289
Merritt, Harold 279, 289
Mess, Max 289
Messang, Lester 64
Mettler, Floyd 100
Metz, Edwin 38
Meyer, Arthur 177, Euene 95, Francis 177, John 289, Millard 269, Russell 201
Meyers, Clarence 289, Clyde 264, 299, Gerald (Tug) 19, Harlan 95
Mickens, Eugene 157
Miles, Herbert 157, Parker 54, Willis 93
Milholland, John 95
Miller, Donald 201, 249, Edward 157, 297, 299, Gerald 289, Gilbert 158, Henry 177, Irwin 20, 297, James Louis 158, Jean 297, John 258, 300, Lloyd D. 57, Lloyd J. 203, Maurice 17, 24,

Morris 289, Paul 106, Paul W. 65, Ralph 264, Ray 262, Raymond 263, Robert 148, 299, Thomas E. 202, 284, Thomas H. 177, Tom 217, Wilbur 66
Millett, Alan 296
Millican, Vincent 87
Milligan, Glenn 203, Raymond 158
Minger, Clarence 210, Earl 210, Robert 210
Minneman, Jacob 66
Mirick, Hansel 202, Russell 289
Moeller, Howard 40
Molter, Michel 153, Omer 95, Tom 95, Wilmer 158, 203
Mondary, Victor 153, 241 Floyd 151
Moody, Alvin 202, George 177, Robert 95
Moon, Howard 289, Lyndon 19, 297
Moore, Arthur 87, 289
Moorehead, James 51, Robert 55
Morand, Clarence (Denny) 153, Lawrence 216, Walter 87, 88
Morehead, Hobart 202, Orville 95
Morgan, Samuel 289
Morison, Samuel Eliot 296
Morling, Chester 236, Edith 137
Morrell, Robert 93

Morris, Edwin 158, L. H. 95, Lawrence 252, Marcus 214, Russell 268, Warren 95
Morrison, Charles 217
Morrow, John 151
Morter, Omer 289
Mosley, Carl 36, Miller, Jr. 241, William 289
Mueller, Howard 41, Paul 19
Mulroy, Jim 299, Paul 216
Munch, Theodore 289
Murdock, Howard 243
Murphy, Earl 158
Murray, Mary F. 300, Patrick G. E. 296, Tom 145, William 296
Murtaugh, Mary 298, Justin 118
Myer, Harold 51, Millard 261
Myers, Clyde 260, 300, Robert 262, 300

N

Naegele, Carl 158
Nagel, Robert 289
Nanz, Henry 266, 298, 300, Robert 123
Nead, William 249
Neal, Colonel 58, Donald 95, Elmer 18
Neary, Roy 40, Slyvester 244, 297, 300, Walter 20, 21, 297

Neff, Joseph 270, Williard 158
Negley, Wilfred 254
Nelson, Fred 289, Walter 158, 299
Newbold, Gilbert 289
Nicholas, Phillip 289
Nields, Daniel 115
Niemeyer, Albert, Jr. 95
Noble, Clyde 289
Nocks, Emery 37, 43, Harry 276, Jackie 236, Ron 297, 300, Thomas 69
Nolte, Clifford 289, Gilbert 16
Nordmeyer, Harry 100, Harry 98, Lester 254
Norman, Glenn 268, William 151
Norris, Alvin 289, Irvin 93, John 54
Nowlin, Charles 276, 289, Dale 243, 300, Lloyd 289, Norman 289, Orin 276, Paul 216, Raymond 289, Robert 103, Walter Eugene 37, Willard 204

O

Obert, Julian 177
Oberting, Leo 95, Oscar 95, Paul 204, Richard 248, Robert 177
O'brien, Anna Cook 295
Ochs, Lester 176, Robert 158
O'Connell, Leroy 289

O'Conner, Thomas 289
Oelker, Robert 177, 297
Ogden, Lew 239
Ohler, Charles (Ted) 204, Robert (Bob) 179
Ohlmansiek, Omer 62
Olcott, Charles 220
Oldfield, Albert 68, Hubert 165
Olman, Curtis 289
Olson, Kenneth 289
O'Neal, Hubert 289
Oppen, Richard 204, 289
Orlamuende, Gerhard 249
Ortman, Eugene 223
O'Shaughnessy, William 281
Owens, Chester 289, George 13

P

Powell, Betty 137, Ollie Lambert 138
Palmer, Donald 36, Ernest 179, 244, Walter 179
Parish, James 278, 279
Parker, Alberta 295, Emmett 19, Frederick 115, 165, Lois 295, Oscar 23, Robert 3, 241, 295, 299, 300, William 278, 279
Parrott, Elmer 289
Parsons, Curtis 289
Pate, Chauncey 289
Patton, George 77
Payton, Cecil 289
Pearson, Donald 100
Pease, Harry 289

Peelman, Herbert 289
Pelgen, Lawrence 276
Pelsor, John 289
Percival, Robert 252
Perkins, Delmar 179
Permar, Eugene 217
Perpington, Robert 205
Perrin, Clifford 101
Peters, Cecil 289, Charles 269, Edwin 205, Frances 205, Henry 205, 299, Morris 289, Robert 219
Petit, Clarence 289
Pettit, James 179
Pfeifer, James 224, 225
Pheister, Fred 10, Robert 79, 81, 101
Phillips, Donald 289
Phipps, Robert 69, William 81, 100
Pieper, Floyd 205, Irwin 101
Pindell, Delmer 240
Pitts, Lyle 263, Margaret 297
Platt, Barbara 298, Elmer 81, William (Bill) 249
Plummer, Henry 67
Plunket, Philip 249
Plunkett, Frank 268
Poellman, Harold 115
Polk, Sally 271, 292, 300
Porter, Howard 223
Poshard, Harvey 172, 299
Pound, Donald 220
Pound, Ralph 9
Powell, Edwin 100, Isaac C. 11, Jesse 249, Paul 212, Woodrow 101
Powers, Edward 213, George 265
Prather, George 62, Martin 205
Pribble, Paul 281
Probst, John 63, 298
Pruss, Norman 172
Purvis, Chester 16
Pyle, Charles 101
Pyles, Walter 244

R

Radar, David (Crockett) 261
Radspinner, John Lester 61
Ramey, Mary 299, Robert 226, Robert (Bob) 226
Randall, Glenn 265
Ransom, Vernon 165
Rardin, Chester 220
Ravenscraft, James 71
Rechenbach, Clayton 87, 101
Redding, John 101
Redman, Charles 266
Redwine, Gordon 101, Roy 12
Reed, Carl S. 260, Earl 172, Edward 241, Raymond 261
Rees, Ellis 16, Margaret 138, Ralph 240, 241, 297, 300
Reese, Phillip 6, 33, Robert 64, 66
Reif, William H. 69
Reisen, Ralph 282
Renck, John 99, 101, 298
Renner, Harold 215, Lester 215
Renschler, Charles 241
Rice, Charles 205, Garnet 222, Harold 101, Joe 65, Joy 299, 300, Robert 100, Tom (Tuck) 30, Wesley 205, William 265
Richardson, Charles 83
Rider, Dan 299, Jacob 226, 227
Riese, Harry 205
Riggs, John 71, Oliver 70
Riley, Charles 165, Edward 101, Lester 206
Rimstidt, Everett 266
Ritter, Don 157, 257, Kenneth 82, 101
Ritzman, William 37
Ritzmann, Arthur 14, Robert 64, 65, Sally 127, Sheila 298, Sheila O'Brien 292, William, Jr. 297
Roache, Fred 18, Robert 100, Russell 83
Robbins, Philip 260
Roberson, Wesley F. 287
Roberts, Theodore 41
Robinson, Bob 151, Marjorie D. 292, Robert (Bob) 266, William 206
Rockwell, Paul 205
Rodenburg, Frederick 165
Rodgers, Howard 206
Rogers, Ward 260
Rohrer, Samuel 174
Rolf, Lynn 62
Rollins, Charles 254
Ropley, Robert 104
Roseburrough, Robert 165
Rosemeyer, Alfred 70, George 70, Robert 104, 240
Rosenbaum, Warren 263
Ross, Carl 42, Dallas 205, Darrell 104, Eugene 174, Harvey 174, L. Eugene 174, Robert 174
Rossen, Lindsey 56
Roush, Floyd 259
Rowe, Fred 165
Ruble, Raymond 16, William (Billy) 100
Rudolph, Harold 145
Ruhlman, Alice 138, Harold (Hal) 148
Rullman, Arnold 260, Edith 300, Elizabeth 300, Louis 260, Norman 174, Russell 254, Theron 260
Rummel, Joseph 241
Rump, Arthur 146, Ralph 150
Rumsey, Delmar 165, Elmer 266, Francis 239, Glenn (Hickory) 226, 227, Gloria 299, 300
Runnels, Merlin 71
Runyan, Eugene (Duke) 151, James 260, Stanley 12, William 67
Rupp, Mary E. 300,

Robert 266, 267, Theodore 174
Rusche, Robert 104
Rush, Lloyd 174
Russell, Charles 71, Edmund 154, Raymond 69
Rutenkroger, Paul 151
Ruth, Edward 100, William 205
Ryan, Arthur 260, Barry 205, Henry 260
Ryle, Jeremy 55, Robert 58 64, 298

S

Sackett, Floyd 215, Forest 260
Sailor, Floyd 215, William 244
Sams, Everett 242
Sandbrink, Lawrence 252, Willis 270, 300
Sappenfield, David 265, Luther 265
Sartin, C. Paul 71, Paul 52, 298, William 21
Satchwell, Anthony 106, James 265
Satchwell, John 206
Satchwill, James 270
Savage, Frank 146, 147, 297, 299, Robert 242, 300
Scarber, John 93
Schaefer, Edward 151, Harry 148, Raymond 62
Schantz, Ralph 248
Scheibel, Sylvester 254, 255
Schiller, Ernest 214

Schilson, Elton 110, Vincent 108
Schman, Leroy 298
Schmeltzer, Donald 236, 300
Schmidt, Clarence 253, Clifford 108, Denver 174, Howard 108, Paul 174, Ronald 174
Schneider, Alfred 152, 153, Charles 253, Robert 98
Schnetzer, James 151
Schoeff, Dale 60, 298, Martha 299, Millard 98, Virgil 98
Schoeppe, E. A. 108
Scholle, Earl 153, Margaret 299, Paul 206, Raymond 98, 253
Schoolcraft, James 108, Joe 108
Schott, John 260, 262, 300, Wallace 206
Schreiber, August (Gus) 10
Schreiner, Kenneth 102
Schuck, Walter 243
Schuette, Leo 217, Verna 299
Schulenberg, Frederick 219, Manuel 62, Theodore 218
Schuler, Clifford 270, Larry 36, Philip 253, Willis 108
Schultz, Keith 298, Luther 55, Marvin 35, 37, 297, Evelyn 298, 299, 300, Evelyn S. 292, Ralph 69, Richard 49, 70

Schuman, A. T. 299
Schuman, Albert 25, 206, 216, 299, Leroy 83, 206, Paul 211, William 262
Schuyler, James 115
Schwartz, Anthony 83, 100
Schwier, Carl 206, David 251
Schwing, Carl 173, Clifford 243, James 98, Robert 35, 36, 297, Vernon 67, William 98
Scott, Stanley 243
Scotti, Tony 242
Scripture, W.C. 115
Scudder, Robert 212, Willard 253
Scwanholtz, Dana 100
Seaman, Harold 247
Seaver, Caroline 299, Dolan 220, John 266, Matthew 31, Spenser 250
Seavers, Stafford 19
Sedam, Dorothy 297
Sedler, James R. 144, 145, Leonard 59 Martha 299, 300, William 108
Seevers, Earl 262, Leroy 81, 102, 298
Seiler, Albert 148
Seitz, Eugene 31, 38, Gene 29, Jerome (Jerry) 31, Jerry 38, Leo (Doc) 22, Leo (Doc), Jr. 22, M. 297, 298, Marie Edwards 122, Orville 102, Wayne 82, 83

Sellers, Albert 148, Leslie 262
Selmeyer, Clarence 253, Melvin 211
Service, Henry 236
Shamblin, Robert 251
Shanks, Glenn 41
Sharp, Chester 98, 217, Elmer 237
Sheldon, Charles 151, Paul 65, Robert 102
Shell, Arthur 215
Shelton, Francis 257
Sherman, George 217
Shilling, Ralph 55, 56, 298
Shilton, Leroy 21, 23
Shinkle, Clifford 102, Raymond 108, Robert 252
Shipper, George 102, Louis 236
Shockley, Robert 253
Shook, Harold 257, Howard 236, Verrell 215, Wayne 108
Short, Ernest 207
Shuman, Floyd 50
Shuter, Glenn 237, Lloyd 217, 299
Siebenthal, Edgar 257
Siebert, William 115
Siemantel, Frank 110, Leonard 255
Simmerman, George 257, Ray 62, Robert 115
Sizemore, George 173, Lee 51, 59, Marvin 298
Skidmore, Charles 245, 275, Clyde 153
Skykes, Carl 299
Slack, Chauncey 110

Slayback, Charles 257, Irvin 257, James 243, Jonas 40, Omer 237, Raymond 103
Slinkard, Robert 217
Small, Joe (Pete) 17, Lytle 37, 43
Smashey, Aubrey 173, Henry 249, Howard 259
Smith, Alan 259, 295, 297, 299, 300, Albert 265, Austin 218, 221, 299, Charles 83, 103, Clarence 83, Clayton 237, Clifford 103, Curtis 84, Elbert 106, Enyard 154, Eric 295, 297, 298, 299, 300, F. L. 173, G. F. 14, James 147, Lester 100, Lloyd 173, Louis 103, Lowell 173, Mark 254, Raymond 265, Richard 265, Robert 259, Russell 207, 299, Terrance 15, Terry 15
Snelling, Forest 212, George 215, Leo 207
Snider, Jack 145
Snow, Hugh 251
Snyder, Carrol 239, Charles 214, Clarence 207, Helen 138, William 251, Williard 173
Snyer, Glenn 214
Sommer, Earl 41, 70
Somser, Clyde 44
Sortwell, Edward 239
Sortwell, George 250, Glenn 37, Raymond 67
Spanagel, Bob 239
Speckman, Gene 103, Rahe 259, Waneta 138, Wilbur 103
Splangler, Dale 173
Spronk, Frederick 40
Stacy, Dick 153
Stacy, Joseph 266
Stadlander, Robert 148
Stadler, Walter 165
Stadtlander, Richard 251, Robert 148, Ruth 299, 300
Stahl, Thomas 151
Stainer, Robert 297
Stalker, George 153, 165
Stamper, Floyd 15
Standriff, John 56, Robert 213, William 151, 206
Steele, Charles 100, 103, Clyde 239, Kathryn 299, Norbert 151, Norman 206, Russel 297
Steele, Russell 17
Steelman, Marvin 103
Stegemiller, Clifford 253
Steigerwald, James 298, Larry 144, 148, 297, 299
Steiner, Carl 65, Floyd 65, Robert 267, 297, 299, 300
Steinmetz, Joseph 159
Steirs, Roger 69
Stenger, Leo 20, 25, Melvin P. 103, Sylvester 254, Victor 58
Stephenson, Joseph 153
Sterling, Dan 152, Joe 34
Steuver, Charles 155, Williard 173
Steven, Edwin 265
Stevens, Carrol 253, Clayton 55, 60, 219, 298, Edgar 258, 259, 275, Floyd 68, Lawrence 151, 164, Leroy 98, Paul 103
Stiegler, Stella 123
Stoll, Lawrence 103
Stone, Hershel 105, Raymond 150
Stoops, Donald 159
Storey, Earl 103
Stover, Lester 159
Strassinger, Paul 86, 103
Strong, William 206
Struckman, Earl 68, Louis 146
Stryker, Al 213, John 17, 213
Stuard, Ray 154
Stutz, Doris 299, Vernon 245, Virgil 245
Sullivan, Charles 69, Earl 267
Summer, Earl 148
Sutton, Carroll 244, 295, Gerald 213, Harley 243, Paul 56, 93
Swales, John 277, Robert 207, Robert (Bud) 207
Sweppenheise, Milred 298
Swift, John 253
Swinford, John 173
Sykes, Carl 67, 298, James 159, Orpha 299, Robert 123

T

Tandy, Joe 58
Tanner, David Glenn 214, Joseph 144, 146, Otis 151
Taylor, Beth Elliott 112, Charles 218, 298, Charles K. 218, Frank L. 177, 178, George 254, James 173, John 118, Louis 81, 94, 105, 106, 298, Roger 39, Wesley 11, 297, Wilbert 101, 105, 298
Teaney, Bernard 148, Charles 148, Leland 150, 151, 299
Teel, Francis 207
Teke, David 300, Linda 295, Ralph 173, Talbert 266, 267, Vern 173
Telker, William 58
Terrill, Edward 146, George 251, Mary J. 299
Tettenhorst, Helen 299
Tettenhorst, Ray 178
Thamann, Mary 299
Thayer, Raymond 22
Thebo, Arthur 219
Theetge, Edward 21, 81
Thomas, Hubert 105, 107, Mary 298, 299, 300, Wayne 248
Thompson, Charles 213,

Finley 178, Mark 295, Willis 147
Thornton, Russell 267
Thuermer, Robert 247, Russell 218
Thurman, Raymond 106, 226, 227
Tibbets, Paul 147
Tibbetts, Clarence (Red) 36, Clyde 67, Raymond 253
Tibbits, Dawson 207, Frank 207, Harry 207
Timberlake, Clarence 38
Tittel, Paul 64, P. 298
Tittle, Paul 59
Todd, Harrison 59, James W. 64, Jess 247, John 251, Lee 68, Luther 109, Margaret 134, Raymond 207, Robert 291, Sharon 300
Trabel, Raymond 68
Tracy, Phillip 106
Transier, Curtis 236, Herman 150, Lee 159
Traue, Fred 213, Richard 249
Trennepohl, Howard 259, Virgil 215, 219, Willie 178
Trester, Eulalie 138, Gordon 255, Leland 16, Raymond 253
Trichter, John 38
Tschaen, George 211
Tschaenn, Charles 178
Tucker, Arthur 153, Delmar 214, Edmon (Eddie) 19

Tufts, Frank 105
Turner, Louis 109, Orville 251, Paul 259, Raymond 54, Robert 253, William 211
Tyler, Donald 107

U

Uhlmansiek, Harley 212, 213, 299
Ullrich, John 147, Suzanne 295, 297, 298, 299, 300
Ulmansiek, Virgil 109
Utter, Norman Lee 255

V

Vastine, Wilford 109
Vetter, Robert 211
Vickroy, Stanley 104, 105, 152 245, 298
Vineup, Curtis W. 210
Vinup, Donald 106, Omer 147
Vogel, Lloyd 105
Vogelsang, Marvin 259, Sylvester 146
Voit, Arch 66
Volgelsang, Sylvester 146
Votaw, Joe 268

W

Wafford, Earl 9, Russell 106
Waitman, Herbert 99
Walcott, Dilver 267

Waldon, Edwin 247, Wanda 300
Walker, Albert 213, Chester 109, George 250, 251, Robert 159
Wallace, Arthur 109, James 109, Joseph 243
Walser, Francis Joe 245, Hobart 146, Howard 243, Joe 300
Walsh, Kenneth 21, 93
Walter, Anthony 207
Walton, Harry 259
Warburton, Earl 109
Ward, Carl 247, Cathy 295, Samuel 212, Tom 295
Ware, Paul 148
Warneford, Gould 239, 300
Warner, Charles 107, Leroy 255, Norman 251
Warren, Anna Probst 131, 138
Washburn, Lester 248
Waters, Lewis 208, Theodore 59, Forrest 91
Watters, Theodore 93
Watts, Cletus 251, Harry 159, 300, Thomas 159, 163, Tom 299
Weaver, Charles 147, Leslie 115, 154, Richard (Dick) 62, Robert 251
Webb, Alfred 208, John 259
Weber, Anthony 211, 226, John 109, Murrell 66, 67, William 67
Webster, O. P. 109
Weddle, James 241
Weddle, Mary 300
Wehmeyer, Albert 207, Ernest 99, Fred 264, Omer 105, 107
Weigert, Wayne 107
Weiler, Wilfred 164
Welch, Kenneth 68
Weldon, Tom 153
Weller, Wilford 99
Wells, Bernice 299, 300, Bob 60, Charles 277, 282, Clayton 8, 11, Gertrude 138, Kenneth 60, Russell 213, William 208, 218
Werner, Arthur Earl 179
Wessel, Clarence 264, Francis 208
West, James 252
Westerkamp, Anthony 259
Westmeyer, Everett 164
Westrich, George 60, Mike 99, 105, Milborn 22, Robert 20, Walter 254
Whaley, Wilford 208, 215
Wheeler, Sam 226
Whitaker, Charles 38, Leroy 93, 99, Louis 148
White, Donald 59, Doris 298, Eugene 219, Joe 70, Ronald 59, Russell 61, Willard 271
Whiteford, Dan 216, 299, 300, Earl 208, John 280, 281

Widolf, Mark 299
Widolff, Cornelius 158, 159
Wiedeman, Norbert 107, Paul 159, 167
Wiegand, Paul 71
Wildridge, Norman 110
Willers, Aurelia 139
William, Carl 60
Williams, Harry 208, Kenneth 164, Wayne 266
Williamson, Jesse 110
Willkie, Jack 164
Willman, John 221
Willoughby, Ferman 37, James 164
Wilson, Clarence 209, Harry 110
Wiltberger, Albert 208, James 208
Wine, Naomi 139
Wingate, Carl 208, Filmore 164, Wilbur 179
Winkle, James 208, James Van 109, Marion Van 109
Winter, Edward 208, Francis 208
Wirth, Robert 265
Witt, George 243, James 261, Rosemary 131, 139, 298
Witte, Clarence 209, Harold 209, Jean 295
Wittenstrom, Leesa 297, 299
Wittrick, Wilma 297
Wittrock, Nicholas 38, William 268, Wilma 300
Wolfram, Frederick 250
Woliung, John 248, Paul 101, 298
Wolker, Elzie 59, Leo 209
Wolking, George 150
Woodward, Leland 166
Workman, George 63, Les 110, William 216, 248
Wullenweber, Clarence 110
Wunderlich, Fred 209, John 265, George 62
Wunker, Robert 92 Swift 210, William 110
Wymond, John 9, 35

Y

Yandles, Jean 139
Yauger, Frank 261, George 260, John 60
York, Donald 70, Everett 210
Young, Richard 261, Rita 300, Rose Mary 139, Roy 254, Vincent 70

Z

Zeh, Kenneth 35
Ziegler, Martha 299
Zimmer, Debbie 297, 298
Zimmerman, Edward 266, Floyd 178
Zinser, Francis 79, 81 92, 102

FAMILY RECORD

NAME	BIRTH Date — Place	DEATH Date — Place

Notes

Notes

NOTES

Annual Memorial Day services at Greendale Cemetery for departed veterans

www.ingramcontent.com/pod-product-compliance
Lightning Source LLC
Chambersburg PA
CBHW080438170426
43195CB00017B/2813